Kaplan Publishing are constantly finding new ways to make a difference to your studies and our exciting online resources really do offer something different to students looking for exam success.

This book comes with free MyKaplan online resources so that you can study anytime, anywhere. This free online resource is not sold separately and is included in the price of the book.

Having purchased this book, you have access to the following online study materials:

CONTENT	ACCA (including FFA,FAB,FMA)		FIA (excluding FFA,FAB,FMA)	
	Text	Kit	Text	Kit
Eletronic version of the book	✓	✓	✓	✓
Check Your Understanding Test with instant answers	✓			
Material updates	✓	✓	✓	✓
Latest official ACCA exam questions*		✓		
Extra question assistance using the signpost icon**		✓		
Question debriefs using clock icon***		✓		
Consolidation Test including questions and answers	✓			

*   Excludes AB, MA, FA, LW, FAB, FMA and FFA; for all other subjects includes a selection of questions, as released by ACCA

**   For ACCA SBR, AFM, APM, AAA only

*** Excludes AB, MA, FA, LW, FAB, FMA and FFA

How to access your online resources

Kaplan Financial students will already have a MyKaplan account and these extra resources will be available to you online. You do not need to register again, as this process was completed when you enrolled. If you are having problems accessing online materials, please ask your course administrator.

If you are not studying with Kaplan and did not purchase your book via a Kaplan website, to unlock your extra online resources please go to www.mykaplan.co.uk/addabook (even if you have set up an account and registered books previously). You will then need to enter the ISBN number (on the title page and back cover) and the unique pass key number contained in the scratch panel below to gain access.

You will also be required to enter additional information during this process to set up or confirm your account details.

If you purchased through Kaplan Flexible Learning or via the Kaplan Publishing website you will automatically receive an e-mail invitation to MyKaplan. Please register your details using this email to gain access to your content. If you do not receive the e-mail or book content, please contact Kaplan Publishing.

Your Code and Information

This code can only be used once for the registration of one book online. This registration and your online content will expire when the final sittings for the examinations covered by this book have taken place. Please allow one hour from the time you submit your book details for us to process your request.

Please scratch the film to access your MyK

D1341099

KAPLAN

PUBLISHING

Please be aware that this code is case-sensitive and you will need to include the dashes within the passcode, but not when entering the ISBN. For further technical support, please visit www.MyKaplan.co.uk

ACC

Applied Knowledge

Diploma in Accounting and Busin

Financial Accounting (FA/FFA)

EXAM KIT

PUBLISHING

British Library Cataloguing-in-Publication Data

A catalogue record for this book is available from the British Library.

Published by:

Kaplan Publishing UK
Unit 2 The Business Centre
Molly Millar's Lane
Wokingham
Berkshire
RG41 2QZ

ISBN: 978-1-78740-099-3

Acknowledgements

These materials are reviewed by the ACCA examining team. The objective of the review is to ensure that the material properly covers the syllabus and study guide outcomes, used by the examining team in setting the exams, in the appropriate breadth and depth. The review does not ensure that every eventuality, combination or application of examinable topics is addressed by the ACCA Approved Content. Nor does the review comprise a detailed technical check of the content as the Approved Content Provider has its own quality assurance processes in place in this respect.

CONTENTS

Section

This document references IFRS® Standards and IAS® Standards, which are authored by the International Accounting Standards Board (the Board), and published in the 2017 IFRS Standards Red Book.

Features in this edition

In addition to providing a wide ranging bank of practice questions, we have also included in this edition:

- Details of the examination format.

- Examples of 'objective test' and 'multi-task' questions that will form part of the examination format.

- Exam-specific information and advice on exam technique.

- Our recommended approach to make your revision for this particular subject as effective as possible.

    This includes step-by-step guidance on how best to use our Kaplan material (Study Text, Pocket Notes and Exam Kit) at this stage in your studies.

You will find a wealth of other resources to help you with your studies on the following sites:

www.MyKaplan.co.uk and www.**acca**global.com/students/

Quality and accuracy are of the utmost importance to us so if you spot an error in any of our products, please send an email to mykaplanreporting@kaplan.com with full details.

Our Quality Co-ordinator will work with our technical team to verify the error and take action to ensure it is corrected in future editions.

INDEX TO QUESTIONS AND ANSWERS

OBJECTIVE TEST QUESTIONS

MULTI-TASK QUESTIONS

LONG-FORM QUESTIONS

EXAM TECHNIQUE

- **Do not skip any of the material** in the syllabus.

- **Read each question** *very* carefully.

- **Double-check your answer** before committing yourself to it.

- Answer **every** question – if you do not know an answer, you don't lose anything by guessing. Think carefully before you **guess**.

- If you are answering a multiple-choice question, **eliminate first those answers that you know are wrong**. Then choose the most appropriate answer from those that are left.

- Remember that **only one answer to a multiple-choice question can be right**. After you have eliminated the ones that you know to be wrong, if you are still unsure, guess. Only guess after you have double-checked that you have only eliminated answers that are *definitely* wrong.

Computer-based exams – tips

- Do not attempt a CBE until you have **completed all study material** relating to it.

- On the ACCA website there is a CBE demonstration. It is **ESSENTIAL** that you attempt this before your real CBE. You will become familiar with how to move around the CBE screens and the way that questions are formatted, increasing your confidence and speed in the actual exam.

- Be sure you understand how to use the **software** before you start the exam. If in doubt, ask the assessment centre staff to explain it to you.

- Questions are **displayed on the screen** and answers are entered using keyboard and mouse. At the end of the exam, you are given a certificate showing the result you have achieved.

- The CBE question types are as follows:

  - Multiple choice – where you are required to choose one answer from a list of options provided by clicking on the appropriate 'radio button'

  - Multiple response – where you are required to select more than one response from the options provided by clicking on the appropriate tick boxes(typically choose two options from the available list

  - Multiple response matching – where you are required to indicate a response to a number of related statements by clicking on the 'radio button' which corresponds to the appropriate response for each statement

  - Number entry – where you are required to key in a response to a question shown on the screen.

- Note that the CBE variant of the examination will not require you to input text, although you may be required to choose the correct text from options available.

- You need to be sure you **know how to answer questions** of this type before you sit the exam, through practice.

EXAM-SPECIFIC INFORMATION

THE EXAM

FORMAT OF THE COMPUTER-BASED EXAM

	Number of marks
35 compulsory objective test questions (2 marks each)	70
2 multi-task questions (15 marks each)	30

Total time allowed: 2 hours

- Two mark questions will usually comprise the following answer types:

    (i) Multiple choice with four options (A, B, C or D)

    (ii) Some MCQs may use a multiple response approach (e.g. identify which two of four available statements are correct, with four options to choose from, each option consisting of a combination of two of the available statements). Remember that only one of the four available options will be correct.

- The multi-task questions will test consolidations and preparation of financial statements. The consolidation question could include a small amount of interpretation.

- The examinations contain 100% compulsory questions and students must study across the breadth of the syllabus to prepare effectively for the examination

- The examination will be assessed by a two hour computer-based examination. You should refer to the ACCA web site for information regarding the availability of the computer-based examination.

PASS MARK

The pass mark for all ACCA Qualification examinations is 50%.

DETAILED SYLLABUS, STUDY GUIDE AND CBE SPECIMEN EXAM

The detailed syllabus and study guide written by the ACCA, along with the specimen exam, can be found at:

accaglobal.com/financial-accounting

KAPLAN'S RECOMMENDED REVISION APPROACH

QUESTION PRACTICE IS THE KEY TO SUCCESS

Success in professional examinations relies upon you acquiring a firm grasp of the required knowledge at the tuition phase. In order to be able to do the questions, knowledge is essential.

However, the difference between success and failure often hinges on your exam technique on the day and making the most of the revision phase of your studies.

The **Kaplan study text** is the starting point, designed to provide the underpinning knowledge to tackle all questions. However, in the revision phase, poring over books is not the answer.

Kaplan online progress tests help you consolidate your knowledge and understanding and are a useful tool to check whether you can remember key topic areas.

Kaplan pocket notes are designed to help you quickly revise a topic area, however you then need to practice questions. There is a need to progress to full exam standard questions as soon as possible, and to tie your exam technique and technical knowledge together.

The importance of question practice cannot be over-emphasised.

The recommended approach below is designed by expert tutors in the field, in conjunction with their knowledge of the examiner.

The approach taken for the Applied Knowledge exams is to revise by topic area.

You need to practice as many questions as possible in the time you have left.

OUR AIM

Our aim is to get you to the stage where you can attempt exam standard questions confidently, to time, in a closed book environment, with no supplementary help (i.e. to simulate the real examination experience).

Practising your exam technique on real past examination questions, in timed conditions, is also vitally important for you to assess your progress and identify areas of weakness that may need more attention in the final run up to the examination.

The approach below shows you which questions you should use to build up to coping with exam standard question practice, and references to the sources of information available should you need to revisit a topic area in more detail.

Remember that in the real examination, all you have to do is:

- attempt all questions required by the exam

- only spend the allotted time on each question, and

- get them at least 50% right!

Try and practice this approach on every question you attempt from now to the real exam.

THE KAPLAN FINANCIAL ACCOUNTING REVISION PLAN

Stage 1: Assess areas of strengths and weaknesses

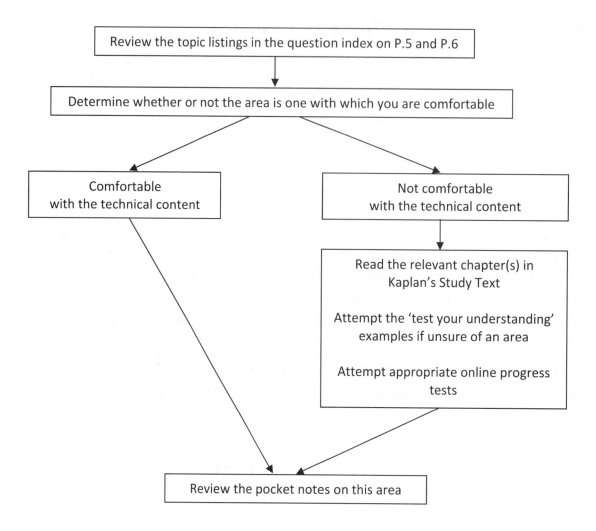

Stage 2: Practice questions

Ensure that you revise all syllabus areas as questions could be asked on anything.

Try to avoid referring to text books and notes and the model answer until you have completed your attempt.

Try to answer the question in the allotted time.

Review your attempt with the model answer. If you got the answer wrong, can you see why? Was the problem a lack of knowledge or a failure to understand the question fully?

KAPLAN PUBLISHING

Fill in the self-assessment box below and decide on your best course of action.

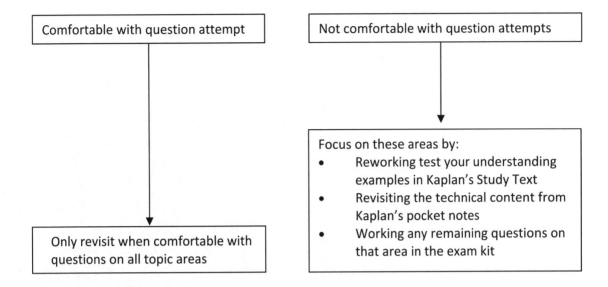

Stage 3: Final pre-exam revision

We recommend that you **attempt at least one two hour mock examination** containing a set of previously unseen exam standard questions.

It is important that you get a feel for the breadth of coverage of a real exam without advanced knowledge of the topic areas covered – just as you will expect to see on the real exam day.

Ideally this mock should be sat in timed, closed book, real exam conditions and could be:

- a mock examination offered by your tuition provider, and/or

- the specimen exam paper in the back of this exam kit.

Section 1

OBJECTIVE TEST QUESTIONS

THE CONTEXT AND PURPOSE OF FINANCIAL REPORTING

1 **Which of the following statements is true?**

  A   The directors of a company are liable for any losses of the company

  B   A sole trader business is owned by shareholders and operated by the proprietor

  C   Partners are liable for losses in a partnership in proportion to their profit share ratio

  D   A company is run by directors on behalf of its members

2 **Which of the following statements best defines a statement of financial position?**

  A   It is a summary of income and expenditure for an accounting period

  B   It is a summary of cash receipts and payments made during an accounting period

  C   It is a summary of assets, liabilities and equity at a specified date

  D   It is a summary of assets and expenses at a specified date

3 **Which of the following statements best defines a statement of profit or loss?**

  A   It is a summary of assets and expenses at a specified date

  B   It is a summary of cash receipts and payments made during an accounting period

  C   It is a summary of assets, liabilities and equity at a specified date

  D   It is a summary of income and expenditure for an accounting period

4 **Which one of the following user groups is likely to require the most detailed financial information?**

  A   The management

  B   Investors and potential investors

  C   Government agencies

  D   Employees

5 **Which of the following statements are true?**

(1) Accounting can be described as the recording and summarising of transactions.

(2) Financial accounting describes the production of a statement of financial position and statement of profit or loss for internal use.

A (1) only

B (2) only

C Both (1) and (2)

D Neither (1) nor (2)

6 **What is the main purpose of financial accounting?**

A To record all transactions in the books of account

B To provide management with detailed analyses of costs

C To enable preparation of financial statements that provides information about an entity's financial performance and position

D To calculate profit or loss for an accounting period

7 **Which one of the following sentences does NOT explain the distinction between financial statements and management accounts?**

A Financial statements are primarily for external users and management accounts are primarily for internal users.

B Financial statements are normally produced annually and management accounts are normally produced monthly.

C Financial statements are more accurate than management accounts.

D Financial statements are audited by an external auditor and management accounts do not normally have an external audit.

8 **Which of the following items is the IFRS Advisory Council is responsible for?**

(1) To give advice to the IASB or to the trustees.

(2) To give advice to the IASB on agenda decisions.

A (1) and (2)

B (1) only

C (2) only

D Neither (1) nor (2)

9 **Which one of the following statements best defines a liability?**

A A liability is an obligation arising from a past transaction or event.

B A liability is a legally binding amount owed to a third party.

C A liability is an obligation arising from a past transaction or event which is expected to be settled by an outflow of economic benefits.

D A liability is anything which results in an outflow of economic benefits from an entity.

10 **State whether each of the following statements is true or false.**

	True	False
International accounting standards are effective only if adopted by national regulatory bodies.		
Accounting standards provide guidance on accounting for all types of transaction.		

11 **Which one of the following statements best defines an expense?**

A An expense is any outflow of economic benefits in an accounting period.

B An expense is an outflow of economic benefits resulting from the purchase of resources in an accounting period.

C An expense is an outflow of economic benefits resulting from a claim by a third party.

D An expense is an outflow of economic benefits in an accounting period as a result of the using up of resources or a fall in the value of an asset.

12 **Which one of the following statements is true in relation to a partnership?**

A A partnership is a separate legal entity

B A partnership is jointly owned and managed by the partners

C A partnership can raise capital by issuing shares to members of the public

D A partnership is able to own property and other assets in its own name

13 **Which one of the following statements is true in relation to a sole trader?**

A A sole trader cannot have any employees

B A sole trader is able to introduce or withdraw capital from the business at any time

C A sole trader has limited liability for the debts of the business

D A sole trader can operate a business from only one location

14 **Which of the following statements is true in relation to a limited liability company?**

A   A limited liability company can incur liabilities in its own name

B   A limited liability company cannot acquire assets in its own name

C   A limited liability company cannot incur liabilities in its own name

D   A limited liability company can be formed on an informal basis by simple agreement between the first shareholders

15 **Which one of the following items could be used to encourage executive directors to operate in the best interests of the company?**

A   They could be awarded a high salary

B   They could receive bonuses based on both individual and company performance

C   The could be entitled to large payment on resignation

D   The could be asked to attend Annual General Meetings of the company

16 **Which one statement relating to partnerships and limited liability companies is true?**

A   Both partnerships and limited liability companies are able to own assets in their own name.

B   The members of a limited liability company have the right to participate in the management of that company, whereas partners do not have the right to participate in the management of their partnership.

C   The partners have the right to participate in the management of the partnership, whereas members of a limited liability company do not have the right to participate in the management of that company.

D   Partnerships are subject to the same regulations regarding introduction and withdrawal of capital from the business as a limited liability company.

17 **Which one of the following items is the most obvious means of achieving public oversight of corporate governance?**

A   The company establishing a comprehensive web site

B   Publication of the Annual Report and Accounts

C   Press announcements of all significant developments

D   Shareholder access to the Annual General Meeting

18 **Which TWO items would you expect to see included within the financial statements of a sole trader?**

A   Issued share capital

B   Revaluation surplus

C   Personal drawings

D   Capital account

19 Which TWO items would you expect to see included within the financial statements of a partnership?

A   Dividends paid

B   Capital accounts

C   Profit appropriation account

D   Share premium account

20 Which body is responsible for the issue of International Financial Reporting Standards?

A   The IFRS Advisory Council

B   The International Financial Reporting Interpretations Committee

C   The International Accounting Standards Board

D   The European Union

21 For each of the following statements, relating to the IASB's Conceptual Framework for Financial Reporting 'the Framework,' identify whether it is true or false.

	True	False
The Conceptual Framework is a financial reporting standard		
The Conceptual Framework assists in harmonising global accounting practices.		
The Conceptual Framework assists national standard setters to develop national standards.		
The Conceptual Framework assists users of financial information to interpret financial statements.		

22 Which one of the following statements best defines an asset?

A   An asset is a resource owned by the entity with a financial value.

B   An asset is a resource controlled by an entity from which future economic benefits are expected to be generated.

C   An asset is a resource controlled by an entity as a result of past events.

D   An asset is a resource controlled by an entity as a result of past events from which future economic benefits are expected to be generated.

23 Which one of the following statements best defines the equity or capital of a business?

A   Equity or capital of a business is represented by the net assets of the business

B   Equity or capital of a business is equivalent to the value of the business

C   Equity or capital of a business is equivalent to the value of the business assets

D   Equity or capital of a business is represented by the total assets of the business

THE QUALITATIVE CHARACTERISTICS OF FINANCIAL INFORMATION

24 For each of the following items, identify whether it is or is not an enhancing qualitative characteristic of useful financial information as stated in the IASB Conceptual Framework.

	An enhancing qualitative characteristic	Not an enhancing qualitative characteristic
Comparability		
Timeliness		
Faithful representation		
Understandability		

25 Which ONE of the following statements is correct?

A   The going concern concept guarantees that a business will continue in operational existence for at least twelve months after the reporting date.

B   To comply with the law, the legal form of a transaction must always be reflected in financial statements.

C   If a non-current asset initially recognised at cost is revalued, the surplus must be credited in the statement of cash flows.

D   In times of rising prices, the use of historical cost accounting tends to understate assets and overstate profits.

26 For each of the following items, identify whether or not it is an enhancing qualitative characteristics of useful financial information as stated in the IASB Conceptual Framework.

	An enhancing qualitative characteristic	Not an enhancing qualitative characteristic
Relevance		
Comparability		
Faithful representation		
Verifiability		

27 **Which of the following statements best explains the principle of faithful representation in relation to the preparation of the annual financial statements?**

   A   Transactions are presented any way that is considered appropriate.

   B   Transactions are presented in such a way as to maximise profit for the year.

   C   Transactions are presented in such a way to maximise asset values in the statement of financial position.

   D   Transactions are presented to reflect their commercial substance of a transaction rather than their legal form.

28 **The accounting concept which dictates that non-current assets should be valued at cost less accumulated depreciation, rather than at their enforced saleable value, is:**

   A   Understandability

   B   Relevance

   C   Comparability

   D   Going concern

29 **Which of the following pairs of items comprise the two fundamental qualitative characteristics of useful financial information?**

   A   Relevance and comparability

   B   Relevance and faithful representation

   C   Faithful representation and understandability

   D   Faithful representation and comparability

30 **Which of the following statements defines the business entity concept?**

   A   The business will continue to operate for the foreseeable future.

   B   A business is always a separate legal entity, distinct from those who own or manage that business.

   C   A business is never a separate legal entity from those who own or manage that business.

   D   Financial transactions are recorded and presented from the perspective of the business, rather than from the perspective of the owners or managers of that business.

THE USE OF DOUBLE-ENTRY AND ACCOUNTING SYSTEMS

DOUBLE ENTRY BOOKKEEPING

31   Oscar runs a sole trader business selling computers. On 12 January 20X7, he employed his daughter as an administrator for the business and took a computer from the store room for her to use in the office.

What is the double entry for this transaction?

A	Dr Drawings	Cr Cost of sales
B	Dr Non-current assets	Cr Cost of sales
C	Dr Cost of sales	Cr Drawings
D	Dr Cost of sales	Cr Non-current assets

32   **Which ONE pair of the following items would appear on the same side of the trial balance?**

A   Drawings and accruals

B   Carriage outwards and prepayments

C   Carriage inwards and rental income

D   Opening inventory and purchase returns

33   **The double-entry system of bookkeeping normally results in which of the following balances on the ledger accounts?**

	Debit balances:	*Credit balances:*
A	Assets and revenues	Liabilities, capital and expenses
B	Revenues, capital and liabilities	Assets and expenses
C	Assets and expenses	Liabilities, capital and revenues
D	Assets, expenses and capital	Liabilities and revenues

34   **Which one of the following states the entries required to account for a reimbursement to the petty cash float of $125 from the bank account?**

A	Dr Petty cash	Cr Cash and bank
B	Dr Cash and bank	Cr Petty cash
C	Dr Drawings	Cr Petty cash
D	Dr Drawings	Cr Cash and bank

35 Sasha has prepared a draft statement of profit or loss for her business as follows:

	$	$
Sales		256,800
Cost of sales		
Opening inventory	13,400	
Purchases	145,000	
Closing inventory	(14,200)	
		(144,200)
Gross profit		112,600
Expenses		(76,000)
Net profit		36,600

Sasha has not yet recorded the following items:

- Carriage in of $2,300
- Discounts received of $3,900
- Carriage out of $1,950

After these amounts are recorded, what are the revised values for gross and net profit of Sasha's business?

	Gross profit	Net profit
	$	$
A	108,350	36,250
B	108,350	28,450
C	110,300	28,450
D	110,300	36,250

36 Elijah started the month with cash at bank of $1,780.

What was the balance carried forward after accounting for the following transactions in June?

(1) Elijah withdrew $200 per week to cover living expenses.

(2) A customer paid for goods with a list price of $600, less trade discount of 5%.

(3) An amount of $400 was received from a credit customer.

(4) Bankings of $1,200 from canteen vending machines.

$ _____

37 After corrections, what should be the balance on the following account?

Bank

	$		$
Overdraft at start of month	1,340	Returns of goods purchased for cash	50
Reimbursement of petty cash float	45	Payments to credit suppliers	990
Receipts from customers	4,400	Rental income	1,300
		Payment of electricity bill	700
		Balance c/f	2,745
	____		____
	5,785		5,785
	____		____

$

38 Andrea started a taxi business by transferring her car, at a value of $5,000, into the business.

What accounting entries are required to record this transaction?

A   Dr Capital $5,000, Cr Car $5,000

B   Dr Car $5,000, Cr Drawings $5,000

C   Dr Car $5,000, Cr Capital $5,000

D   Dr Drawing $5,000 Cr Car $5,000

39 Which one of the following statements best describes the purpose of a purchase order?

A   It is issued to a supplier to request supply of goods from them on terms specified within the order.

B   It is issued to a customer to confirm the supply of goods to them on terms specified in the order.

C   It is issued to a supplier as notification of payment.

D   It confirms the price that will be charged by a supplier for goods supplied.

40 Which one of the following statements best describes the purpose of a goods despatched note (delivery note)?

A   It is issued by a customer returning faulty goods to their supplier.

B   It is issued by a customer to their supplier and specifies the quantity and type of goods they require to be despatched.

C   It is issued by a supplier to their customer and specifies the quantity and type of goods delivered to that customer.

D   It is issued by a supplier to their customer and specifies what goods will be provided to them at a specified future date.

41   **An invoice is best defined by which one of the following statements?**

A   An invoice is raised by a business and confirms only the amount due to be paid for goods and services provided.

B   An invoice is raised by business and issued to a supplier as recognition of goods and services received from that supplier.

C   An invoice is raised by a business and issued to a customer to confirm amounts not yet paid.

D   An invoice is raised by a business and issued to a customer to request payment for goods and services provided.

42   **With reference to the accounting equation, state whether each of the following statements is true or false.**

	True	False
Business assets will always equal business liabilities		
Business assets will always exceed business liabilities		
Business assets include proprietor's capital		
Business liabilities include proprietor's capital		

43   **With reference to the journal, state whether each of the following statements is true or false?**

	True	False
The journal records all bank and cash transactions		
The journal records all accounting transactions		
The journal is a book of prime entry		
The journal records all credit sales transactions		

44   During the year, Ferguson made the following accounting entries to account for the depreciation charge relating to motor vehicles:

Debit Accumulated depreciation – motor vehicles $5,000

Credit Depreciation expense – motor vehicles $5,000

What are the journal entries required to account correctly for the depreciation charge for motor vehicles for the year?

A   Debit Motor vehicles $5,000, and Credit Accumulated depreciation $5,000

B   Debit Depreciation Expense $10,000, and Credit Accumulated depreciation $10,000

C   Debit Depreciation expense $5,000, and Credit Accumulated depreciation $5,000

D   Debit Accumulated depreciation $10,000, and Credit Depreciation expense $10,000

45 During the year, Redknapp made the following accounting entries to account for the increase in the allowance for receivables:

Debit Trade receivables' ledger control account $4,300

Credit Allowance for receivables $4,300

What journal entries are required to adjust the above accounting entries to increase the allowance for receivables for the year?

A   Debit Trade receivables' ledger control, and Credit Irrecoverable debts

B   Debit Allowance for receivables, and Credit Irrecoverable debts

C   Debit Irrecoverable debts and allowance for receivables expense, and Credit Trade receivables' ledger control

D   Debit Irrecoverable debts, and Credit Allowance for receivables

46 During the year, Allardyce made the following accounting entries to account for the cash proceeds received upon disposal of an item of machinery:

Debit Bank $2,500

Credit Sales revenue $2,500

What are the journal entries required to account correctly for the disposal proceeds received upon disposal of the item of machinery?

A   Debit Accumulated depreciation $2,500, and Credit Disposal of machinery $2,500

B   Debit Sales revenue $2,500, and Credit Bank $2,500

C   Debit Disposal of machinery $2,500, and Credit Machinery asset $2,500

D   Debit Sales revenue $2,500, and Credit Disposal of machinery $2,500

47 Pardew is unsure of the accounting entries required to account for a contra between the receivables ledger control and payables ledger control accounts for $1,250.

What are the journal entries required to account correctly for a contra between the trade receivables' and trade payables' ledger control accounts?

A   Debit Trade payables' ledger control $1,250, and Credit Trade receivables' ledger control $1,250

B   Debit Trade payables' ledger $1,250, and Credit Trade receivables' ledger $1,250

C   Debit Trade receivables' control $1,250, and Credit Trade payables' control $1,250

D   Debit Trade receivables' ledger $1,250, and Credit Trade payables' ledger $1,250

48 **What are the journal entries required to correctly account for the depreciation charge for the year of $3,500 relating to buildings?**

A   Debit Depreciation expense $3,500, and Credit Buildings $3,500

B   Debit Buildings $3,500, and Credit Accumulated depreciation $3,500

C   Debit Depreciation expense $3,500 and Credit Accumulated depreciation $3,500

D   Debit Accumulated depreciation $3,500, and Credit Depreciation expense $3,500

49 **What are the accounting entries required to account for settlement discount received of $250 from a credit supplier?**

A   Debit Discount received $250, and Credit Trade payables' control $250

B   Debit Trade payables' control $250, and Credit Discount received $250

C   Debit Discount received $250, and Credit Trade payables' control $250

D   Debit Trade payables' control $250, and Credit Revenue $250

50 Pardew made the following accounting entries to account for the purchase of goods on credit from a supplier:

Debit Trade payables' ledger control account $3,200

Credit Purchases $3,200

What are the journal entries required to account correctly for the purchase of the goods on credit from a supplier?

A   Debit Purchases $3,200, and Credit Trade receivables' control $3,200

B   Debit Purchases $3,200, and Credit Trade payables' control $3,200

C   Debit Purchases $3,200, and Credit Suspense $3,200

D   Debit Purchases $6,400, and Credit Trade payables' control $6,400

51 Bob used the following balances to prepare his financial statements as at 30 April 20X3.

	$	$
Receivables	6,000	
Bank loan		3,000
Bank overdraft		2,500
Drawings	4,100	
Capital 1 May 20X2		12,500
Purchases and revenue	19,200	22,000
Rent	5,400	
Bank interest	825	
Heat and light	4,475	
	_____	_____
	40,000	40,000
	_____	_____

The business does not hold inventory. No further adjustments were required.

What was Bob's closing capital as at 30 April 20X3?

$ [   ]

LEDGER ACCOUNTS, BOOKS OF PRIME ENTRY AND JOURNALS

52 **State whether each of the following items is one of the books of prime entry.**

	A book of prime entry	Not a book of prime entry
Sales day book		
Trial balance		
The journal		
Accounts receivable ledger		

53 The petty cash balance at 30 November 20X9 was $25. The following transactions occurred during November 20X9:

(1) Refreshments were purchased at a cost of $7.25.

(2) Travel expenses of $12.75 were reimbursed to an employee.

(3) The cleaner was paid $15.

What was the petty cash float at 1 November 20X9?

A $25

B $60

C $35

D $50

54 **Which ONE of the following explains the imprest system of operating petty cash?**

A   Weekly expenditure cannot exceed a set amount

B   The exact amount of expenditure is reimbursed at intervals to maintain a fixed float

C   All expenditure out of the petty cash must be properly authorised

D   Regular equal amounts of cash are transferred into petty cash at intervals

55 You are given the following figures for sales and receivables:

	20X7	20X6
	$	$
Receivables at year end	74,963	69,472
Sales	697,104	
Total cash received from customers	686,912	
Specific allowance for receivables	2,014	1,578
Irrecoverable debts written off	1,697	

What was the value of sales returns during 20X7?

$ [   ]

56 Ignatius operates the imprest system for petty cash. At 1 July there was a float of $150, but it was decided to increase this to $200 from 31 July onwards. During July, the petty cashier received $25 from staff for using the photocopier and a cheque for $90 was cashed for an employee. In July, cheques were drawn for $500 for petty cash.

How much cash was paid out as cash expenses by the petty cashier in July?

$ [   ]

57 **Which ONE of the following might explain a debit balance on a payables ledger account?**

A   The business took a settlement discount to which it was not entitled and paid less than the amount due

B   The business mistakenly paid an invoice twice

C   The book-keeper failed to enter a contra with the receivables ledger

D   The book-keeper failed to post a cheque paid to the account

58 Allister's payables' ledger control account has a balance at 1 October 20X8 of $34,500 credit. During October, credit purchases were $78,400, cash purchases were $2,400 and payments made to suppliers, excluding cash purchases, and after deducting settlement discounts of $1,200, were $68,900. Purchase returns were $4,700.

What was the closing balance on the payables' ledger control account?

$ [   ]

59 The entries in a receivables' ledger control account for the first accounting period were:

Sales	$250,000
Bank	$225,000
Returns	$2,500
Irrecoverable debts	$3,000
Returned unpaid cheque	$3,500
Contra payables ledger account	$4,000

What is the balance on the receivables' ledger control account at the end of the accounting period?

$ [   ]

60 **In which book of prime entry would a business record the part-exchange value received for a vehicle traded in when purchasing a new vehicle?**

A   The sales daybook

B   The cash payments book

C   The journal

D   The non-current asset register

61 **Mike wrongly paid Norman $250 twice for goods purchased on credit. Norman subsequently reimbursed Mike for the overpayment of $250. How should Mike account for the reimbursement received from Norman?**

A   Debit Cash received, and   Credit Sales

B   Debit Cash received, and   Credit Discount received

C   Debit Cash received, and   Credit Trade receivables' control account

D   Debit Cash received, and   Credit Trade payables' control account

62 **What are the accounting entries required to record sales on credit of $10,000, on which sales tax is applied at the rate of 20%?**

A   Debit Trade receivables' control account $12,000, Credit Sales revenue $10,000 and Credit Sales tax $2,000

B   Debit Trade receivables' control account $10,000, Credit Sales revenue $8,000 and Credit Sales tax $2,000

C   Debit Sales revenue $10,000, Debit Sales tax $2,000 and Credit Suspense $12,000

D   Debit Sales revenue $8,000, Debit Sales tax $2,000 and Credit Suspense $10,000

63 **What are the accounting entries required to record the purchase of goods for resale on credit with a gross invoice value of $1,541, which includes sales tax at the rate of 15%. The business is registered to account for sales tax.**

A   Debit Purchases $1,309.85, Debit Sales tax $231,15, and Credit Trade payables' control $1,541.00

B   Debit Purchases $1,340, Debit Sales tax $201, and Credit Trade payables' control $1,541

C   Debit Purchases $1,541.00, Debit Sales tax $231.15, and Credit Trade payables' control $1,772.15

D   Debit Purchases $1,772.15, Credit Sales tax $231.15 and Credit Trade payables' control $1,541.00

64 **Which one of the following best describes the purpose of a purchase invoice?**

A   It is issued by a supplier as a request for payment

B   It is sent to supplier as a request for a supply

C   It is issued by supplier listing details of recent transactions

D   It is sent to the supplier as notification of payment

65 **In which book of prime entry would discounts received be recorded?**

A   Cash received book

B   Cash payments book

C   Sales day book

D   Purchases day book

66 **Simran uses the imprest method of accounting for petty cash. She counted the petty cash and there was $66·00 in hand. There were also the following petty cash vouchers:**

	$
Sundry purchases	22.00
Loan to sales manager	10.00
Purchase of staff drinks	19.00
Sundry sales receipts	47.00

What is Simran's imprest amount?

$ [   ]

RECORDING TRANSACTIONS AND EVENTS

SALES AND PURCHASES AND SALES TAX

67 Erin is registered for sales tax. During May, she sold goods with a list price of $600, excluding sales tax, to Kyle on credit. As Kyle was buying a large quantity of goods, Erin deducted trade discount of 5% of the normal list price.

If sales tax is charged at 15%, what will be the gross value of the sales invoice prepared by Erin?

$ [   ]

68 At 1 December 20X5, Laurel owes the sales tax authorities $23,778. During the month of December, she recorded the following transactions:

- Sales of $800,000 exclusive of 17.5% sales tax.
- Purchases of $590,790 inclusive of sales tax of 17.5%.

What is the balance on Laurel's sales tax account at the end of December?

$ [   ]

69 If sales (including sales tax) amounted to $27,612.50, and purchases (excluding sales tax) amounted to $18,000, what would be the balance on the sales tax account, assuming all transactions are subject to sales tax at 17.5%?

$ [   ]

70 In the quarter ended 31 March 20X2, Chas had taxable sales, net of sales tax, of $90,000 and taxable purchases, net of sales tax, of $72,000.

If the rate of sales tax is 10%, how much sales tax is payable to the tax authority?

A $1,800 receivable

B $2,000 receivable

C $1,800 payable

D $2,000 payable

71 A summary of the transactions of Ramsgate, who is registered to account for sales tax at 17.5% on all transactions, shows the following for the month of August 20X9:

Outputs $60,000 (exclusive of tax)

Inputs $40,286 (inclusive of tax)

At the beginning of the period Ramsgate owed $3,400 to the authorities, and during the period he paid $2,600 to them.

What is the amount due to the tax authorities at the end of the month?

$ [   ]

72 **Which one of the following statements best explains the sales account?**

A   It is credited with the total of sales made, including sales tax

B   It is credited with the total of sales made, excluding sales tax

C   It is credited with the total purchases made, including sales tax

D   It is credited with the total expenses, excluding sales tax

73 A business sold goods that had a net value of $600 to Lucid.

What entries are required by the seller to record this transaction if sales tax is applied at 17.5%?

A   Dr Lucid $600, Dr Sales tax $105, Cr Sales $705

B   Dr Lucid $705, Cr Sales tax $105, Cr Sales $600

C   Dr Lucid $600, Cr Sales tax $105, Cr Sales $600

D   Dr Sales $600, Dr Sales tax $105, Cr Lucid $705

74 Laker, a customer, returned goods to Streamer that had a net value of $200.

What entries are required by Streamer to record this transaction if transactions are subject to sales tax is payable at 17.5%?

A   Dr Returns inward $200, Dr Sales tax $35, Cr Laker $235

B   Dr Returns inward $235, Cr Sales tax $35, Cr Laker $200

C   Dr Purchases $200, Dr Sales tax $35, Cr Laker $235

D   Dr Laker $235, Cr Returns inward $200, Cr Sales tax $35

75 Stung, which is registered to account for sales tax, purchased furniture on credit at a cost of $8,000, plus sales tax of $1,200.

What are the correct accounting entries to record this transaction?

		$		$
A	Debit Furniture	9,200	Credit Supplier	9,200
B	Debit Furniture	8,000	Credit Sales tax	1,200
			Credit Supplier	6,800
C	Debit Furniture	8,000	Credit Supplier	9,200
	Debit Sales tax	1,200		
D	Debit Furniture	8,000	Credit Supplier	8,000

76   State whether each of the following statements is true or false.

	True	False
Sales tax is a form of indirect taxation		
If input tax exceeds output tax the difference is payable to the tax authorities		
Sales tax is included in the reported sales and purchases of a sales tax registered business		
Sales tax cannot be recovered on some purchases		

77   Based upon the following information, what was the cost of purchases?

	$
Opening trade payables	142,600
Cash paid	542,300
Discounts received	13,200
Goods returned	27,500
Closing trade payables	137,800

$ [   ]

78   You are given the following information:

Receivables at 1 January 20X3	$10,000
Receivables at 31 December 20X3	$9,000
Total receipts during 20X3 (including cash sales of $5,000)	$85,000

Based upon the available information, what was the sales revenue figure for 20X3?

$ [   ]

79   P is a sole proprietor whose accounting records are incomplete. All the sales are cash sales and during the year $50,000 was banked, including $5,000 from the sale of a business car. He paid $12,000 wages in cash from the till and withdrew $2,000 per month as drawings. The cash in the till at the beginning and end of the year was $300 and $400 respectively.

What was the value of P's sales revenue for the year?

A $80,900

B $81,000

C $81,100

D $86,100

80   The following transactions took place during Alan's first month of trading:

- Credit sales of $121,000 exclusive of sales tax
- Credit purchases of $157,110 inclusive of sales tax
- Cash payments to credit suppliers of $82,710 inclusive of sales tax

All transactions are subject to sales tax at 20%.

What was the balance on Alan's sales tax account at the end of his first month of trading?

A $1,985DR

B $1,985CR

C $15,770DR

D $15,770CR

81   **Which one of the following statements is correct?**

A   Carriage inwards and carriage outwards are both accounted for as an expense in the statement of profit or loss.

B   Carriage inwards and carriage outwards are both accounted for as income in the statement of profit or loss.

C   Carriage inwards is treated as an expense and carriage outwards is treated as income in the statement of profit or loss.

D   Carriage inwards is treated as income and carriage outwards is treated as an expense in the statement of profit or loss.

82   Jupiter returned unsatisfactory goods to Saturn. The goods had been sold on credit by Saturn at $100 plus sales tax of $20.

What accounting entries are required by Saturn to record the return of goods?

A   Dr Purchases $100, Dr Sales tax $20, Cr Jupiter $120

B   Dr Returns outward $100, Dr Sales tax $20, Cr Jupiter $120

C   Dr Returns inward $100, Dr Sales tax $20, Cr Jupiter $120

D   Dr Jupiter $120, Cr Returns outward $100, Cr Sales tax $20

83   Eric is registered for sales tax. During October, he sold goods with a tax exclusive price of $800 to Kevin on credit. As Kevin is buying a large quantity of goods, Eric reduced the price by 8%. Eric accounts for sales tax on all transactions at 25%.

What was the gross value of the sales invoice for Kevin prepared by Eric?

$

84 ABC Co sold goods with a list price of $1,000 to Smith which was subject to trade discount of 5% and early settlement discount of 4% if the invoice was paid within 7 days. The normal credit period available to credit customers is 30 days from invoice date. At the point of sale, Smith was not expected to take advantage of early settlement terms offered.

If Smith subsequently paid within 7 days and was eligible for the settlement discount, what accounting entries should be made by ABC Co to record settlement of the amount outstanding?

A   Debit Cash $950, Debit Revenue $50 and Credit Trade receivables $1,000

B   Debit Cash $950, Credit Revenue $38 and Credit Trade receivables $912

C   Debit Cash $912, Debit Revenue $38 and Credit Trade receivables $950

D   Debit Cash $912, and Credit Trade receivables $912

85 ABC Co sold goods with a list price of $2,500 to Jones which was subject to trade discount of 5% and early settlement discount of 4% if the invoice was paid within 7 days. The normal credit period available to credit customers is 30 days from invoice date. At the point of sale, Jones was expected to take advantage of the early settlement terms.

If Jones subsequently paid within 7 days and was eligible for the settlement discount, what accounting entries should be made by ABC Co to record settlement of the amount outstanding?

A   Debit Cash $2,280, Debit Revenue $95 and Credit Trade receivables $2,375

B   Debit Cash $2,280 and Credit Trade receivables $2,280

C   Debit Cash $2,375, Debit Revenue $125 and Credit Trade receivables $2,500

D   Debit Cash $2,500, and Credit Trade receivables $2,500

86 ABC Co sold goods with a list price of $4,500 to Black which was subject to trade discount of 5% and early settlement discount of 4% if the invoice was paid within 7 days. The normal credit period available to credit customers is 30 days from invoice date. At the point of sale, Black was expected to take advantage of the early settlement terms offered.

If, on this occasion, Black did not pay within 7 days and was not eligible for the settlement discount, what accounting entries should be made by ABC Co to record settlement of the amount outstanding?

A   Debit Cash $4,104, Debit Revenue $396 and Credit Trade receivables $4,500

B   Debit Cash $4,275, Debit Discount received $171 and Credit Trade receivables $4,104

C   Debit Cash $4,275 and Credit Trade receivables $4,275

D   Debit Cash $4,275, Credit Trade receivables $4,104 and Credit Revenue $171

87 ABC Co sold goods with a list price of $3,700 to White which was subject to trade discount of 5% and early settlement discount of 4% if the invoice was paid within 7 days. The normal credit period available to credit customers is 30 days from invoice date. At the point of sale, White was not expected to pay early and take advantage of the early settlement terms offered.

If, as expected, White did not pay within the settlement discount period, what accounting entries should be made by ABC Co to record settlement of the amount outstanding?

A   Debit Cash $3,515, and Credit Trade receivables $3,515

B   Debit Cash $3,515, Credit Discount received $140.60 and Credit Trade receivables $3,374.40

C   Debit Cash $3,374.40 and Credit Trade receivables $3,374.40

D   Debit Cash $3,515, Debit Revenue $185 and Credit Trade receivables $3,700

88 ABC Co sold goods with a list price of $1,400 to Green which was subject to trade discount of 4% and early settlement discount of 5% if the invoice was paid within 7 days. The normal credit period available to credit customers is 30 days from invoice date. At the point of sale, Green was expected to take advantage of the early settlement discount terms offered.

If, on this occasion, Green did not pay within the settlement discount period, what accounting entries should be made by ABC Co to record settlement of the amount outstanding?

A   Debit Cash $1,400 Credit Trade receivables $1,400

B   Debit Cash $1,344, Credit Trade receivables $1,276.80 and Credit Revenue $67.20

C   Debit Cash $1,344 and Credit Trade receivables $1,344

D   Debit Cash $1,276.80, and Credit Trade receivables $1,276.80

INVENTORY

89 An item of inventory was purchased for $500. It is expected to be sold for $1,200 although $250 will need to be spent on it in order to achieve the sale. To replace the same item of inventory would cost $650.

At what value should this item of inventory be included in the financial statements?

$ [   ]

90 In the year ended 31 August 20X4, Aplus' records show closing inventory of 1,000 units compared to 950 units of opening inventory.

Which of the following statements is true assuming that prices have fallen throughout the year?

A   Closing inventory and profit are higher using FIFO rather than AVCO

B   Closing inventory and profit are lower using FIFO rather than AVCO

C   Closing inventory is higher and profit lower using FIFO rather than AVCO

D   Closing inventory is lower and profit higher using FIFO rather than AVCO

91 Appleby buys and sells inventory during the month of August as follows:

		No. of units	$
Opening inventory		100	2.52/unit
4 August	Sales	20	
8 August	Purchases	140	2.56/unit
10 August	Sales	90	
18 August	Purchases	200	2.78/unit
20 August	Sales	180	

Which one of the following statements is true?

A   Closing inventory is $19.50 higher when using the FIFO method instead of the periodic weighted average.

B   Closing inventory is $19.50 lower when using the FIFO method instead of the periodic weighted average.

C   Closing inventory is $17.50 higher when using the FIFO method instead of the periodic weighted average.

D   Closing inventory is $17.50 lower when using the FIFO method instead of the periodic weighted average.

92 David performs an inventory count on 30 December 20X6 ahead of the 31 December year end. He counts 1,200 identical units, each of which cost $50. On 31 December, David sold 20 of the units for $48 each.

What figure should be included in David's statement of financial position for inventory at 31 December 20X6?

$ [   ]

93 **Identify whether each of the following statements relating to the accounting treatment of inventory and work in progress in financial statements is true or false.**

	True	*False*
Inventory should be valued at the lower of cost, net realisable value and replacement cost.		
When valuing work in progress, materials costs, labour costs and variable and fixed production overheads must be included.		
Inventory items can be valued using either first in, first out (FIFO) or weighted average cost.		
An entity's financial statements must disclose the accounting policies used in measuring inventories.		

94 Kiera's interior design business received a delivery of fabric on 29 June 20X6 and was included in the inventory valuation at 30 June 20X6. As at 30 June 20X6, the invoice for the fabric had not been accounted for.

Based upon the available information, what effect(s) will this have on Kiera's profit for the year ended 30 June 20X6 and the inventory valuation at that date?

(1)   Profit for the year ended 30 June 20X6 will be overstated.

(2)   Inventory at 30 June 20X6 will be understated.

(3)   Profit for the year ended 30 June 20X7 will be overstated.

(4)   Inventory at 30 June 20X6 will be overstated.

A   (1) and (2)

B   (2) and (3)

C   (1) only

D   (1) and (4)

95 **What journal entry is required to record goods taken from inventory by the owner of a business for personal use?**

A   Dr Drawings   Cr Purchases

B   Dr Sales   Cr Drawings

C   Dr Drawings   Cr Inventory

D   Dr Inventory   Cr Drawings

96 A business had an opening inventory of $180,000 and a closing inventory of $220,000 in its financial statements for the year ended 31 December 20X5.

Which of the following accounting entries are required to account for opening and closing inventory when preparing the financial statements of the business?

		Debit	Credit
		$	$
A	Inventory account	180,000	
	Statement of P/L		180,000
	Statement P/L	220,000	
	Inventory account		220,000
B	Statement of P/L	180,000	
	Inventory account		180,000
	Inventory account	220,000	
	Statement of P/L		220,000
C	Inventory account	40,000	
	Purchases account		40,000
D	Purchases account	40,000	
	Inventory account		40,000

97 Ajay's annual inventory count took place on 7 July 20X6. The inventory value on this date was $38,950. During the period from 30 June 20X6 to 7 July 20X6, the following took place:

Sales $6,500

Purchases $4,250

The mark up is 25% on cost.

What is Ajay's inventory valuation at 30 June 20X6?

$ _____

98 Inventory movements for product X during the last quarter were as follows:

Opening inventory at 1 January was 6 items valued at $15 each.

January	Purchases	10 items at $19.80 each
February	Sales	10 items at $30 each
March	Purchases	20 items at $24.50
	Sales	5 items at $30 each

What was gross profit for the quarter, if inventory is valued using the continuous weighted average cost method?

$ _____

99 Your firm values inventory using the periodic weighted average cost method. At 1 October 20X8, there were 60 units in inventory valued at $12 each. On 8 October, 40 units were purchased for $15 each, and a further 50 units were purchased for $18 each on 14 October. On 21 October, 75 units were sold for $1,200.

What was the value of closing inventory at 31 October 20X8?

$ _____

100 Percy Pilbeam is a book wholesaler. On each sale, commission of 4% is payable to the selling agent. The following information is available in respect of total inventories of three of his most popular titles at his financial year-end:

	Cost $	Selling price $
Henry VII – Shakespeare	2,280	2,900
Dissuasion – Jane Armstrong-Siddeley	4,080	4,000
Pilgrim's Painful Progress – John Bunion	1,280	1,300

What is the value of these inventories in Percy's statement of financial position?

A $7,368

B $7,400

C $7,560

D $7,640

101 An organisation's inventory at 1 July was 15 units at a cost of $3.00 each. The following movements occur:

3 July 20X4	5 units sold at $3.30 each
8 July 20X4	10 units bought at $3.50 each
12 July 20X4	8 units sold at $4.00 each

What was the value of closing inventory at 31 July, if the FIFO method of inventory valuation is used?

A $31.50

B $36.00

C $39.00

D $41.00

102 **What would be the effect on an entity's profit for the year of discovering that inventory with cost of $1,250 and a net realisable value of $1,000 had been omitted from the original inventory valuation?**

A   An increase of $1,250

B   An increase of $1,000

C   A decrease of $250

D   No effect at all

103 S Co sells three products – Basic, Super and Luxury. The following information was available at the year-end:

	Basic	Super	Luxury
	$ per unit	$ per unit	$ per unit
Original cost	6	9	18
Estimated selling price	9	12	15
Selling and distribution costs	1	4	5
	units	units	units
Units in inventory	200	250	150

What was the valuation of inventory at the year-end?

$ ☐

104 **In times of rising prices, the valuation of inventory using the first in, first out method, as opposed to the weighted average cost method, will result in which ONE of the following combinations?**

	Cost of sales	Profit	Closing inventory
A	Lower	Higher	Higher
B	Lower	Higher	Lower
C	Higher	Lower	Higher
D	Higher	Higher	Lower

105 If an entity uses the periodic weighted average cost method to value closing inventory, which of the following statements is true?

A   Unit average cost is recalculated each time there is a purchase of inventory

B   Unit average cost is recalculated each time there is a sale of goods

C   Unit average cost is calculated once only at the end of an accounting period

D   Unit average cost is recalculated each time there is a purchase or a sale

106 If an entity uses the continuous weighted average cost method to value closing inventory, which of the following statements is true?

A   Unit average cost is recalculated each time there is a purchase of inventory

B   Unit average cost is calculated once only at the end of an accounting period

C   Unit average cost is recalculated each time there is a sale of goods

D   Unit average cost is recalculated each time there is a purchase or a sale

107 If an entity uses the continuous weighted average cost method to value closing inventory, what is the value of closing inventory based upon the following information?

2 Feb   Purchased 10 units at a cost of $5.00 per unit

5 Feb   Sold 6 units at a price of $8 per unit

7 Feb   Purchased 10 units at a cost of $6.50 per unit

$ [   ]

108 If an entity uses the periodic weighted average cost method to value closing inventory, what is the value of closing inventory based upon the following information?

12 Apr   Purchased 10 units at a cost of $5.00 per unit

15 Apr   Sold 6 units at a price of $8 per unit

17 Apr   Purchased 10 units at a cost of $6.50 per unit

$ [   ]

109 Using the periodic weighted average cost method to value closing inventory, what is the value of cost of sales for April based upon the following information?

1 Apr   Opening inventory 4 units at a cost of $4.00 per unit

12 Apr   Purchased 10 units at a cost of $5.00 per unit

15 Apr   Sold 6 units at a price of $8 per unit

17 Apr   Purchased 10 units at a cost of $6.00 per unit

25 Apr   Sold 8 units at a price of $8.50 per unit

$ [   ]

110 Using the continuous weighted average cost method to value closing inventory, what is the value of cost of sales for April based upon the following information?

1 Apr   Opening inventory 4 units at a cost of $4.00 per unit

12 Apr   Purchased 10 units at a cost of $5.00 per unit

15 Apr   Sold 6 units at a price of $8 per unit

17 Apr   Purchased 10 units at a cost of $6.00 per unit

25 Apr   Sold 8 units at a price of $8.50 per unit

$ [   ]

TANGIBLE NON-CURRENT ASSETS

111 The non-current asset register shows a carrying amount for non-current assets of $85,600; the ledger accounts include a cost balance of $185,000 and an accumulated depreciation balance of $55,000.

Which one of the following statements may explain the discrepancy?

A   The omission of an addition of land costing $30,000 from the ledger account and the omission of the disposal of an asset from the register (cost $25,600 and accumulated depreciation at disposal $11,200).

B   The omission of the revaluation of an asset upwards by $16,600 and the depreciation charge of $20,000 from the ledger account and the omission of the disposal of an asset with a carrying amount of $41,000 from the register.

C   The omission of the disposal of an asset from the ledger accounts (cost $25,600 and accumulated depreciation at disposal $11,200) and the omission of an addition of land costing $30,000 from the register.

D   The omission of an upwards revaluation by $16,400 from the register and the accidental debiting of the depreciation charge of $28,000 to the accumulated depreciation ledger account.

112 Laurie bought an asset on the 1st January 20X4 for $235,000. He has depreciated it at 30% using the reducing balance method. On 1st January 20X7, Laurie revalued the asset to $300,000.

What accounting entries should Laurie post to record the revaluation?

		$		$
A	Dr Non-current assets – cost	65,000	Cr Revaluation surplus	219,395
	Dr Accumulated depreciation	154,395		
B	Dr Non-current assets – cost	65,000	Cr Revaluation surplus	276,500
	Dr Accumulated depreciation	211,500		
C	Dr Revaluation surplus	219,395	Dr Non-current assets – cost	65,000
			Dr Accumulated depreciation	154,395
D	Dr Revaluation surplus	276,500	Dr Non-current assets – cost	65,000
			Dr Accumulated depreciation	211,500

113 **Which ONE of the following statements is true in relation to the non-current asset register?**

A   It is an alternative name for the non-current asset ledger account.

B   It is a list of the physical non-current assets rather than their financial cost.

C   It is a schedule of planned maintenance of non-current assets for use by the plant engineer.

D   It is a schedule of the cost and other information about each individual non-current asset.

114 The plant and equipment account in the records of C Co for the year ended 31 December 20X6 is shown below:

Plant and equipment – cost

	$		$
Balance b/f	960,000		
1 July Cash	48,000	30 Sept Disposals	84,000
		Balance c/f	924,000
	————		————
	1,008,000		1,008,000
	————		————

C Co's policy is to charge straight line depreciation at 20% per year on a pro rata basis.

What should be the charge for depreciation in C Co's statement of profit or loss for the year ended 31 December 20X6?

$ [   ]

115 On 1 January 20X7, Z Co purchased an item of plant. The invoice showed:

	$
Cost of plant	48,000
Delivery to factory	400
One year warranty covering breakdown	800
	————
	49,200
	————

Modifications to the factory building costing $2,200 were necessary to enable the plant to be installed.

What amount should be capitalised for the plant in Z Co's accounting records?

$ [   ]

116 A non-current asset was purchased at the beginning of Year 1 for $2,400 and depreciated at 20% per annum using the reducing balance method. At the beginning of Year 4 it was sold for $1,200.

The result of this was:

A   a loss on disposal of $240.00

B   a loss on disposal of $28.80

C   a profit on disposal of $28.80

D   a profit on disposal of $240.00

117 A business' non-current assets had a carrying amount of $125,000. An asset which had cost $12,000 was sold for $9,000, at a profit of $2,000.

What is the revised carrying amount of non-current assets?

A $113,000

B $118,000

C $125,000

D $127,000

118 W Co bought a new printing machine from abroad. The cost of the machine was $80,000. The installation costs were $5,000 and the employees received training on how to use the machine, at a cost of $2,000. Before using the machine to print customers' orders, pre-production safety testing was undertaken at a cost of $1,000.

What should be the cost of the machine in W Co's statement of financial position?

$ _____

119 A non-current asset was disposed of for $2,200 during the last accounting year. It had been purchased exactly three years earlier for $5,000, with an expected residual value of $500, and had been depreciated on the reducing balance basis, at 20% per annum.

What was the profit or loss on disposal?

A $360 loss

B $150 loss

C $104 loss

D $200 profit

120 At the end of its financial year, Tanner Co had the following non-current assets:

Land and buildings at cost	$10.4 million
Land and buildings: accumulated depreciation	$0.12 million

Tanner Co decided to revalue its land and buildings at the year-end to $15 million.

What will be the value of the revaluation surplus if the revaluation is accounted for?

$ _____

FA (FFA): FINANCIAL ACCOUNTING

121 **Which ONE of the following items should be accounted for as capital expenditure?**

    A   The cost of painting a building

    B   The replacement of broken windows in a building

    C   The purchase of a car by a car dealer for re-sale

    D   Legal fees incurred on the purchase of a building

122 F Co purchased a car for $12,000 on 1 April 20X1 which has been depreciated at 20% each year straight line, assuming no residual value. F Co's policy is to charge a full year's depreciation in the year of purchase and no depreciation in the year of sale. The car was traded in for a replacement vehicle on 1 August 20X4 for an agreed figure of $5,000.

What was the profit or loss on the disposal of the vehicle for the year ended 31 December 20X4?

    A   Loss $2,200

    B   Loss $1,400

    C   Loss $200

    D   Profit $200

123 At 30 September 20X2, the following balances existed in the records of Lambda Co:

Plant and equipment:

Cost $860,000

Accumulated depreciation $397,000

During the year ended 30 September 20X3, plant with a written down value of $37,000 was sold for $49,000. The plant had originally cost $80,000. Plant purchased during the year cost $180,000. It is Lambda Co's policy to charge a full year's depreciation in the year of acquisition of an asset and none in the year of sale, using a rate of 10% on the straight line basis.

What was the carrying amount that should appear in Lambda Co's statement of financial position at 30 September 20X3 for plant and equipment?

$ [   ]

124 **Which of the following statements best describes depreciation?**

    A   It is a means of spreading the payment for non-current assets over a period of years.

    B   It is a decline in the market value of the assets.

    C   It is a means of spreading the net cost of non-current assets over their estimated useful life.

    D   It is a means of estimating the amount of money needed to replace the assets.

32   KAPLAN PUBLISHING

125 On 1 January 20X8, Wootton has a building in its books which cost $380,000 with a carrying amount of $260,000. On 1 July 20X8, the asset was valued at $450,000 and Wootton wishes to include that valuation in its books. Wootton's accounting policy is to depreciate buildings at the rate of 3% on a straight-line basis.

What was depreciation charge included in the statement of profit or loss for the year ended 31 December 20X8?

$ [   ]

126 A car was purchased by a newsagent business in May 20X1 as follows:

	$
Cost	10,000
Vehicle tax – 1 year	150
Total	10,150

The business adopted a date of 31 December as its year-end.

The car was traded in for a replacement vehicle in August 20X5 at an agreed value of $5,000.

It was depreciated at 25 per cent per annum using the reducing-balance method, charging a full year's depreciation in the year of purchase and none in the year of sale.

What was the profit or loss on disposal of the vehicle during the year ended December 20X5?

A   Profit: $718

B   Profit: $781

C   Profit: $1,788

D   Profit: $1,836

127 **The reducing balance method of depreciating non-current assets is more appropriate than the straight-line method when:**

A   there is no expected residual value for the asset

B   the expected life of the asset is not capable of being estimated

C   the asset is expected to be replaced in a short period of time

D   the asset decreases in value less in later years than in the early years of use

128 SSG bought a machine at a cost of $40,000 on 1 January 20X1. The machine had an expected useful life of six years and an expected residual value of $10,000. The machine was depreciated using the straight-line basis on a monthly basis. At 31 December 20X4, the machine was sold for $15,000.

What was the profit or loss on disposal for inclusion in the financial statements for the year ended 31 December 20X4?

$ [   ]   Profit / loss*   * Delete which does not apply

129 Liza bought a guillotine for her framing business for $20,000 on 1 July 20X7. She expected the guillotine to have a useful life of ten years and a residual value of $500. On 1 July 20X8, Liza revised these estimates and now believes the guillotine to have a remaining useful life of 5 years and no residual value.

What was the depreciation charge for the year ended 30 June 20X9?

$ [   ]

130 The following information of P Co is available for the year ended 31 October 20X2:

Property	$
Cost as at 1 November 2011	102,000
Accumulated depreciation as at 1 November 20X1	(20,400)
	————
	81,600

On 1 November 20X1, P Co revalued the property to $150,000.

P Co's accounting policy is to charge depreciation on a straight-line basis over 50 years. On revaluation there was no change to the overall useful economic life. It has also chosen not to make an annual transfer of the excess depreciation on revaluation between the revaluation surplus and retained earnings.

What should be the balance on the revaluation surplus and the depreciation charge as shown in P Co's financial statements for the year ended 31 October 20X2?

	Depreciation charge $	Revaluation surplus $
A	3,750	68,400
B	3,750	48,000
C	3,000	68,400
D	3,000	48,000

131 A business has an accounting year end of 31 March. It purchased a truck on 1 April 20X3 at a total cost of $21,000, including $1,000 for one year of insurance cover.

At the date of purchase, the truck had an estimated useful life to the business of eight years, and had an estimated residual value of $3,000. The truck was traded in for a replacement vehicle on 31 March 20X8 at an agreed valuation of $10,000. The truck was depreciated on a straight-line basis, with a pro-rated charge in the year of acquisition and disposal.

Calculate the profit or loss on disposal of the truck.

$ [   ] Profit / loss*   * Delete which does not apply

132   Complete the following statement by making one choice from each option available.

When an entity has revalued a non-current asset, it is (Option 1)...............to account for excess depreciation arising on the revaluation. When excess depreciation is accounted for, the accounting adjustment is reflected in (Option 2)...........................

Option 1   compulsory/optional
Option 2   profit or loss/other comprehensive income/the statement of changes in equity

133   A business has an accounting year end of 30 June. It purchased an item of plant on 1 April 20X5 as follows:

	$
Cost	15,000
3 year maintenance agreement	450
Total	15,450

At the date of purchase, the item of plant and equipment had an estimated useful life to the business of five years and an estimated residual value of $2,000. This item of plant was traded in for a replacement item on 30 September 20X8 at an agreed valuation of $5,000.

It has been depreciated at 20 per cent per annum on a straight-line basis, with a pro-rated charge in the year of acquisition and disposal.

Calculate the profit or loss on disposal of the item of plant.

$ [   ]   Profit / loss*   * Delete which does not apply

INTANGIBLE ASSETS

134   Which ONE of the following statements is correct?

A   If all the conditions specified in IAS 38 Intangible assets are met, the directors can chose whether to capitalise the development expenditure or not.

B   Amortisation of capitalised development expenditure will appear as an item in an entity's statement of changes in equity.

C   Capitalised development costs are shown in the statement of financial position as non-current assets.

D   Capitalised development expenditure must be amortised over a period not exceeding five years.

135   Complete the following statement by selecting the appropriate wording from the choice available.

When accounting for intangible assets using the revaluation model, movements in the carrying amount are..

A   accounted for in other comprehensive income and other components of equity

B   accounted for in the statement of profit or loss only

C   accounted for in other comprehensive income only

D   accounted for on other components of equity only

136 **What is the correct accounting treatment for an intangible asset with an indefinite useful life?**

    A   It is recognised at cost for as long as the entity has the intangible asset.

    B   It is recognised at cost and is subject to an annual impairment review.

    C   It is recognised at cost and the entity must make an estimate of estimated useful life so that it can be amortised.

    D   It cannot be recognised as an intangible asset as it would not be possible to calculate an annual amortisation charge.

137 **Identify whether or not each of the following items should be capitalised as intangible assets from the following list.**

	Capitalised	Not capitalised
Employment costs of staff conducting research activities		
Cost of constructing a working model of a new product		
Materials and consumables costs associated with conducting scientific experiments		
Licence purchased to permit production and sale of a product for ten years		

138 **Complete the following statement by selecting the appropriate wording from the choice available.**

When accounting for intangible assets using the cost model, annual impairment charges are:

    A   accounted for in other comprehensive income and other components of equity

    B   accounted for in the statement of profit or loss only

    C   accounted for in other comprehensive income only

    D   accounted for on other components of equity only

139 **Classify each of the following costs as either a research expense or as an intangible asset.**

	Research expense	Intangible asset
Market research costs		
Patented product design costs		
Product advertising		
Employee training costs		

140 Which one of the following statements best defines an intangible asset?

A   An intangible asset is an asset with no physical substance

B   An intangible asset is always generated internally by a business

C   An intangible asset is an asset which cannot be sold

D   An intangible asset is a purchased asset which has no physical substance

141 Geranium is engaged in the following research and development projects:

Identify how the costs of each project should be accounted for in the financial statements.

	Written off as an expense	*Capitalised as an asset*
Project 1 – It is applying a new technology to the production of heat resistant fabric. Upon completion, the fabric will be used in the production of uniforms for the emergency services. Geranium has sufficient resources and the intention to complete the project.		
Project 2 – It is testing whether a particular substance can be used as an appetite suppressant. If this is the case, it is expected be sold worldwide in chemists and pharmacies.		
Project 3 – It is developing a material for use in kitchens which is self-cleaning and germ resistant. A competitor is currently developing a similar material and, for this reason, Geranium is unsure whether its project will be completed.		

142 Merlot Co is engaged in a number of research and development projects during the year ended 31 December 20X5:

Project A – A project to investigate the properties of a chemical compound. Costs incurred on this project during the year ended 31 December 20X5 were $34,000.

Project B – A project to develop a new process which will save production time in the manufacture of widgets. This project commenced on 1 January 20X5 and met the capitalisation criteria on 31 August 20X5. The cost incurred during 20X5 was $78,870 to 31 August and $27,800 from 1 September.

Project C – A development project which was completed on 30 June 20X5. Development costs incurred up to 31 December 20X4 were $290,000, with a further $19,800 incurred between January and June 20X5. Production and sales of the new product commenced on 1 September and are expected to last 36 months.

What amount should be expensed to the statement of profit or loss and other comprehensive income of Merlot Co in respect of these projects in the year ended 31 December 20X5?

$ _____

143 Identify which THREE of the following statements are true in relation to application of IAS 38 Intangible Assets.

	True
Research costs should be expensed to the statement of profit or loss.	
All types of goodwill can be capitalised.	
Capitalised development costs that no longer meet the criteria specified by IAS 38 must be written off to the statement of profit or loss.	
Capitalised development costs are amortised from the date the assets is available to use or sell.	
Research costs written off can be re-capitalised when the developed asset is feasible.	
Only purchased intangibles can be capitalised.	

ACCRUALS AND PREPAYMENTS

144 Leddley owns two properties which it rents to tenants. In the year ended 31 December 20X6, it received $280,000 in respect of property 1 and $160,000 in respect of property 2. Balances on the prepaid and accrued income accounts were as follows:

	31 December 20X6	*31 December 20X5*
Property 1	13,400 Dr	12,300 Cr
Property 2	6,700 Cr	5,400 Dr

What amount should be credited to the statement of profit or loss for the year ended 31 December 20X6 in respect of rental income?

$ [   ]

145 Troy Co has a property rental business and received cash totalling $838,600 from tenants during the year ended 31 December 20X6.

Figures for rent in advance and in arrears at the beginning and end of the year were:

	31 December 20X5	*31 December 20X6*
	$	$
Rent received in advance	102,600	88,700
Rent in arrears (all subsequently received)	42,300	48,400

What amount should appear in Troy Co's statement of profit or loss for the year ended 31 December 20X6 for rental income?

$ [   ]

146 Details of B Co's insurance policy are shown below:

Premium for year ended 31 March 20X6 paid April 20X5 $10,800

Premium for year ending 31 March 20X7 paid April 20X6 $12,000

What figures should be included in the B Co's financial statements for the year ended 30 June 20X6?

	Statement of profit or loss	Statement of financial position
	$	$
A	11,100	9,000 prepayment
B	11,700	9,000 prepayment
C	11,100	9,000 accrual
D	11,700	9,000 accrual

147 Vine Co sublets part of its office accommodation to earn rental income. The rent is received quarterly in advance on 1 January, 1 April, 1 July and 1 October. The annual rent has been $24,000 for some years, but it was increased to $30,000 from 1 July 20X5.

What amounts for rent should appear in Vine Co's financial statements for the year ended 31 January 20X6?

	Profit or loss	Statement of financial position
A	$27,500	$5,000 in accrued income
B	$27,000	$2,500 in accrued income
C	$27,000	$2,500 in prepaid income
D	$27,500	$5,000 in prepaid income

148 On 1 May 20X0, A commenced business and paid an annual rent charge of $1,800 for the period to 30 April 20X1.

What is the charge to the statement of profit or loss and the entry in the statement of financial position for the accounting period ended 30 November 20X0?

A $1,050 charge to statement of profit or loss and prepayment of $750 in the statement of financial position.

B $1,050 charge to statement of profit or loss and accrual of $750 in the statement of financial position.

C $1,800 charge to statement of profit or loss and no entry in the statement of financial position.

D $750 charge to statement of profit or loss and prepayment of $1,050 in the statement of financial position.

149 At 1 September, the motor expenses account showed 4 months' insurance prepaid of $80 and fuel costs accrued of $95. During September, the outstanding fuel bill was paid, plus further bills of $245. At 30 September there was a further outstanding fuel bill of $120.

What was the expense included in the statement of profit or loss for motor expenses for September?

$ [   ]

150 The electricity account for the year ended 30 June 20X3 was as follows:

	$
Opening balance for electricity accrued at 1 July 20X2	300
Payments made during the year:	
1 August 20X2 for three months to 31 July 20X2	600
1 November 20X2 for three months to 31 October 20X2	720
1 February 20X3 for three months to 31 January 20X3	900
30 June 20X3 for three months to 30 April 20X3	840

What was the expense charged to the statement of profit or loss for the year ended 30 June 20X3 and the accrual at 30 June 20X3?

Accrued at June 20X3   P&L a/c expense

$ [   ] $ [   ]

151 The annual insurance premium for S for the period 1 July 20X3 to 30 June 20X4 was $13,200, which is 10% more than the previous year. Insurance premiums are paid on 1 July.

What is the statement of profit or loss charge for insurance for the year ended 31 December 20X3?

$ [   ]

152 Farthing's year-end is 30 September. On 1 January 20X6 Farthing took out a loan of $100,000 with annual interest of 12%. The interest is payable in equal instalments on the first day of April, July, October and January in arrears.

How much should be charged to the statement of profit or loss account for the year ended 30 September 20X6, and how much should be accrued on the statement of financial position?

	Statement of profit or loss	Statement of financial position
A	$12,000	$3,000
B	$9,000	$3,000
C	$9,000	Nil
D	$6,000	$3,000

153 On 1 January 20X3, a business had prepaid insurance of $10,000. On 1 August 20X3, it paid, in full, the annual insurance invoice of $36,000, to cover the twelve months to 31 July 20X4.

What was the amount charged in the statement of profit or loss and the amount shown in the statement of financial position for the year ended 31 December 20X3?

	Statement of profit or loss	*Statement of financial position*
	$	$
A	5,000	24,000
B	22,000	23,000
C	25,000	21,000
D	36,000	15,000

154 **Which of the following statements is false?**

A Accruals decrease profit

B Accrued income decreases profit

C A prepayment is an asset

D An accrual is a liability

155 On 9 October, Parker paid his heat and power bill for the three months ended 30 September 20X4. The bill included a meter rental charge of $60 for the three months ending 31 December 20X4 and a usage charge of $135 for the three month period to 30 September 20X4. Parker has an accounting year end date of 31 October 20X4.

Which TWO of the following adjustments are required in relation to the heat and power expense as at 31 October 20X4?

A Accrual of $40

B Accrual of $45

C Prepayment of $40

D Prepayment of $45

IRRECOVERABLE DEBTS AND ALLOWANCES FOR RECEIVABLES

156 In the statement of financial position at 31 December 20X5, Boris reported net receivables of $12,000. During 20X6 he made sales on credit of $125,000 and received cash from credit customers amounting to $115,500. At 31 December 20X6, Boris decided to write off debts of $7,100 and increase the specific allowance for receivables by $950 to $2,100.

What was the net receivables figure reported in the statement of financial position at 31 December 20X6?

A $12,300

B $13,450

C $14,400

D $15,550

157 The following balances relate to Putney:

	$
Receivables at 1.1.X8	34,500
Cash received from credit customers	247,790
Contra with payables	1,200
Cash sales	24,000
Irrecoverable debts	18,600
Increase in allowance for receivables	12,500
Discounts received	15,670
Receivables at 31.12.X8	45,000

What is the revenue figure reported by Putney in the year ended 31 December 20X8?

A $275,690

B $278,090

C $320,690

D $302,090

158 The following account has been extracted from the general ledger of Purdey:

Receivables ledger control account

	$		$
Balance b/f	84,700	Irrecoverable debts	4,300
Contra with payables ledger control account	5,000	Increase in allowance for receivables	6,555
Discounts received	21,100	Cash received from credit customers	625,780
Credit sales	644,000		
Cash sales	13,500	Balance c/f	131,665
	768,300		768,300

After amendment, what is the correct receivables' balance carried forward?

A $100,175

B $93,620

C $89,320

D $97,920

159 Newell's receivables ledger control account shows a balance at the end of the year of $58,200 before making the following adjustments:

(i) Newell decides to write off debts amounting to $8,900 as he believes they are irrecoverable.

(ii) He also decides to make specific allowance for Carroll's debt of $1,350, Juff's debt of $750 and Mary's debt of $1,416.

Newell's allowance for receivables at the previous year end was $5,650.

What is the charge to the statement of profit or loss in respect of the above information?

A $6,766

B $11,034

C $6,829

D $10,971

160 At 1 July 20X5, V Co's allowance for receivables was $48,000. At 30 June 20X6, trade receivables amounted to $838,000. It was decided to write off $72,000 of these debts and adjust the specific allowance for receivables to $60,000.

What are the final amounts for inclusion in V Co's statement of financial position at 30 June 20X6?

	Trade receivables	Allowance for receivables	Net balance
	$	$	$
A	838,000	60,000	778,000
B	766,000	60,000	706,000
C	766,000	108,000	658,000
D	838,000	108,000	730,000

161 In the year ended 30 September 20X8, Fauntleroy had sales of $7,000,000. The year-end receivables amounted to 5% of annual sales. At the year end, Fauntleroy's specific allowance for receivables equated to 4% of receivables. He also identified that this amount was 20% higher than at the previous year end.

During the year irrecoverable debts amounting to $3,200 were written off and debts amounting to $450 and previously written off were recovered.

What was the irrecoverable debt expense for the year?

A $5,083

B $5,550

C $5,583

D $16,750

162 On 1 January 20X3 Tipton's trade receivables were $10,000. The following relates to the year ended 31 December 20X3:

	$
Credit sales	100,000
Cash receipts	90,000
Contra with payables	800
Discounts received	700

Cash receipts include $1,000 in respect of a receivable previously written off.

What was the value of receivables at 31 December 20X3?

A $19,300

B $20,200

C $20,800

D $20,700

163 G Co has been notified that a customer has been declared bankrupt. G Co had previously made allowance for this receivable.

Which of the following is the correct double entry?

	Dr	*Cr*
A	Allowance for receivables	Receivables' ledger control account
B	Receivables' ledger control account	Irrecoverable debts account
C	Irrecoverable debts account	Receivables' ledger control account
D	Receivables' ledger control account	Allowance for receivables

164 Headington Co is owed $37,500 by its customers at the start, and $39,000 at the end, of its year ended 31 December 20X8.

During the period, cash sales of $263,500 and credit sales of $357,500 were made, contras with the payables ledger control account amounted to $15,750 and discounts received $21,400. Irrecoverable debts of $10,500 were written off. Headington Co also identified that the increase in the specific allowance for receivables required at 31 December 20X8 was $8,750.

How much cash was received from credit customers during the year ended 31 December 20X8?

A $329,750

B $593,175

C $593,250

D $614,650

165 The sales revenue of J Co was $2 million and its receivables were 5% of sales. J Co wishes to have a specific allowance for receivables of $4,000, which would make the allowance one-third higher than the current allowance.

How will the profit for the period be affected by the change in allowance?

A   Profit will be reduced by $1,000

B   Profit will be increased by $1,000

C   Profit will be reduced by $1,333

D   Profit will be increased by $1,333

166 Abacus Co started the year with total receivables of $87,000 and an allowance for receivables of $2,500.

During the year, two specific debts were written off, one for $800 and the other for $550. A debt of $350 that had been written off as irrecoverable in the previous year was paid during the year. At the year-end, total receivables were $90,000 and the allowance for receivables was $2,300.

What is the charge to the statement of profit or loss for the year in respect of irrecoverable debts and allowance for receivables?

A $800

B $1,000

C $1,150

D $1,550

167 **An increase in the allowance for receivables results in:**

A   an increase in net current assets

B   a decrease in net current assets

C   An increase in sales

D   A decrease in drawings

168 At the end of 20X7, Chester's receivable's balance is $230,000. He wishes to make specific allowance for Emily's debt of $450 and Lulu's debt of $980. Irrecoverable debts of $11,429 should be written off.

What amount should be charged or credited to the statement of profit or loss in respect of irrecoverable debts and the allowance for receivables if the allowance at the start of the year was $11,700?

A $1,159 Dr

B $1,230 Dr

C $200 Cr

D $12,930 Dr

169 Which ONE of the following is not a benefit of providing credit to customers?

A It may result in increased sales

B It may encourage customer loyalty

C It may attract new customers

D It may improve the cash flow of the business

170 Which ONE of the following best explains the purpose of an aged receivables analysis?

A To ensure that credit is not extended to unapproved customers

B To ensure that credit customers regularly purchase goods from the business

C To keep track of outstanding debts and identify overdue amounts to follow up

D To keep track of customer addresses

171 On 31 March 20X4, the balance on the receivables control account of P Co was $425,700. The book-keeper has identified that the following adjustments for receivables are required:

Irrecoverable debt recovered $2,000

Specific allowance required $2,400

It was decided that amounts totalling $8,466 should be written off as irrecoverable. The allowance for receivables on 1 April 20X3 was $1,900.

What was the expense for irrecoverable debts and allowance for receivables for the year ended 31 March 20X4?

$ [   ]

PROVISIONS AND CONTINGENCIES

172 For each of the items noted below, identify whether or not a provision is required in accordance with IAS 37 Provisions, Contingent Liabilities and Contingent Assets?

	Provision required	Provision not required
A retail outlet has a policy of providing refunds over and above the statutory requirement to do so. This policy is well publicised and customers have made use of this facility in the past.		
A customer has made a legal claim against an entity, claiming that faulty goods sold to them caused damage to their property. The entity's lawyers have advised that the claim will possibly succeed and, if it does, compensation of $10,000 will be payable.		

173 **Which of the following statements about the requirements relating to IAS 37 Provisions, Contingent Liabilities and Contingent Assets are correct?**

(1)   A contingent asset should be disclosed by note if an inflow of economic benefits is probable.

(2)   No disclosure of a contingent liability is required if the possibility of a transfer of economic benefits arising is remote.

(3)   Contingent assets must not be recognised in financial statements unless an inflow of economic benefits is virtually certain to arise.

A   All three statements are correct

B   (1) and (2) only

C   (1) and (3) only

D   (2) and (3) only

174 The following items need to be considered in finalising the financial statements of Q Co:

(1)   Q Co gives warranties on its products. Q Co's statistics show that about 5% of sales give rise to a warranty claim.

(2)   Q Co has guaranteed the overdraft of another entity. The likelihood of a liability arising under the guarantee is assessed as possible.

What is the correct action to be taken in the financial statements of Q Co for these items?

	Create a provision	*Disclose by note only*	*No action*
A	(1)	(2)	
B		(1)	(2)
C	(1) and (2)		
D		(1) and (2)	

175 **Which one the following statements relating to the requirements of IAS 37 Provisions, Contingent Liabilities and Contingent Assets is correct?**

A   A contingent asset must always be recognised and accounted for in the financial statements.

B   A contingent asset must always be disclosed in the notes to the financial statements.

C   A contingent liability must always be disclosed in the notes to the financial statements if it is regarded as possible.

D   A contingent liability must always be disclosed in the notes to the financial statements if it is regarded as probable.

176 Which one the following statements relating to the requirements of IAS 37 Provisions, Contingent Liabilities and Contingent Assets is correct?

A   A contingent asset must be recognised and accounted for in the financial statements if it is regarded as probable.

B   A contingent asset must never be recognised in the financial statements.

C   A contingent liability must either be recognised and accounted for in the financial statements, or disclosed in the notes to the financial statements.

D   A contingent liability may not be required to be accounted for or disclosed in the notes to the financial statements under certain circumstances.

177 Which of the following statements are correct in relation to provisions and liabilities?

(1)   A provision will always be classified as falling due for payment within twelve months of the reporting date, whereas a liability may be classified as either current or non-current.

(2)   A provision requires judgement and estimation to quantify the amount and/or the date of payment, whereas a liability is normally capable of precise calculation and the date of payment can be determined.

(3)   A provision meets the definition of a liability, but is subject to uncertainty regarding the exact amount or date of the future outflow of economic benefits.

A   (1) and (2)

B   (2) and (3)

C   (3) and (1)

D   None of the above

178 Driller Co undertakes oil and gas exploration activities. One of the conditions of the operating licence is that Driller must make good any damage caused to the local environment as a result of its exploration activities. As at the year-end date of 31 August 20X4, Driller Co estimated that the cost of rectifying damage already caused at current exploration sites at $5 million. At that date Driller Co estimated that that the cost of rectifying expected future damage at current exploration sites at an additional $20 million. Driller Co also estimated that all current exploration sites will operate until 20X7 or beyond that date.

How should this information be reported in the financial statements of Driller Co for the year ended 31 August 20X4?

A   There should be a provision classified as a current liability for $5 million

B   There should be a provision classified as a current liability for $25 million

C   There should be a provision classified as a non-current liability for $5 million

D   There should be a provision classified as a non-current liability for $25 million

179 Recently, users of a new perfume have suffered blistering of the skin along with considerable pain and discomfort. Following investigation by the manufacturer, Fleur Co, it appears that product contamination occurred during the bottling process which was performed by Bottler. Fleur Co's legal representatives have advised it that it is probable that customers will make valid compensation claims totalling $3 million and that it is probable Fleur Co will be able to successfully counter-claim against Bottler for the same amount.

How should this information be reported in the financial statements of Fleur Co for the year ended 31 August 20X4?

A   There should be a provision for $3 million only recognised in the statement of financial position.

B   There should be a provision and an asset, each for $3 million, recognised in the statement of financial position.

C   No provision or asset should be recognised in the statement of financial position as the two amounts cancel each other.

D   There should be a provision for $3 million in the statement of financial position and a disclosure note only to deal with the contingent asset of the amount which may be recovered from Bottler.

180 Electrode manufactures vacuum cleaners and allows customers three months from the date of purchase to return cleaners if they are dissatisfied with the product for any reason. At 31 May 20X8, Electrode included a provision of $10,000 in the financial statements relating to the expected return of cleaners which had been sold before the year-end date. At 31 May 20X9, Electrode estimated that the amount of the provision should be changed to $13,000.

How should this information be accounted for in the financial statements for the year ended 31 May 20X9?

	Dr	Cr
A	Other comprehensive income $3,000	Provision $3,000
B	Provision $3,000	Other comprehensive income $3,000
C	Profit or loss $3,000	Provision $3,000
D	Provision $3,000	Profit or loss $3,000

181 During the year ended 30 April 20X7 Doolittle experienced a number of difficulties with employees. On 1 April 20X7 Doolittle dismissed an employee and subsequently received notice of a claim for unfair dismissal amounting to $50,000. Another employee suffered personal injury on 30 March 20X7 whilst operating machinery at work. On 30 May Doolittle received notice of a claim from that employee for compensation of $100,000. Doolittle's legal representatives have advised that the claim for unfair dismissal will probably be successful and result in a compensation award of $50,000 to the employee. They also advised that the compensation claim for injury suffered is regarded as possible, but not probable, that compensation will be payable. In the event that compensation was payable for personal injury suffered, an amount of $100,000 is a reliable estimate.

How should this information be accounted for in the financial statements of Doolittle for the year ended 30 April 20X7?

A   A provision should be recognised in the financial statement for $50,000 only.

B   A provision should be recognised in the financial statements for $50,000 plus a disclosure note included of the possible compensation payment relating to the personal injury claim.

C   A provision should be recognised in the financial statements for $150,000 only.

D   A provision should be recognised in the financial statements for $150,000 and a disclosure note included of the possible compensation payment relating to the personal injury claim.

CAPITAL STRUCTURE AND FINANCE COSTS

182 State whether each of the following statements is true or false.

	True	*False*
A rights issue capitalises the entity's reserves, which can be a disadvantage, as this can reduce the amount of reserves available for future dividends.		
A rights issue is offered to the entity's existing shareholders and is usually at a discounted price compared to the nominal value of a share.		

183 Which TWO items within the statement of financial position would change immediately following the issue of redeemable preference shares?

Selection

Cash

Retained earnings

Finance cost

Equity

Long-term debt

184 The statement of financial position of Cartwright Co shows closing retained earnings of $320,568. The statement of profit or loss showed profit of $79,285. Cartwright Co paid last year's dividend of $12,200 during the year and proposed a dividend of $13,500 at the year end. This had not been approved by the shareholders at the end of the year.

What is the opening retained earnings balance?

A $241,283

B $387,653

C $254,783

D $253,483

185 The following extract is from the statement of profit or loss of Gearing for the year ended 30 April 20X5:

	$
Profit before tax	68,000
Tax	(32,000)
Profit for the year	36,000

In addition to the profit above:

(1)   Gearing Co paid a dividend of $21,000 during the year.

(2)   A gain on revaluation of land resulted in a revaluation surplus of $18,000.

What total amount will be added to retained earnings at the end of the financial year?

$

186 **Which ONE of the following items would you exclude from the statement of changes in equity?**

A   Issued share capital

B   Bank loans

C   Revaluation surplus

D   Dividends paid

187 **Which TWO of the following statements are true?**

A   Redeemable preference shares are classified as a liability on the statement of financial position.

B   Irredeemable preference shares are classified as a liability on the statement of financial position.

C   Redeemable preference shares are classified as equity on the statement of financial position.

D   Irredeemable preference shares are classified as equity on the statement of financial position.

188 **Which ONE of the following statements is true in relation to a rights issue of shares by an entity?**

    A   No cash is received by the entity as a result of making the rights issue

    B   The entity issues shares for cash at market price of the shares

    C   The entity issues shares for cash at a price less than the market price of the shares

    D   None of the above

189 **Which ONE of the following statements is true in relation to a bonus issue of shares by an entity?**

    A   The entity issues shares for cash at a price less than the market price of the shares

    B   The entity issues shares for cash at market price of the shares

    C   No cash is received by the entity as a result of making the bonus issue

    D   None of the above

190 **State whether each of the following statements is true or false.**

	True	*False*
Dividends paid by an entity are excluded from the statement of changes in equity		
Dividends received by an entity are included in the statement of changes in equity.		
Dividends received by an entity are excluded from the statement of changes in equity.		
Dividends paid by an entity are included in the statement of changes in equity.		

191 **When an entity pays a dividend, what accounting entries are required to account for the transaction?**

	Debit	*Credit*
A	Share capital	Bank
B	Share premium	Bank
C	Retained earnings	Bank
D	Profit or loss	Bank

192 An entity made an issue of 20,000 $1 equity shares at a price of $1.75. What accounting entries are required to record the issue of shares?

> *Debit*   *Credit*

A   Debit Bank $35,000, and Credit Share capital $35,000

B   Debit Share capital $20,000, Debit Share premium $15,000 and Credit Bank $35,000

C   Debit Bank $35,000, Credit Share premium $20,000 and Credit Share capital $15,000

D   Debit Bank $35,000, Credit Share capital $20,000 and Credit Share premium $15,000

193 An entity, Taylor, has issued equity share capital of 250,000 shares with a nominal value of $0.50 each and a share premium account balance of $100,000.

What accounting entries are required if Taylor was to make a bonus issue of one share for four held?

	Debit		Credit	
A	Share capital	$62,500	Share premium	$62,500
B	Share premium	$31,250	Share capital	$31,250
C	Share capital	$31,250	Share premium	$31,250
D	Share capital	$62,500	Share premium	$62,500

194 Which of the following would you exclude from the statement of changes inequity?

A   Share premium

B   Revaluation reserve

C   Irredeemable preference shares

D   Redeemable preference shares

195 Which of the following statements are correct?

(1)   A limited company will always have both an issued share capital and a share premium account.

(2)   A limited company will always have an issued share capital account, and may also have a share premium account.

(3)   A limited company will always have ether a share premium account or a revaluation surplus account.

A   (1) only

B   (2) only

C   (1) and (3) only

D   (2) and (3) only

PREPARING A TRIAL BALANCE

FROM TRIAL BALANCE TO FINANCIAL STATEMENTS

196 Lord has extracted the following balances from his accounting records:

	$
Property, plant and equipment	209,000
Inventory	4,600
Payables	6,300
Receivables	5,900
Bank overdraft	790
Loan	50,000
Capital	100,000
Drawings	23,000
Sales	330,000
Purchases	168,200
Sales returns	7,000
Discounts received	?
Sundry expenses	73,890

He has forgotten to extract the balance on the discounts received account.

What was the balance on the discounts received account?

$ [   ]

197 Identify whether each of the following statements is true or false.

	True	False
The trial balance provides a check that no errors exist in the accounting records of a business.		
The trial balance is one of the financial statements prepared annually by an entity for its shareholders.		

198 Which of the following are limitations of the trial balance?

(1) It does not include all final figures to be included in the financial statements.

(2) It does not identify all errors of commission.

(3) It does not identify in which accounts errors have been made.

A   (1) and (2)

B   (2) and (3) only

C   All three

D   None of the above

199 The following is an extract from the trial balance of Gardeners:

	$	$
Non-current assets	50,000	
Inventory	2,600	
Capital		28,000
Receivables and payables	4,500	5,000
Allowance for receivables		320
Cash	290	
Purchases and Sales revenue	78,900	120,000
Rental expense	3,400	
Sundry expenses	13,900	
Bank interest		270
	153,590	153,590

The following items have not yet been accounted for:

- Rent of $200 was prepaid.
- Inventory valuation at the end of the accounting period was $1,900.
- The allowance for receivables should be amended to $200.

What was the profit for the year?

$ [   ]

200 The following year-end adjustments are required to a set of draft financial statements:

- Closing inventory of $45,700 to be recorded.

- Depreciation at 20% straight line to be charged on assets with a cost of $470,800.

- An Irrecoverable debt of $230 to be written off.

- Deferred income of $6,700 to be recorded.

What is the impact on net assets of these adjustments?

A $55,390 increase

B $55,390 decrease

C $41,990 decrease

D $41,990 increase

201 The following is an extract from the trial balance of Ardvark Co:

	Dr	Cr
	$	$
Premises and accumulated depreciation	500,000	120,000
Inventory		23,000
Share capital	200,000	
Retained earnings		105,000
Receivables and payables	43,500	35,900
Carriage in		1,500
Allowance for receivables		3,400
Bank overdraft	1,010	
Sales revenue		500,080
Purchases	359,700	
Sales returns	10,300	
Sundry expenses	14,000	
Suspense		339,630
	1,128,510	1,128,510

After making corrections for errors in the list of balances, what is the revised balance on the suspense account?

A $15,710 Dr

B $14,730 Dr

C $13,390 Dr

D $33,630 Dr

202 The following is the extract of Jenny's trial balance as at 31 December 20X7:

The policy of the business is to charge depreciation at 10% per annum on a straight line basis.

	DR	CR
	$	$
Plant and machinery	50,000	
Plant and machinery accumulated depreciation		15,000

What is the depreciation charge to the statement of profit or loss for the year ended 31 December 20X7 and the closing carrying amount as at 31 December 20X7?

	Depreciation charge	Carrying amount
	$	$
A	3,500	31,500
B	5,000	30,000
C	5,000	45,000
D	3,500	30,000

203 The following is the extract of Jordan's trial balance as at 31 December 20X7:

	DR
	$
Rent	22,000
Insurance	30,000

The following notes have been provided:

(i) The monthly rent charge is $2,000.

(ii) The annual insurance charge for the above year is $28,000.

What is the charge for rent and insurance for the year and the closing accrual and prepayment?

		Charge for the year $		Closing balance $
A	Rent	22,000	Rent prepayment	2,000
	Insurance	28,000	Insurance prepayment	2,000
B	Rent	22,000	Rent accrual	2,000
	Insurance	30,000	Insurance prepayment	2,000
C	Rent	24,000	Rent accrual	2,000
	Insurance	28,000	Insurance prepayment	2,000
D	Rent	24,000	Rent accrual	2,000
	Insurance	30,000	Insurance accrual	2,000

204 The following is the extract of Jim's trial balance as at 31 December 20X7:

	DR	CR
	$	$
Receivables	29,600	
Allowance for receivables		3,100
Irrecoverable debts	1,600	

The following notes are provided.

(i) Additional irrecoverable debts of $3,000 were identified at the year end.

(ii) It has been decided to make an allowance for receivables of $2,660 on the adjusted receivables at the year end.

What was the total irrecoverable debts expense (irrecoverable debts and allowances for receivables) for the year ended 31 December 20X7 and the closing net receivables balance as at 31 December 20X7?

	Irrecoverable debts expense $	Net receivables $
A	4,160	23,940
B	5,040	23,940
C	2,560	21,830
D	4,000	19,800

205 The following is the extract of Julian's trial balance as at 31 December 20X7:

	DR $	CR $
Motor vehicles	50,000	
Motor vehicles accumulated depreciation		21,875

The policy of the business is to charge depreciation at 25% per annum on a reducing balance basis.

What is the statement of profit or loss depreciation charge for the year ended 31 December 20X7 and the closing carrying amount as at 31 December 20X7?

Calculations to be rounded to the nearest $.

	Depreciation charge $	Carrying amount $
A	12,500	15,625
B	7,031	42,969
C	12,500	37,500
D	7,031	21,094

206 **Which TWO of the following errors could cause the total of the debit column and the total of the credit column of the trial balance not to agree?**

	Selection
A casting error of $300 made when totalling the sales day book	
A transposition error made when posting the total of cash payments into the general ledger	
Discount received was included in the trial balance as a debit balance	
A cheque paid to a supplier recorded was debited to cash and correctly recognised in trade payables	

CONTROL ACCOUNT RECONCILIATIONS

207 **What is the most important reason for producing a trial balance prior to preparing the financial statements?**

A   It confirms the accuracy of the ledger accounts

B   It provides all the figures necessary to prepare the financial statements

C   It shows that the ledger accounts contain debit and credit entries of an equal value

D   It enables the accountant to calculate any adjustments required

208 A payables' ledger control account showed a credit balance of $768,420. The payables' ledger totalled $781,200.

Which one of the following possible errors could account in full for the difference?

A   A contra against a receivables' ledger debit balance of $6,390 has been entered on the credit side of the payables' ledger control account.

B   Cash purchases cash purchases of $28,400 was entered to the debit side of the payables' ledger control account instead of the correct figure for discounts received of $15,620.

C $12,780 cash paid to a supplier was entered on the credit side of the supplier's account on the payables' ledger.

D   The total of discounts received $6,390 has been entered on the credit side of the payables' ledger control account.

209 The payables' ledger control account below contains a number of errors:

Payables' ledger control account

	$		$
Balance b/f	318,600	Purchases	1,268,600
Cash paid to suppliers	1,367,000	Contras against debit balances in receivables ledger	48,000
Purchase returns	41,200	Discounts received	8,200
		Balance c/f	402,000
	1,726,800		1,726,800

All items relate to credit purchases.

What should be the closing balance on the payables' ledger control account when all the errors are corrected?

A $122,800

B $139,200

C $205,200

D $218,500

210 Ordan received a statement from one of its suppliers, Alta, showing a balance due of $3,980. The amount due according to the payables' ledger account of Ordan was only $230.

Comparison of the statement and the ledger account revealed the following differences:

(1) A cheque sent by Ordan for $270 has not been recorded in Alta's statement.

(2) Alta has not recorded goods returned by Ordan $180.

(3) Ordan made a contra entry, reducing the amount due to Alta by $3,200, for a balance due from Alta in Ordan's receivables ledger. No such entry has been made in Alta's records.

What difference remains between the two entities' accounting records after adjusting for these items?

A $460

B $640

C $6,500

D $100

211 A business had a receivables' ledger control account did not agree with the total of the balances on the receivables' ledger. An investigation revealed that the sales day book had been overcast by $10.

What effect will this have on the receivables' ledger control account?

A The control account should be credited with $10

B The control account should be debited with $10

C The control account should be credited with $20

D The control account should be debited with $20

212 A supplier sent Lord a statement showing a balance outstanding of $14,350. Lord's records show a balance outstanding of $14,500.

The reason for this difference could be that:

A The supplier sent an invoice for $150 which Lord has not yet received

B The supplier has allowed Lord $150 cash discount which you had omitted to enter in your ledgers

C Lord has paid the supplier $150 which he has not yet accounted for

D Lord has returned goods worth $150 which the supplier has not yet accounted for

213 Which of the following items would NOT lead to a difference between the total of the balances on the receivables' ledger and the balance on the receivables' ledger control account?

A An error in totalling the sales day book

B An error in totalling the receipts column of the cash book

C An overstatement of an entry in a customer's account

D An entry posted to the wrong customer's account

214 A receivables' ledger control account showed a debit balance of $37,642. The individual customers' accounts in the receivables' ledger showed a total of $35,840.

The difference could be due to:

A   Undercasting the sales day book by $1,802

B   Overcasting the sales returns day book by $1,802

C   Entering cash receipts of $1,802 on the debit side of a customer's account

D   Entering a contra with the payables ledger control account of $901 on the debit side of the receivables ledger control account

215 Tarbuck has received a statement of account from one of its suppliers, showing an outstanding balance due to it of $1,350. On comparison with the ledger account, the following was identified:

- The ledger account shows a credit balance of $260.
- The supplier has disallowed a cash discount of $80 due to late payment of an invoice.
- The supplier has not yet allowed for goods returned at the end of the period of $270.
- Cash in transit of $830 has not been received by the supplier.

Following consideration of these items, what was the unreconciled difference between the statement of account from the supplier and Tarbuck's ledger account?

A $70

B $90

C $430

D $590

216 The purchases day book of Arbroath has been undercast by $500, and the sales day book has been overcast by $700. Arbroath maintains payables and receivables ledger control accounts as part of the double-entry bookkeeping system.

The effect of correcting these errors will be to:

A   Make adjustments to the ledger balances of the individual customers and suppliers, with no effect on profit

B   Make adjustments to the ledger balances of the individual customers and suppliers, with a decrease in profit of $1,200

C   Make adjustments to the control accounts, with no effect on profit

D   Make adjustments to the control accounts, with a decrease in profit of $1,200

217 For the month of November 20X0 Figgin's purchases totalled $225,600 plus sales tax of $33,840. A total of $259,440 was credited to the payables ledger control account as $254,940.

Which of the following adjustments is correct?

	Control account	List of suppliers' balances
A	$4,500 Cr	No adjustment
B	$4,500 Cr	Increase by $4,500
C	$29,340 Dr	No effect
D	$33,840 Dr	Increase by $4,500

218 In reconciling the receivables' ledger control account with the list of receivables ledger balances of SK, the following errors were found:

(1) The sales day book had been overcast by $370.

(2) A total of $940 from the cash receipts book had been recorded in the receivables ledger control account as $490.

What adjustments must be made to correct the errors?

A Credit sales control account $820. Decrease total of receivables ledger balances by $820

B Credit sales control account $820. No change in total of receivables ledger balances.

C Debit sales control account $80. No change in total of receivables ledger balances

D Debit sales control account $80. Increase total of receivables ledger balances by $80

219 Mark is a sole trader who has provided the following information relating to transactions with credit customers and suppliers for the year ended 30 April 20X5:

	$
Trade receivables 1 May 20X4	200,000
Trade payables 1 May 20X4	130,000
Cash received from customers	576,800
Cash paid to suppliers	340,000
Discount received	3,500
Contra between payables and receivables	3,800
Trade receivables 30 April 20X5	240,000
Trade payables 30 April 20X5	150,000

What was the cost of Mark's purchases for the year ended 30 April 20X5?

$ _____

BANK RECONCILIATIONS

220 The cash book of Worcester shows a credit balance of $1,350. Cheques of $56 have been written to suppliers but not yet cleared the bank; uncleared lodgements amount to $128. The bank has accidentally credited Worcester's account with interest of $15 due to another customer. A standing order of $300 has not been accounted for in the general ledger.

What is the balance on the bank statement?

A $993 Cr

B $993 Dr

C $1,707 Cr

D $1,707 Dr

221 Jo's bank ledger account shows a balance of $190 credit. Her bank statement reports a balance of $250 credit.

Which of the following will explain the difference in full?

A   Unpresented cheques of $100 and an uncleared lodgement of $30

B   Unpresented cheques of $150, the misposting of a cash receipt of $130 to the wrong side of the cash account and unrecorded bank interest received of $30

C   An unrecorded direct debit of $30, a dishonoured cheque of $70 and an uncleared lodgement of $40

D   An unrecorded standing order of $60, an unpresented cheque of $110 and a bank error whereby Jo's account was accidentally credited with $110

222 State whether each of the following statements is true or false.

	True	False
When preparing a bank reconciliation, unpresented cheques must be deducted from a balance of cash at bank shown in the bank statement.		
A cheque from a customer paid into the bank but dishonoured must be corrected by making a debit entry in the cash book.		
An error by the bank must be corrected by an entry in the cash book.		
An overdraft is a debit balance in the bank statement.		

223 The following bank reconciliation statement has been prepared by an inexperienced bookkeeper at 31 December 20X5:

	$
Balance per bank statement (overdrawn)	38,640
Add: Lodgements not credited	19,270
	57,910
Less: Unpresented cheques	14,260
Balance per cash book	43,650

What should the final cash book balance be when all the above items have been properly accounted for?

A $43,650 overdrawn

B $33,630 overdrawn

C $5,110 overdrawn

D $72,170 overdrawn

224 A bank reconciliation statement for Dallas at 30 June 20X5 is being prepared. The following information is available:

(1)   Bank charges of $2,340 have not been entered in the cash book.

(2)   The bank statement shows a balance of $200 Dr.

(3)   Unpresented cheques amount to $1,250.

(4)   A direct debit of $250 has not been recorded in the ledger accounts.

(5)   A bank error has resulted in a cheque for $97 being debited to Dallas' account instead of Dynasty's account.

(6)   Cheques received but not yet banked amounted to $890.

The final balance in the cash book after all necessary adjustments should be:

A $463 Dr

B $463 Cr

C $63 Cr

D $63 Dr

225 The following information relates to a bank reconciliation:

(1) The bank balance in the cash book before taking the items below into account was $8,970 overdrawn.

(2) Bank charges of $550 on the bank statement have not been entered in the cash book.

(3) The bank has credited the account in error with $425 which belongs to another customer.

(4) Cheque payments totalling $3,275 have been entered in the cash book but have not been presented for payment.

(5) Cheques totalling $5,380 have been correctly entered on the debit side of the cash book but have not been paid in at the bank.

What was the balance as shown by the bank statement before taking the items above into account?

A $8,970 overdrawn

B $11,200 overdrawn

C $12,050 overdrawn

D $17,750 overdrawn

226 Sharmin's bank statement at 31 October 20X8 shows a balance of $13,400. She subsequently discovers that the bank has dishonoured a customer's cheque for $300 and has charged bank charges of $50, neither of which is recorded in the cash book.

There are unpresented cheques totalling $1,400 and an automatic receipt from a customer of $195 has been recorded as a credit in Sharmin's cash book.

Sharmin's cash balance, prior to correcting the errors and omissions, was:

A $11,455

B $11,960

C $12,000

D $12,155

227 Wimborne's bank statement shows a balance of $715 overdrawn. The statement includes bank charges of $74 which have not been entered in the cash book. There are also unpresented cheques totalling $824 and lodgements not yet credited of $337. In addition the bank statement erroneously includes a dividend receipt of $25 belonging to another customer.

The bank overdraft in the statement of financial position should be:

A $253

B $1,177

C $1,202

D $1,227

228 The cash book shows a bank balance of $5,675 overdrawn at 31 August 20X5. It is subsequently discovered that a standing order for $125 has been entered twice, and that a dishonoured cheque for $450 has been debited in the cash book instead of credited.

The correct bank balance should be:

A $5,100 overdrawn

B $6,000 overdrawn

C $6,250 overdrawn

D $6,450 overdrawn

229 An organisation's cash book had an opening balance of $485 credit. During the following week, the following transactions took place:

Cash sales $1,450 including sales tax of $150.

Receipts from credit customers of $2,400.

Payments to suppliers of debts of $1,800 less 5% cash discount.

Dishonoured cheques from customers amounting to $250.

What was the resulting balance in the cash book after the transactions had been recorded?

A $1,255 debit

B $1,405 debit

C $1,905 credit

D $2,375 credit

230 The bank statement at 31 October 20X7 showed an overdraft of $800. On reconciling the bank statement, it was discovered that a cheque drawn in favour of Smith for $80 had not been presented for payment, and that a cheque for $130 from a customer had been dishonoured on 30 October 20X7, but that this had not yet been notified to you by the bank.

The correct bank balance to be shown in the statement of financial position at 31 October 20X7 is:

A $1,010 overdrawn

B $880 overdrawn

C $750 overdrawn

D $720 overdrawn

231 Your firm's cash book at 30 April 20X8 showed a balance at the bank of $2,490. Comparison with the bank statement at the same date revealed the following differences:

	$
Unpresented cheques	840
Bank charges not in cash book	50
Receipts not yet credited by the bank	470
Dishonoured cheque not in cash book	140

What was the correct bank balance at 30 April 20X8?

A $1,460

B $2,300

C $2,580

D $3,140

232 Your firm's cash book shows a credit bank balance of $1,240 at 30 April 20X9. On comparison with the bank statement, you determine that there are unpresented cheques totalling $450, and a receipt of $140 which has not yet been passed through the bank account. The bank statement shows bank charges of $75 which have not been entered in the cash book.

What was the balance on the bank statement?

A $1,005 overdrawn

B $930 overdrawn

C $1,475 in credit

D $1,550 in credit

233 **Which of the following is not an 'unrecorded difference' when reconciling the balance on the cash book to the amount shown in the bank statement?**

A   A standing order

B   Bank interest

C   An uncleared lodgement

D   A BACS receipt

234 An entity has prepared its bank reconciliation at 31 March 2014 taking the following information into account:

	$		$
Outstanding lodgements	5,000	Unpresented cheques	2,800

Bank charges included in the bank statement but not recorded in the cash book were $125.

The adjusted cash book balance per the bank reconciliation was a debit balance of $1,060.

What was the balance as shown on the bank statement at 31 March 2014?

A $1,140 debit

B $1,140 credit

C $1,265 debit

D $1,265 credit

CORRECTION OF ERRORS AND SUSPENSE ACCOUNTS

235 A trial balance shows a total of debits of $347,800 and a total of credits of $362,350.

(1)   A credit sale of $3,670 was incorrectly entered in the sales day book as $3,760.

(2)   A non-current asset with a carrying amount of $7,890 was disposed of for $9,000. The only accounting entry was to debit cash.

(3)   The allowance for receivables was increased from $8,900 to $10,200. The allowance account was debited in error.

After adjusting for the errors above, what is the balance on the suspense account?

A $26,150 debit

B $26,060 debit

C $26,240 debit

D $2,950 credit

236 The trial balance of Kelvin does not balance.

Which TWO of the following errors could explain this, assuming that Kelvin maintains control accounts for its receivables and payables within the double entry system?

(1)   The sales day book was undercast by $100.

(2)   Discounts received were credited to sales revenue account.

(3)   An opening accrual was omitted from the rent account.

(4)   The debit side of the cash account was undercast.

A   (1) and (2)

B   (2) and (3)

C   (3) and (4)

D   (1) and (4)

237 The trial balance of MHSB does not balance at the year end.

What type of error may explain this?

A   Extraction error

B   Error of commission

C   Compensating error

D   An error of principle

238 The trial balance of Butler Co shows total debts of $125,819 and total credits of $118,251.

Which of the following explains the difference in full?

A   Carriage inwards of $3,784 has been shown on the wrong side of the trial balance.

B   Discounts received of $3,784 have been credited to the payables ledger control account.

C   The sales day book has been undercast by $7,568.

D   An opening accrual of $7,568 has been omitted from the rental expense account.

239 **Which one of the following journals is correct according to its narrative?**

		Debit	Credit
		$	$
A	Mr Smith personal account	100,000	
	Directors' remuneration		100,000
	Bonus allocated to account of managing director (Mr Smith)		
B	Purchases	14,000	
	Wages	24,000	
	Repairs to buildings		38,000
	Transfer of costs of repairs to buildings carried out by employees using materials from inventory		
C	Sales commission paid	2,800	
	Wages and salaries		2,800
	Correction of error: sales commission paid incorrectly debited to wages and salaries account.		
D	Suspense account	20,000	
	Rent receivable		10,000
	Rent payable		10,000
	Correction of error: rent received credited in error to rent payable account.		

240 The trial balance of Koi did not balance, and a suspense account was opened for the difference.

Which of the following errors would require an entry to the suspense account to correct them?

(1) A cash payment to purchase a motor van had been correctly entered in the cash book but had been debited to the motor expenses account.

(2) The debit side of the wages account had been undercast.

(3) The total of the discounts received column in the cash book had been posted to the payables ledger control account correctly and debited to the purchases account.

(4) A refund to a credit customer had been recorded by debiting the cash book and crediting the customer's account.

A   (1) and (2)

B   (2) and (3)

C   (3) and (4)

D   (2) and (4)

241 An entity's trial balance failed to agree, and a suspense account was opened for the difference.

Subsequent investigation revealed that cash sales of $13,000 had been debited to the purchases account and an entry on the credit side of the cash book for the purchase of some machinery costing $18,000 had not been posted to the plant and machinery account.

Which two of the following journal entries would correct the errors?

		Debit	Credit
		$	$
(1)	Purchases	13,000	
	Sales revenue		13,000
(2)	Purchases	13,000	
	Sales revenue	13,000	
	Suspense account		26,000
(3)	Suspense account	26,000	
	Purchases		13,000
	Sales revenue		13,000
(4)	Plant and machinery	18,000	
	Suspense account		18,000
(5)	Suspense account	18,000	
	Plant and machinery		18,000

A   (1) and (4)

B   (2) and (5)

C   (3) and (4)

D   (3) and (5)

This information is relevant to questions 242 and 243.

Co's draft financial statements for 20X5 showed a profit of $630,000. However, the trial balance did not agree, and a suspense account appeared in the company's financial statements.

Subsequent checking revealed the following errors:

(1)   The cost of an item of plant $48,000 had been entered in the cash book and in the plant account as $4,800. Depreciation at the rate of 10% per year ($480) had been charged.

(2)   Bank charges of $440 appeared in the bank statement in December 20X5 but had not been entered in the company's records.

(3)   One of the directors paid $800 due to a supplier in K Co's payables ledger by a personal cheque. The bookkeeper recorded a debit in the supplier's ledger account but did not complete the double entry for the transaction (K Co does not maintain a payables ledger control account).

(4)   The payments side of the cash book had been understated by $10,000.

Note: in the exam, all questions will be independent, and not based on a common scenario.

---

242   Which of the above items would require an entry to the suspense account to correct them?

   A   All four items

   B   (3) and (4) only

   C   (2) and (3) only

   D   (1), (2) and (4) only

243   What would the K Co's profit be after the correction of the above errors?

   A $634,760

   B $624,760

   C $624,440

   D $625,240

244   The trial balance of Flo Co does not agree and a suspense account has been opened.

Inventory bought at a sales tax inclusive cost of $4,700 has been credited to the payables ledger control account. The sales tax, at 17.5%, has been recorded in the sales tax account and the total $4,700 has been recorded in the purchases account.

What entry is required to correct the error?

   A   Dr Payables ledger control account $700   Cr Suspense account $700

   B   Dr Payables ledger control account $822.50   Cr Suspense account $822.50

   C   Dr Suspense account $700   Cr Purchases $700

   D   Dr Suspense account $822.50   Cr Purchases $822.50

---

245 The draft financial statements of Galahad's business for the year ended 31 July 20X0 show a profit of $54,250 prior to the correction of the following errors:

(1) Cash drawings of $250 have not been accounted for.

(2) Debts amounting to $420, which were provided against in full during the year, should have been written off as irrecoverable.

(3) Rental income of $300 has been classified as interest receivable.

(4) On the last day of the accounting period, $200 in cash was received from a customer, but no bookkeeping entries have been made.

What is the correct profit of Galahad for the year ended 31 July 20X2?

A $53,580

B $53,830

C $54,250

D $55,830

246 Weagan's trial balance at 31 October 20X9 is out of agreement, with the debit side totalling $500 less than the credit side. During November, the following errors are discovered:

- The credit side of the sales account for October had been undercast by $150.

- Rent received of $240 had been credited to the rent payable account.

- The allowance for receivables, which decreased by $420, had been recorded in the allowance for receivables account as an increase.

Following the correction of these errors, the balance on the suspense account would be:

A $190 Cr

B $670 Cr

C $1,190 Cr

D $1,490 Dr

247 **Which ONE of the following is an error of principle?**

A   A gas bill credited to the gas account and debited to the bank account.

B   The purchase of a non-current asset credited to the asset at cost account and debited to the supplier's account.

C   The purchase of a non-current asset debited to the purchases account and credited to the supplier's account.

D   The payment of wages debited and credited to the correct accounts, but using the wrong amount.

248 The trial balance of C did not agree, and a suspense account was opened for the difference. Checking in the bookkeeping system revealed a number of errors:

Error

(1) $4,600 paid for motor van repairs was correctly treated in the cash book but was credited to motor vehicles asset account.

(2) $360 received from Brown, a customer, was credited in error to the account of Green.

(3) $9,500 paid for rent was debited to the rent account as $5,900.

(4) The total of the discount received column in the cash book, $325, had been credited in error to the purchases account.

(5) No entries had been made to record a cash sale of $100.

Which of the errors above would require an entry to the suspense account as part of the process of correcting them?

A Errors (3) and (4) only

B Errors (1) and (3) only

C Errors (2) and (5) only

D Errors (2) and (3) only

249 Drive incurred bank charges of $40, which was then credited to the bank interest receivable account.

What was the effect upon profit for the year of recording the bank charges in this way?

A Profit will be unchanged

B Profit will be overstated by $80

C Profit will be understated by $80

D Profit will be understated by $40

250 A suspense account was opened when a trial balance failed to agree. The following errors were subsequently discovered:

Error

(1) A gas bill of $420 had been recorded in the Gas account as $240.

(2) A payment of $50 for stationery of $50 had been credited to Discounts received.

(3) Interest received of $70 had been entered in the bank account only.

If the errors when corrected clear the suspense account, what was the original balance on the suspense account?

A debit $210

B credit $210

C debit $160

D credit $160

251 The book-keeper of High Hurdles was instructed to make a contra entry for $270 between the supplier account and the customer account for Greyfold. He recorded the transaction by debiting the customer account and crediting the supplier account with $270. The business accounts do not include control accounts.

Which of the following statements is correct?

A   Unless the error is corrected, profit will be over-stated by $540

B   Unless the error is corrected, net assets will be over-stated by $270

C   Unless the error is corrected, net assets will be over-stated by $540

D   The errors should be corrected, but neither the profit nor the net assets are over-stated

252 **Which one of the following errors would lead to creation of a suspense account?**

A   Sales returns were credited to the Purchase returns account and debited to Receivables.

B   The total of the sales day book has been totalled incorrectly before being posted to the ledger accounts.

C   Discounts received have been dealt with correctly in the Payables ledger control account, but credited to the Purchases account.

D   Purchases from the purchases day book have been credited to Sales and dealt with correctly in the Payables ledger control account.

253 Pelle had a balance on his suspense account of $1,820 credit. He discovered the following errors:

(1)   Sundry income of $1,750 has been recorded in the sundry income account as $1,570.

(2)   Sales of $2,800 from the sales day book have been posted to the receivables ledger control account, but no other entry has been made.

(3)   The purchases day book was undercast by $950.

What was the balance on the suspense account after Pelle has corrected the above errors?

$ [   ]

254 Marlon created a suspense account with a debit balance of $1,250 in order to balance his trial balance. He subsequently investigated and found the following errors:

(1)   The closing balance of the purchase ledger control account at the year-end had been undercast by $160.

(2)   Cash received of $450 from customers has only been entered into the cash account.

(3)   The purchase returns day book has been overcast by $300.

What is the remaining debit balance on the suspense account after the errors have been corrected?

$ [   ]

255 At 30 September 20X8, the following require items inclusion in MCD Co's financial statements:

(1) On 1 September 20X8, MCD Co received $5,000 as a deposit for goods which were despatched to the customer on 15 October 20X8.

(2) On 1 August 20X8, MCD Co paid an insurance premium of $5,000 for the six month period commencing 1 July 20X8.

(3) On 1 April 20X8, MCD Co raised a five-year bank loan of $12,000 which is repayable in a single capital sum at the end of the loan term. Interest is payable on the loan annually in arrears at 5% per annum.

For these items, what was the effect of these transactions total figures included in the MCD Co's statement of financial position at 30 September 20X8?

A	Current assets	$17,000	Current liabilities	$2,800
B	Current assets	$19,500	Current liabilities	$10,300
C	Current assets	$14,500	Current liabilities	$5,300
D	Current assets	$7,500	Current liabilities	$5,300

256 The statement of profit or loss for a business for the year ended 31 July 20X8 showed a net profit of $57,400. It was later discovered that a suite of office furniture had been purchased on 1 February 20X8 at a cost of $15,500 had been charged to the office expenses account. The suite of office furniture had an estimated useful life of ten years with an estimated residual value of $1,500. Depreciation is charged on a monthly basis, commencing with the month of purchase.

What was the net profit for the year ended 31 July 20X8 after adjusting for this error?

$ [   ]

PREPARING BASIC FINANCIAL STATEMENTS

STATEMENT OF FINANCIAL POSITION AND STATEMENT OF PROFIT OR LOSS AND OTHER COMPREHENSIVE INCOME

257 Arthur had net assets of $19,000 at 30 April 20X7. During the year to 30 April 20X7, he introduced $9,800 additional capital into the business and his profit for the year was $8,000. During the year ended 30 April 20X7 he withdrew $4,200.

What was the balance on Arthur's capital account at 1 May 20X6?

A $5,400

B $13,000

C $16,600

D $32,600

258 The following information relates to Minnie's hairdressing business in the year ended 31 August 20X7:

	$
Expenses	7,100
Opening inventory	1,500
Closing inventory	900
Purchases	12,950
Gross profit	12,125
Inventory drawings of shampoo	75

What was the value of sales revenue of the business for the year ended 31 August 20X7?

A $32,700

B $25,600

C $25,675

D $25,750

259 Astral Co has a debit balance relating to income tax of $500 included in its trial balance extracted on 30 June 20X4. Astral estimated that its income tax liability for the year ended 30 June 20X4 was $8,000.

What amounts should be included in Astral Co's financial statements for the year ended 30 June 20X4?

	Statement of profit or loss	Statement of financial position
A	$8,000	$8,000
B	$8,500	$8,000
C	$7,500	$8,500
D	$8,000	$7,500

260 **The capital of a business would change as a result of:**

A   a supplier being paid by cheque

B   raw materials being purchased on credit

C   non-current assets being purchased on credit

D   wages being paid in cash

261 A draft statement of financial position has been prepared for Lollipop, a sole trader. It is now discovered that a loan due for repayment by Lollipop fourteen months after the reporting date has been included in trade payables.

The necessary adjustment will:

A   have no effect on net current assets

B   increase net current assets

C   reduce net current assets

D   increase current assets but reduce net current assets

262 The profit of a business may be calculated by using which one of the following formulae?

A Opening capital – drawings + capital introduced – closing capital

B Closing capital + drawings – capital introduced – opening capital

C Opening capital + drawings – capital introduced – closing capital

D Closing capital – drawings + capital introduced – opening capital

263 Which accounting concept requires that amounts of goods taken from inventory by the proprietor of a business are treated as drawings?

A Accruals

B Prudence

C Separate entity

D Substance over form

264 The following information is available about Andrew's business at 30 September 20X6:

	$
Motor van	14,000
Loan (repayable in 4 equal annual instalments starting 1 January 20X7)	100,000
Receivables	23,800
Bank balance (a debit on the bank statement)	3,250
Accumulated depreciation	7,000
Payables	31,050
Inventory	12,560
Petty cash	150
Rent due	1,200
Allowance for receivables	1,500

What are the correct figures for current liabilities and current assets?

	Current liabilities $	Current assets $
A	34,300	35,010
B	32,250	38,260
C	57,250	38,260
D	60,500	35,010

265 The following transactions relate to Max's business:

1 May	Purchase of goods for resale on credit	$300
2 May	Max injects long term capital into the business	$1,400
3 May	Payment of rent made	$750
5 May	Max withdraws cash from the business	$400
7 May	Goods which had cost $600 were sold on credit	1,200

At the start of the week, the assets of the business were $15,700 and liabilities amounted to $11,200.

At the end of the week, what was the amount of Max's capital?

A $5,350

B $1,400

C $850

D $1,000

266 **State the amount that will be included in other comprehensive income of Zappa Co for the year ended 30 June 20X4 based upon the following information.**

There was a revaluation surplus of $70,000 arising on revaluation of land and buildings during the year.

The depreciation charge for the year relating to buildings was $20,000. Zappa Co does not make an annual transfer of 'excess depreciation' between revaluation surplus and retained earnings.

During the year, there was a gain on disposal on disposal of motor vehicles of $1,000.

$ [   ]

267 **State the total amount that will be charged as an expense in the statement of profit or loss of Clapton Co or the year ended 30 September 20X6 based upon the following information.**

Clapton Co incurred development expenditure during the year of $50,000.

The amortisation charge on intangible assets for the year was $15,000.

During the year, there was a loss on disposal on disposal of plant and equipment of $3,000.

$ [   ]

268 On 1 January 20X8 Baker Co revalued its property to $100,000. At the date of the revaluation, the asset was accounted for at a cost of $80,000, and had accumulated depreciation $16,000. The property had an expected useful life of fifty years from the date of purchase and nil residual value.

What was the amount of the 'excess depreciation' transfer required from revaluation surplus to retained earnings at 31 December 20X8 as a result of accounting for the revaluation?

$ [   ]

269   On 1 January 20X8 Hendrix Co revalued its property to $200,000. Up to the date of the revaluation, the asset had been accounted for at a cost of $160,000, and had accumulated depreciation $40,000. The property had an expected useful life of fifty years from the date of purchase and nil residual value.

What are the accounting entries required to record the property revaluation in the accounting records?

	Debit	$	Credit	$
A	Non-current asset - property	$200,000	Revaluation surplus	$200,000
B	Revaluation surplus	$80,000	Non-current asset - property	$40,000
			Accumulated dep'n	$40,000
C	Non-current asset - property	$40,000	Revaluation surplus	$40,000
D	Non-current asset - property	$40,000	Revaluation surplus	$80,000
	Accumulated dep'n	$40,000		

270   **The following information is relevant to Wimbledon:**

	$
Opening inventory	12,500
Closing inventory	17,900
Purchases	199,000
Distribution costs	35,600
Administrative expenses	78,800
Audit fee	15,200
Carriage in	3,500
Carriage out	7,700
Depreciation	40,000

Depreciation is to be split in the ratio 70:30 between the factory and the office. All office expenses are classified as administrative expenses.

Based upon the available information, what was Wimbledon's cost of sales?

A $233,600

B $221,600

C $225,100

D $237,100

271 Brown Co had $100,000 50c shares and $400,000 8% irredeemable preference shares in issue. A dividend of 3c per ordinary share and half of the preference dividend was paid during the year.

Which of the following statements is/are true?

(1) An ordinary dividend of $3,000 was paid during the year.

(2) A preference dividend of $16,000 was accrued at the year end.

A (1) only

B (2) only

C Neither (1) nor (2)

D Both (1) and (2)

272 At 1 October 20X6, Ozber Co's capital structure was as follows:

	$
Ordinary shares of 25c	100,000
Share premium	30,000

On 10 January 20X7, in order to raise finance for expansion, Ozber Co made a 1 for 4 rights issue at $1.15. The issue was fully taken up. This was followed by a 1-for-10 bonus issue on 1 June 20X7.

What was the balance on the share premium account after these transactions?

A $17,500

B $21,250

C $107,500

D $120,000

273 In which TWO financial statements, complied in accordance with IFRS Standards, would you expect to find dividends paid?

Selection

Statement of profit or loss and other comprehensive income

Statement of financial position

Statement of cash flows

Statement of changes in equity

274 Where in the financial statements should tax on profit for the current period, and unrealised surplus on revaluation of properties in the year, be separately disclosed?

	Tax on profit for the current period	*Unrealised surplus on revaluation of properties*
A	Statement of profit or loss and other comprehensive income	Statement of cash flows
B	Statement of changes in equity	Statement of profit or loss and other comprehensive income
C	Statement of profit or loss and other comprehensive income	Statement of profit or loss and other comprehensive income
D	Statement of cash flows	Statement of cash flows

275 The following information is available about L Co's dividends:

Sept 20X5	Final dividend for the year ended 30 June 20X5 paid (declared August 20X5)	$100,000
March 20X6	Interim dividend for the year ended 30 June 20X6 paid	$40,000
Sept 20X6	Final dividend for the year ended 30 June 20X6 paid (declared August 20X6)	$120,000

What figures, if any, should be disclosed in L Co's statement of profit or loss and other comprehensive income for the year ended 30 June 20X6 and its statement of financial position at that date?

	Statement of profit or loss and other comprehensive income	*Statement of financial position*
A	$160,000 deduction	$120,000
B	$140,000 deduction	Nil
C	Nil	$120,000
D	Nil	Nil

276 Classify each of the following statements as either true or false.

	True	*False*
An entity may make a rights issue if it wished to raise more equity capital.		
A rights issue might increase the share premium account whereas a bonus issue is likely to reduce it.		
A rights issue will always increase the number of shareholders in an entity whereas a bonus issue will not.		
A bonus issue will result in an increase in the market value of each share		

(1)

277 Florabundi Co's trial balance at 31 December 20X8 included a credit balance of $3,400 on its tax liability account, having already settled the tax liability for the year ended 31 December 20X7 during the year. Florabundi Co estimated that its income tax charge arising on its profits for the year ended 31 December 20X8 at $67,900.

What amounts should be included in Florabundi Co's financial statements for the year ended 31 December 20X8 in respect of tax?

	Statement of profit or loss	*Statement of financial position*
A	$67,900 tax charge	$67,900 tax payable
B	$64,500 tax charge	$64,500 tax payable
C	$64,500 tax charge	$67,900 tax payable
D	$71,300 tax charge	$67,900 tax payable

278 **Classify the following assets and liabilities as current or non-current in Albatross Co's financial statements:**

	Current	*Non-current*
A sale has been made on credit to a customer. They have agreed to terms stating that payment is due in 12 months' time.		
A bank overdraft facility of $30,000 is available under an agreement with the bank which extends 2 years.		
Albatros Co purchases a small number of shares in another entity which it intends to trade.		
A bank loan has been taken out with a repayment date 5 years hence.		

279 Extracts from the accounting records of Andratx Co relating to the year ended 31 December 20X6 are as follows:

Revaluation surplus	$230,000
Ordinary interim dividend paid	$12,000
Profit before tax	$178,000
Estimated tax liability for year	$45,000
8% $1 Preference shares	$100,000
Under provision for tax in previous year	$5,600
Proceeds of issue of 2,000 $1 ordinary Shares	$5,000
Final ordinary dividend proposed	$30,000

What was the total of equity reported in the statement of changes in equity at 31 December 20X6?

A $312,400

B $356,000

C $348,000

D $342,400

280 Which of the following statements is/are true in relation to a preference share?

(1) They carry voting rights.

(2) Their dividend is paid out in priority to an ordinary dividend.

(3) Their dividend is related to profits.

A   All three statements

B   (1) and (2)

C   (2) and (3)

D   (2) only

281 Bangeroo Co, issues 100,000 3% $1 redeemable preference shares during the year ended 30 September 20X8 at 98c per share.

What are the correct accounting entries to account for this transaction?

		Debit		Credit
		$		$
A	Cash	$98,000	Liability	$98,000
B	Cash	$98,000	Share capital	$100,000
	Share premium	$2,000		
C	Cash	$98,000	Share capital	$98,000
D	Cash	$98,000	Share capital	$100,000
	Statement of profit or loss	$2,000		

282 The nominal value paid by the shareholder plus further amounts that they have agreed to pay in the future' best describes:

A   Paid up share capital

B   Called up share capital

C   Authorised share capital

D   Issued share capital

283 Which TWO of the following statements are advantages of a bonus issue?

	Selection
It is the cheapest way for an entity to raise finance through the issuing of shares	
It makes the shares in the entity more marketable	
The total reserves of the entity will increase	
Issued share capital is brought more into line with assets employed in the entity	

284   Argonaut Co issued $400,000 12% loan notes for $380,000 on 1 August 20X6.

What accounting entries are required in the year ended 30 September 20X6?

A	Dr Cash	$400,000
	Cr Non-current liabilities	$400,000
	And	
	Dr Interest	$7,600
	Cr Current liabilities	$7,600
B	Dr Cash	$380,000
	Cr Non-current liabilities	$380,000
	And	
	Dr Interest	$8,000
	Cr Current liabilities	$8,000
C	Dr Cash	$400,000
	Cr Non-current liabilities	$400,000
	And	
	Dr Interest	$8,000
	Cr Current liabilities	$8,000
D	Dr Cash	$380,000
	Cr Non-current liabilities	$380,000
	And	
	Dr Interest	$7,600
	Cr Current liabilities	$7,600

285   Revenue reserves would decrease if an entity:

A   Sets aside profits to pay future dividends

B   Transfers amounts into 'general reserves'

C   Issues shares at a premium

D   Pays dividends

286   Radar Co has accounted for the revaluation of buildings in its financial statements for the year ended 31 December 20X4. The increase in carrying amount of the property was $50,000, with a depreciation charge for the year of $13,000. Radar Co accounts for excess depreciation and this has been calculated at $2,000.

For each of the following items, identify where in the statement of profit or loss and other comprehensive income each item would be included, or if it would be omitted completely from that statement.

A   Profit or loss

B   Other comprehensive income

C   Omitted from the statement of profit or loss and other comprehensive income

Choice: A, B or C

Excess depreciation on revaluation

Increase in carrying amount of a property

Depreciation charge

287 Saturn Co disposed of a property that had been revalued in an earlier accounting period. The details relating to this property are as follows:

	$000
Carrying amount at disposal date	150
Disposal proceeds	165
Revaluation surplus at disposal date	15

How should the property disposal be accounted for in Saturn's financial statements?

A   Gain on disposal of $15,000 included in profit or loss for the year only.

B   Gain on disposal of $30,000 included in profit or loss for the year only.

C   Gain on disposal of $15,000 included in profit or loss for the year and revaluation gain of $15,000 included in other comprehensive income for the year.

D   Gain on disposal of $15,000 included in profit or loss for the year and a transfer within the statement of changes in equity of $15,000 from revaluation surplus to retained earnings.

288 Starstruck Co estimated that its income tax liability for the year ended 30 September 20X6 was $15,000. The income tax charge disclosed in the statement of profit or loss for the year ended 30 September 20X6 was $14,200.

Which of the following statements is true?

A   The difference between the statement of profit or loss charge and the liability in the statement of financial position is the result of an adjustment relating to an under provision in an earlier year.

B   The difference between the statement of profit or loss charge and the liability in the statement of financial position is the result of an adjustment relating to an overprovision in an earlier year.

C   It is not possible to state whether the difference between the statement of profit or loss charge and the liability in the statement of financial position is due to an underprovision or overprovision in an earlier year.

D   There is no relationship between the amounts included in the statement of financial position and statement of profit or loss relating to income tax.

289 Details of two of Clooney's transactions in the year ended 31 August 20X7 were as follows:

(1)   Clooney sold a machine to a customer, Pitt, on 28 August 20X7. Pitt is responsible for installation and operation of the machine following delivery.

(2)   Clooney sold a number of food mixers to Damon, on credit. Damon collected the food mixers from Clooney on 26 August 20X7. Damon has not yet paid for the goods purchased.

For which of the transactions should sales revenue be recognised?

A   (1) only

B   (2) only

C   Both (1) and (2)

D   Neither (1) nor (2)

290 Kaplin publishes study materials and runs courses for students studying for professional accountancy examinations. Details of two transactions that occurred in December 20X8 were as follows:

(1) Ten students enrolled on a course due to commence in January 20X9 at a price of $1,000 per student and each student paid their fees in advance. If sold separately, the study materials would be sold for $200 and the course of ten lectures would be sold for a total of $800. The study materials are issued on the first day of the course.

(2) Kaplin sold study materials to forty self-study students at a price of $400 per student who will receive no further support with their studies, which were delivered to students prior to 31 December 20X8.

What sales revenue should Kaplin recognise in the financial statements for the year ended 31 December 20X8?

$ _____

291 Vostok sells computer games and is the sole distributor of a new game 'Avalanche'. Customer demand for the new game has resulted in lots of advance orders pending release of the game later in the year. As at 31 July 20X2, Vostok had received customer orders and deposits received amounting to $500,000. Vostok anticipates that all orders will be despatched to customers by 1 December 20X2.

What sales revenue can Vostok recognise in the financial statements for the year ended 31 July 20X2?

$ _____

292 Scrubber provides contract cleaning services in commercial office premises. Scrubber charges each business an annual fee of $1,200, based upon providing an agreed level of service each month. In one office block there are twelve businesses which use Scrubber to provide cleaning services. At 1 April 20X5 four businesses had paid one month in advance and two customers were in one month in arrears. With effect from 31 August 20X5, one customer terminated their agreement with Scrubber, whilst two additional contracts were signed to take effect from 1 December 20X5. At 31 March 20X6, the same four businesses had paid one month in advance and two customers were in arrears by one month. Each annual service contract is regarded as a contract which gives rise to obligations which are satisfied over a period of time.

What sales revenue can Scrubber recognise in the financial statements for the year ended 31 March 20X6?

$ _____

293 Hamilton provides internet and website support services to its customers. On 1 September 20X7, Hamilton agreed a three-year support service agreement with a customer at a total price of $2,250.

How much revenue can be recognised from this transaction for the year ended 31 March 20X8?

$ _____

294 At 1 January 20X8, Clarinet Co had an estimated income tax liability of $2,350. This liability was settled by a payment of $2,050 made In March 20X8. Due to challenging trading conditions, Clarinet Co made a loss for the year ended 31 December 20X8 and expects to recover a repayment of income tax of $2,120 during 20X9.

What amounts should be included in Clarinet Co's financial statements for the year ended 31 December 20X8 for income tax?

	Statement of profit or loss	Statement of financial position
A	$2,420 tax charge	$1,820 tax recoverable asset
B	$2,120 tax credit	$2,120 tax payable
C	$2,420 tax credit	$2,120 tax recoverable asset
D	$1,820 tax charge	$2,120 tax recoverable asset

295 Banjo Co estimated that its income tax liability on the profit for the year ended 30 June 20X5 was $16,940. This liability was settled in February 20X6 by a payment of $17,500. Having made a trading loss for the year ended 30 June 20X6, Banjo Co estimated that it would receive repayment of income tax of $4,500 during the following accounting period.

What amounts should be included in Banjo Co's financial statements for the year ended 30 June 20X6 for income tax?

	Statement of profit or loss	Statement of financial position
A	$3,940 tax credit	$4,500 tax recoverable asset
B	$4,500 tax credit	$4,500 tax payable
C	$3,940 tax charge	$4,500 tax payable
D	$5,060 tax credit	$4,500 tax recoverable asset

DISCLOSURE NOTES

296 **Which of the following should be disclosed in the notes to the financial statements relating to intangible assets?**

(1) Accumulated amortisation charges at the start and at the end of the reporting period.

(2) A reconciliation of the movement in the net carrying amount of intangible assets for the reporting period.

(3) A statement from the directors, explaining whether or not they believe that capitalised development costs will be recovered at some future date.

A (1) only

B (2) only

C (1) and (2)

D (2) and (3)

297 **Which of the following would be a suitable accounting policy note for disclosure in the financial statements relating to intangible assets?**

    A   The entity has some intangible assets accounted for using the cost model and other intangible assets accounted for using the valuation model, based upon the judgement of the directors. All intangible assets are written off over their expected useful lives to the business.

    B   The entity accounts for intangible assets using the cost model. All intangible assets are amortised over their expected useful lives to the business, between five and fifteen years, on a straight-line basis.

    C   The entity accounts for intangible assets using the valuation model, based upon a valuation estimated by the directors. All changes in the carrying valuation from one reporting date to the next are accounted for in the statement of profit or loss.

    D   The entity uses the same accounting policy for tangible and intangible non-current assets.

298 **Which of the following would be a suitable accounting policy note for disclosure in the financial statements relating to land and buildings?**

    A   Land and buildings are accounted for at cost and are written off over their expected useful life of fifty years on a straight-line basis.

    B   Land and buildings are accounted for at cost and are not depreciated as the directors believe that the market value of land and buildings will increase over time.

    C   Land and buildings are accounted for at cost, and the buildings are written off over their expected useful life of fifty years on a straight-line basis.

    D   The entity uses the same accounting policy for land and buildings as it does for intangible assets.

299 **Which of the following would be a suitable accounting policy note for disclosure in the financial statements relating to inventory?**

    A   Inventory is valued at the lower of total cost and total net realisable value.

    B   Inventory is valued at the lower of cost and net realisable value for each separate product or item.

    C   Inventory is valued at the higher of cost and net realisable value for each separate product or item.

    D   Inventory is valued at cost for each separate product or item.

300 **Is the following statement true or false?**

Non-adjusting events can be ignored when preparing the annual financial statements and supporting disclosure notes.

    A   True

    B   False

301 **When dealing with non-adjusting events what information should be disclosed in the notes to the financial statements?**

(1)   The nature of the event.

(2)   The names of those with responsibility for the event.

(3)   The geographical location of the event.

(4)   An estimate of the financial effect of the event.

A   (1) and (2)

B   (1), (3) and (4)

C   (2), (3) and (4)

D   (1) and (4)

302 **In relation to non-current assets, identify for each of the following items whether it should be disclosed in the notes to the financial statements.**

	Disclosed	Not disclosed
Reconciliation of carrying amounts of non-current assets at the beginning and end of period.		
Useful lives of assets or depreciation rates used.		
Increases in asset values as a result of revaluations in the period.		
Depreciation expense for the period.		

303 IAS 1 Presentation of Financial Statements requires certain items to be presented on the face of the statement of profit or loss for the year.

Which THREE of the following items must be disclosed on the face of the statement of profit or loss for the year?

Selection

Revenue

Closing inventory

Finance costs

Dividends paid

Tax expense

Depreciation charge for the year

304 **Which ONE of the following statements is true in relation to disclosure requirements?**

A   Disclosure requirements consist only of monetary disclosures

B   Disclosure requirements consist only of narrative disclosures

C   Disclosure requirements consist of both monetary and narrative disclosures

D   Disclosure notes do not form part of the annual financial statements

305 When considering disclosures required in the financial statements relating to property, plant and equipment, is the following statement true or false?

The estimated useful lives of the property plant and equipment and the depreciation rates used must be disclosed.

A   True

B   False

306 When making disclosures required in the financial statements relating to provisions, which of the following needs to be disclosed?

(1)   The nature of the obligation.

(2)   Expected timing of any payment.

(3)   The name of the party to whom the obligation is owed.

(4)   The nature of any uncertainties which may affect the amount to be paid.

A   (1), (2) and (3)

B   (2), (3) and (4)

C   (1), (3) and (4)

D   (1), (2), and (4)

307 When considering disclosures required in the financial statements in relation to provisions, is the following statement true or false?

An entity need only state the carrying amount of the obligation at the beginning and end of the accounting period, without providing a reconciliation of the movement in the provision during the year.

A   True

B   False

308 In relation to non-current assets, which of the following items must be disclosed in the notes to the financial statements of an entity which complies with international accounting standards?

(1)   The depreciation charge on property, plant and equipment for the year.

(2)   The amortisation charge on intangible assets for the year.

(3)   The date of any revaluation of property plant and equipment made during the accounting year.

(4)   Whether an independent valuer was used in the revaluation of property, plant and equipment during the accounting year.

A   (1), (2) and (3) only

B   (2), (3) and (4) only

C   (1), (3) and (4) only

D   (1), (2), (3) and (4)

309   How are intangible assets disclosed in the statement of financial position?

   A   Cost only without any recognition of amortisation or impairment

   B   Cost or valuation – amortisation – impairment = Carrying amount

   C   The amortisation amount only

   D   At the disposal proceeds value

EVENTS AFTER THE REPORTING PERIOD

310   Ribblesdale Co has prepared financial statements for the year ended 30 September 20X8. The financial statements were approved by the directors on 12 January 20X9 and issued to the shareholders on 20 February 20X9.

   State whether each of the following items are adjusting or non-adjusting events after the reporting period.

	Adjusting	Non-adjusting
A flood on 3 October 20X8 that destroyed a relatively small quantity of inventory which had cost $1,700.		
A credit customer with a balance outstanding at 30 September 20X8 was declared insolvent on 20 December 20X8.		
Inventory valued at a cost of $800 at 30 September 20X8 was sold for $650 on 11 November 20X8.		
A dividend on ordinary shares of 4c per share was declared on 1 December 20X8.		

311   **Which of the following statements are correct based upon the requirements of IAS 10 Events after the Reporting Period?**

   (1)   Details of all adjusting events must be disclosed by note to the financial statements.

   (2)   A material loss arising from the sale, after the reporting date of inventory valued at cost at the statement of financial position date must be reflected in the financial statements.

   (3)   If the market value of property, plant and equipment falls materially after the reporting date, the details must be disclosed by note.

   (4)   Events after the reporting period are those that occur between the statement of financial position date and the date on which the financial statements are approved.

   A   (1) and (2) only

   B   (1), (3) and (4) only

   C   (2) and (3) only

   D   (2), (3) and (4) only

312 Brakes Co had a reporting date of 30 September 20X8. The financial statements for that year were approved by the directors on 14 December 20X8 and issued to the shareholders on 17 January 20X9. Details of several events which occurred after the reporting date of 30 September 20X8 are as follows:

(1) On 3 October 20X8 a fire destroyed all inventory on the premises with the consequence that it was unlikely Brakes would be able to continue as a going concern.

(2) A credit customer with an outstanding balance at 30 September 20X8 was declared bankrupt on 12 December 20X8.

(3) An ordinary dividend of 6c per share was declared on 1 December 20X8.

(4) Inventory valued at a cost of $800 at the year-end was sold for $650 on 11 November 20X8.

Which of the above are non-adjusting events?

A   All are non-adjusting events

B   (3) only is a non-adjusting event

C   (3) and (4) only are non-adjusting events

D   (1) and (3) only are non-adjusting events

313 **Where there are material non-adjusting events, a note to the financial statements should disclose:**

A   The nature of the event and the estimated financial effect

B   A letter from the solicitor

C   Nothing

D   Where the event took place

314 **Viola has an accounting year-end of 31 January 20X4. Which of the following events, if they occurred before the financial statements were approved, would be classified as adjusting events in accordance with IAS 10 Events after the Reporting Period?**

(1) Viola paid an equity dividend of $10,000 on 28 February 20X4. The dividend had been proposed by the directors on 20 January 20X4.

(2) Notification of a compensation claim from a customer was received on 15 February 20X4 which related to a faulty product sold by Viola in January 20X4.

(3) Viola received notification on 5 February 20X4 that a major credit customer was insolvent.

A   (1), (2) and (3) are adjusting events

B   (2) and (3) are adjusting events

C   (1) and (3) are adjusting events

D   (2) only is an adjusting event

REVENUE FROM CONTRACTS WITH CUSTOMERS

315 Rep Co is preparing its financial statements for the year ended 30 September 20X4. During that year, Rep Co acted as an agent on behalf of Zip Co and arranged a sale of goods on 1 August 20X4 at a price of $80,000. Rep Co is entitled to 10% commission upon receipt of cash from the customer. The customer paid for the goods on 28 September 20X4.

How much revenue can be recognised by Rep Co in its statement of profit or loss for the year ended 30 September 20X4?

$ [   ]

316 Loc Co sells machines, and also offers installation and technical support services. The selling price of each product is shown below.

Sale price of machine	$750
Installation	$100
One year service support agreement	$120

Cox Co purchased a machine, along with the installation service and the service agreement on 1 October 20X5. The machine was delivered and installed on 1 October 20X5 and the service support agreement also commenced from that date.

How much can Loc Co recognise as revenue for the year ended 31 December 20X5?

$ [   ]

317 **Which one of the following items has been included correctly in Hat Co's revenue for the year ended 31 March 20X5?**

A Hat Co negotiated a sale at a value of $200,000 on behalf of a client, Res Co, one of its clients. Hat Co is entitled to 10% commission on the agreed sale price and has recognised revenue of $200,000 in its financial statements.

B Hat Co entered into a contract to supply consultancy services to Cap Co for a three year term for a total fee of $300,000. The contract commenced on 1 July 20X4, and Hat Co recognised revenue of $100,000 on this transaction in its financial statements.

C On 1 November 20X4 Hat Co purchased goods at a cost of $50,000 and sold those goods to Far Co for $75,000 on 20 January 20X5. Hat Co recognised revenue of $75,000 on this contract in its financial statements.

D On 1 December 20X4 Hat Co purchased goods at a cost of $25,000 and sold those goods to Ber Co for $50,000 on 10 January 20X5. Hat Co recognised revenue of $25,000 on this contract in its financial statements.

318 Which one of the following items is not part of the 'five step' approach for revenue recognition as outlined in IFRS 15 Revenue from Contracts with Customers?

A   Allocate the total price between the separate performance obligations in the contract

B   All contracts must be in writing

C   Recognise revenue when a performance obligation is satisfied

D   Identify the contract

319 Identify whether each of the following items is an acceptable basis for recognition of revenue in the financial statements of an entity.

	True	False
On any reasonable basis		
At a point in time		
Annually		
Over a period of time		

STATEMENTS OF CASH FLOWS

320 Extracts from the financial statements of Deuce Co showed balances as follows:

	20X9	20X8
$1 Share capital	300,000	120,000
Share premium	260,000	100,000

A bonus issue of 1 share for every 12 held at the 20X8 year-end occurred during the year and loan notes of $300,000 were issued at par. Interest of $12,000 was paid during the year.

What is the net cash inflow from financing activities?

A $480,000

B $605,000

C $617,000

D $640,000

321 Nobus Co is producing its statement of cash flows for the year ended 31 December 20X5. The accountant has identified the following balances in the financial statements:

	$
Interest accrual b/f	4,900
Interest accrual c/f	1,200
Interest payable	20,000
Interest receivable	13,000
Preference dividend payable b/f	120,000
Preference dividends payable c/f	140,000
Dividends (statement of changes in equity)	600,000

What is the net cash flow from investing activities?

$	Inflow / outflow*	* delete which does not apply

322 Which of the following items could appear as items in an entity's statement of cash flows?

(1)   A bonus issue of shares.

(2)   A rights issue of shares.

(3)   The revaluation of non-current assets.

(4)   Dividends paid.

A   All four items

B   (1), (3) and (4) only

C   (2) and (4) only

D   (3) only

323 A draft statement of cash flows contains the following:

	$m
Profit before tax	22
Depreciation	8
Increase in inventories	(4)
Decrease in receivables	(3)
Increase in payables	(2)
	___
Net cash inflow from operating activities	21
	___

Which TWO of the following corrections need to be made to the calculations?

Selection

Depreciation should be deducted, not added

Increase in inventories should be added, not deducted

Decrease in receivables should be added, not deducted

Increase in payables should be added, not deducted

324 Where, in an entity's financial statements, complying with International accounting standards, should you find the proceeds of non-current assets sold during the period?

A   Statement of cash flows and statement of financial position

B   Statement of changes in equity and statement of financial position

C   Statement of profit or loss and other comprehensive income and cash flow statement

D   Statement of cash flows only

325 The figures below have been prepared for inclusion in the statement of cash flows of Bamboo.

Tax and dividends paid	$87,566
Increase in payables	$13,899
Decrease in inventory	$8,900
Redemption of loans	$300,000
Increase in receivables	$6,555
Reduction in cash and cash equivalents	$3,211
Depreciation charge	$10,600
Payments to acquire non-current assets	$47,999
Proceeds from sale of non-current assets	$13,100

What is the cash generated from operations?

A $331,688

B $338,110

C $425,676

D $419,254

326 A business's bank balance increased by $750,000 during its last financial year. During the same period it issued shares, raising $1 million and repaid a loan of $750,000. It purchased non-current assets for $200,000 and charged depreciation of $100,000. Receivables and inventory increased by $575,000.

What was the profit for the year?

A $1,175,000

B $1,275,000

C $1,325,000

D $1,375,000

327 A business had non-current assets with a carrying amount of $50,000 at the start of the financial year. During the year the business sold assets that had cost $4,000 and had been depreciated by $1,500. Depreciation for the year was $9,000. The carrying amount of assets at the end of the financial year was $46,000.

How much cash has been invested in non-current assets during the year?

A $4,000

B $7,500

C $9,000

D $10,000

328 A business has made a profit of $8,000 but its bank balance has reduced by $5,000.

Which one of the following statements could be a possible explanation for this situation?

A   Depreciation charge of $3,000 and an increase in inventories of $10,000

B   Depreciation charge of $6,000 and the repayment of a loan of $7,000

C   Depreciation charge of $12,000 and the purchase of new non-current assets for $25,000

D   The disposal of a non-current asset for $13,000 less than its carrying amount

329 A Co made a profit for the year of $18,750, after accounting for depreciation of $1,250. During the year, non-current assets were purchased for $8,000, receivables increased by $1,000, inventories decreased by $1,800 and payables increased by $350.

What was A Co's increase in cash and bank balances during the year?

A $10,650

B $10,850

C $12,450

D $13,150

330 A statement of cash flows prepared in accordance with the indirect method reconciles profit before tax to cash generated from operations.

Which of the following lists of items consists only of items that would be ADDED to profit before tax?

A   Decrease in inventory, depreciation charge, profit on sale of non-current assets

B   Increase in payables, decrease in receivables, profit on sale of non-current assets

C   Loss on sale of non-current assets, depreciation charge, increase in receivables

D   Decrease in receivables, increase in payables, loss on sale of non-current assets

331 In relation to statements of cash flows, identify whether each of the following statements are true or false.

	True	False
The direct method of calculating net cash from operating activities leads to a different figure from that produced by the indirect method, but this is balanced elsewhere in the statement of cash flows.		
An entity making high profits must necessarily have a net cash inflow from operating activities.		
Profits and losses on disposals of non-current assets appear as items under investing activities in the statement of cash flows.		

332 The movement on the plant and machinery account for X is shown below:

Cost b/f	$10,000
Additions	$2,000
Disposals	($3,000)
Cost c/f	$9,000
Depreciation b/f	$2,000
Charge for the year	$1,000
Disposals	($1,500)
Depreciation c/f	$1,500
Carrying amount b/f	$8,000
Carrying amount c/f	$7,500

The profit on the sale of the machine was $500. What figures would appear in the statement of cash flows of X under the heading of 'Investing activities'?

A Movement on plant account $500 and profit on disposal of $500

B Movement on plant account $500 and proceeds on sale of plant $2,000

C Purchase of plant $2,000 and profit on disposal of $500

D Purchase of plant $2,000 and proceeds on sale of plant $2,000

333 Which one of the following is not an advantage of the statement of cash flows?

A It highlights the effect of non-cash transactions

B It helps an assessment of the liquidity off a business

C The numbers within it cannot be manipulated through the adoption of beneficial accounting policies

D It helps users to estimate future cash flows

334 Grainger makes all sales for cash and is preparing its statement of cash flows using the direct method. Grainger has compiled the following information:

Cash sales		$212,500
Cash purchases		$4,600
Cash expenses		$11,200
Payables at start and at the end of the year	$12,300	and $14,300
Credit purchases		$123,780
Wages and salaries due at start and at the end of the year	$1,500	and $2,300
Wages and salaries expense		$34,600
Inventory at start and ay the end of the year	$23,000	and $$17,800

What is the cash generated from operations by Grainger?

A $35,520

B $46,320

C $74,920

D $41,120

335 Howard Co provided the following extracts from the statement of financial position for the years ended 31 December:

	20X6	20X7
	$000	$000
Accumulated profits	72,000	82,000
10% Loan notes	30,000	40,000
Tax payable	12,000	15,000
Dividends payable	1,200	1,600

All dividends were declared and proposed **before** the year end. There was no adjustment for under/over provision for tax in the year ended 31 December 20X7. No interim dividends were paid during the year. The additional 10% loan notes were issued on 1 January 20X7.

What is Howard Co's operating profit (profit before interest and tax) for the year ended 31 December 20X7?

A $29,600

B $27,200

C $30,600

D $102,600

336 In the year ended 31 May 20X2, Galleon purchased non-current assets at a cost of $140,000, financing them partly with a new loan of $120,000. Galleon also disposed of non-current assets with a carrying amount of $50,000, making a loss of $3,000. Cash of $18,000 was received from the disposal of investments during the year.

What is Galleons net cash inflow or outflow from investing activities to include in the statement of cash flows?

$	Inflow / outflow*

* delete which does not apply

337 The following is an extract from the financial statements of Pompeii at 31 October:

	20X7 $000	20X6 $000
Equity and liabilities:		
Share capital	120	80
Share premium	60	40
Retained earnings	85	68
	265	188
Non-current liabilities:		
Bank loan	100	150
	365	338

What was Pompeii's net cash inflow or outflow from financing activities to include in the statement of cash flows for the year ended 31 October 20X7?

$	Inflow / outflow*	* delete which does not apply

338 Carter Co has non-current assets with a carrying amount of $2,500,000 on 1 December 20X7. During the year ended 20 November 20X8, the following occurred:

(1) Depreciation of $75,000 was charged to the statement of profit or loss.

(2) Land and buildings with a carrying amount of $1,200,000 were revalued to $1,700,000.

(3) An asset with a carrying amount of $120,000 was disposed of for $150,000.

The carrying amount of non-current assets at 30 November 20X8 was $4,200,000.

What amount should be shown for the purchase of non-current assets in the statement of cash flows of Carter Co for the year ended 30 November 20X8?

$	Inflow / outflow*	* delete which does not apply

339 Which THREE of the following items would you expect to see included within the operating activities section of a statement of cash flows prepared using the direct method?

	Selection
Payments made to suppliers	
Increase or decrease in receivables	
Receipts from customers	
Increase or decrease in inventories	
Increase or decrease in payables	
Finance costs paid	

340 When comparing two statements of cash flows, one prepared using the direct method and the other prepared using the indirect method, the only differences between the two statements relate to the presentation of items within 'cash flows from operating activities'.

Is the above statement true or false?

A   True

B   False

341 When preparing a statement of cash flows using the direct method in accordance with IAS 7, the depreciation charge for the year is disclosed as an adjustment to reported profit for the year within 'cash flows from operating activities'.

Is the above statement true or false?

A   True

B   False

INCOMPLETE RECORDS

342 The following information is available about the transactions of Razil, a sole trader who does not keep proper accounting records:

	$
Opening inventory	77,000
Closing inventory	84,000
Purchases	763,000
Gross profit margin	30%

Based on this information, what was Razil's sales revenue for the year?

A $982,800

B $1,090,000

C $2,520,000

D $1,080,000

343 On 1 September 20X8, Winston had inventory of $380,000. During the month, sales totalled $650,000 and purchases $480,000. On 30 September 20X8 a fire destroyed some of the inventory. The undamaged goods were valued at $220,000. The business operates with a standard gross profit margin of 30%.

Based on this information, what is the cost of the inventory destroyed in the fire?

A $185,000

B $140,000

C $405,000

D $360,000

344 You have been provided with the following incomplete and incorrect extract from the statement of profit or loss of a business that trades at a mark-up of 25% on cost:

	$	$
Sales		174,258
Less: Cost of goods sold:		
Opening inventory	12,274	
Purchases	136,527	
Closing inventory	X	
	———	
		(X)
		———
Gross profit		X
		———

Having discovered that the sales revenue figure should have been $174,825 and that purchase returns of $1,084 and sales returns of $1,146 have been omitted, what should be the amount for closing inventory?

A $8,662

B $8,774

C $17,349

D $17,458

345 A fire in the offices of Lewis has destroyed most of the accounting records. The following information has been retrieved:

	$
Sales	630,000
Opening inventory	24,300
Closing inventory	32,750
Opening payables	29,780
Closing payables	34,600

Gross profit for the period should represent a mark-up of 40%.

What was the total cash paid to suppliers in the year?

A $463,270

B $381,630

C $391,270

D $453,630

346 Pioneer's annual inventory count took place on 6 January 20X6. The value of inventory on this date was $32,780. During the period from 31 December 20X5 to 6 January 20X6, the following events occurred:

Sales $8,600
Purchases $4,200

The value of inventory at 31 December 20X5 was $34,600.

What is the gross margin of Pioneer?

A   70%

B   72%

C   30%

D   43%

347 Harry has a mark-up of 25% on cost of sales. The following information is also available:

	$
Receivables at start of year	6,340
Receivables at end of year	5,200
Cash at start of year	620
Cash at end of year	500
Total cash payments	16,780

The only receipts during the year consisted of cash and cheques received from customers.

What is the gross profit for the year?

A $3,880

B $3,152

C $3,560

D $3,104

348 During September, Edel had sales of $148,000, which made a gross profit of $40,000. Purchases amounted to $100,000 and opening inventory was $34,000.

The value of closing inventory was:

A $24,000

B $26,000

C $42,000

D $54,000

349 **The gross profit mark-up is 40% if:**

A   sales are $120,000 and gross profit is $48,000

B   sales are $120,000 and cost of sales is $72,000

C   sales are $100,800 and cost of sales is $72,000

D   sales are $100,800 and cost of sales is $60,480

350 Many of the records of G have been destroyed by fire. The following information is available for the period under review.

(1) Sales totalled $480,000.

(2) Inventory at cost was opening $36,420, closing $40,680.

(3) Trade payables were opening $29,590, closing $33,875.

(4) Gross profit for the period should represent a mark-up on cost of 50%.

What was the total of cash paid to suppliers for the period under review?

A $239,975

B $315,715

C $319,975

D $328,545

351 Pike runs an angling shop in the south of Spain. He spends all of his spare time fishing and consequently has kept no accounting records in the year ended 31 August 20X5. He knows that he has taken $6,800 cash out of his business during the year plus bait which cost the business $250. He can also remember putting his $20,000 winnings on the Spanish lottery into the business in March.

Pike knows that at the last year end his business had assets of $40,000 and liabilities of $14,600. He has also calculated that the assets of the business at 31 August 20X5 are worth $56,000, and the liabilities $18,750.

What profit or loss has Pike made in the year?

A $1,100 profit

B $1,100 loss

C $1,350 profit

D $1,350 loss

352 Ives makes and sells handmade pottery. He keeps all finished items in a storeroom at the back of his workshop on the banks of the River Flow. In August 20X5, freak weather conditions led to extensive flooding, and Ives lost pottery which had cost $3,400 and had a retail value of $5,750.

Ives was insured for loss of inventory due to flooding.

What double entry is required to record the loss of inventory?

	Dr	Cr
A	Expense (P/L) $5,750	Cost of sales (P/L) $5,750
B	Current asset (SFP) $5,750	Cost of sales (P/L) $5,750
C	Expense (P/L) $3,400	Cost of sales (P/L) $3,400
D	Current asset (SFP) $3,400	Cost of sales (P/L) $3,400

PREPARING SIMPLE CONSOLIDATED FINANCIAL STATEMENTS

353 At 1 January 20X4 Yogi acquired 80% of the share capital of Bear for $1,400,000. At that date the share capital of Bear consisted of 600,000 ordinary shares of 50c each and its reserves were $50,000. The fair value of the non-controlling interest was valued at $525,000 at the date of acquisition.

In the consolidated statement of financial position of Yogi and its subsidiary Bear at 31 December 20X8, what amount should appear for goodwill?

A $1,575,000

B $630,000

C $1,050,000

D $450,000

354 At 1 January 20X8 Tom acquired 80% of the share capital of Jerry for $100,000. At that date the share capital of Jerry consisted of 50,000 ordinary shares of $1 each and its reserves were $30,000. At 31 December 20X9 the reserves of Tom and Jerry were as follows:

Tom $400,000

Jerry $50,000

In the consolidated statement of financial position of Tom and its subsidiary Jerry at 31 December 20X9, what amount should appear for group reserves?

A $400,000

B $438,000

C $416,000

D $404,000

355 At 1 January 20X6 Fred acquired 75% of the share capital of Barney for $750,000. At that date the share capital of Barney consisted of 20,000 ordinary shares of $1 each and its reserves were $10,000. The fair value of the non-controlling interest was valued at $150,000 at 1 January 20X6.

In the consolidated statement of financial position of Fred and its subsidiary Barney at 31 December 20X9, what amount should appear for goodwill?

A $150,000

B $720,000

C $870,000

D $750,000

356 At 1 January 20X6 Gary acquired 60% of the share capital of Barlow for $35,000. At that date the share capital of Barlow consisted of 20,000 ordinary shares of $1 each and its reserves were $10,000. At 31 December 20X9 the reserves of Gary and Barlow were as follows:

Gary $40,000

Barlow $15,000

At the date of acquisition the fair value of the non-controlling interest was valued at $25,000.

In the consolidated statement of financial position of Gary and its subsidiary Barlow at 31 December 20X9, what amount should appear for non-controlling interest?

A $25,000

B $27,000

C $28,000

D $31,000

357 At 1 January 20X8 Williams acquired 65% of the share capital of Barlow for $300,000. At that date the share capital of Barlow consisted of 400,000 ordinary shares of 50c each and its reserves were $60,000. At 31 December 20X9 the reserves of Williams and Barlow were as follows:

Williams $200,000

Barlow $75,000

The fair value of the non-controlling interest was valued at $50,000 at the date of acquisition.

In the consolidated statement of financial position of Williams and its subsidiary Barlow at 31 December 20X9, what amount should appear for non-controlling interest?

A $55,250

B $50,000

C $76,250

D $5,250

358 The following are extracts from the statements of financial position of Dora and Diego:

	Dora $000	Diego £000
Current assets		
Inventory	200	100
Receivables	540	160
Cash	240	80
Current liabilities		
Payables	320	180

Dora's statement of financial position includes a receivable of $40,000 due from Diego.

In the consolidated statement of financial position what will be the correct amounts for receivables and payables?

	Payables	Receivables
A	$460,000	$660,000
B	$306,000	$660,000
C	$294,000	$694,000
D	$294,000	$654,000

359 Salt owns 70% of Pepper and sells goods to Pepper valued at $1,044 at a mark-up of 20%. 40% of these goods were sold on by Pepper to external parties at the year end.

What is the provision for unrealised profit (PURP) adjustment in the group financial statements?

A $69.60

B $104.40

C $125.28

D $83.52

360 Stress acquired 100% of the ordinary share capital of Full on 1 October 20X7 when Full's retained earnings stood at $300,000. Full's statement of financial position at 30 September 20X9 was as follows:

Assets	$000	Equity and reserves	$000
Property, plant and equipment	1,800	Share capital	1,600
Current assets	1,000	Retained earnings	500
		Current liabilities	700
	2,800		2,800

On 1 October 20X7 the fair value of land included within Full's non-current assets was $400,000 greater than the carrying amount. Stress had non-current assets at 30 September 20X9 at a carrying amount of $2.2m.

What is the total amount for non-current assets that will appear on the consolidated statement of financial position at 30 September 20X9?

$ [   ]

The following data relate to questions 361 to 363.

Hard acquired 80% of the ordinary share capital of Work on 1 April 20X8. The summarised statement of profit or loss for the year-ended 31 March 20X9 is as follows:

	Hard	Work
	$000	$000
Revenue	120,000	48,000
Cost of sales	84,000	40,000
Gross profit	36,000	8,000
Distribution costs	5,000	100
Administration expenses	7,000	300
Profit from operations	24,000	7,600
Investment income	150	–
Finance costs	–	400
Profit before tax	24,150	7,200
Tax	6,000	1,200
Profit for the year	18,150	6,000

During the year Hard sold Work some goods for $24m, these had originally cost $18m. At the year-end Work had sold half of these goods to third parties.

Note: in the exam, all questions will be independent, and not based on a common scenario.

361 **What is the provision for unrealised profit (PURP) adjustment for the year-ended 31 March 20X9?**

   A $1,000,000

   B $6,000,000

   C $3,000,000

   D $7,000,000

362 **What is the total share of group profit attributable to non-controlling interest?**

   A $1,200,000

   B $4,800,000

   C $3,630,000

   D $1,440,000

363 **What is the total amount for revenue and cost of sales to be shown in the consolidated statement of profit or loss for the year-ended 31 March 20X9?**

	Sales	Cost of sales
A	$144,000,000	$100,000,000
B	$168,000,000	$97,400,000
C	$192,000,000	$100,600,000
D	$144,000,000	$103,000,000

The following data relate to questions 364 to 365

Really acquired 75% of the ordinary share capital of Hard on 1 January 20X9 when Hard had retained losses of $112,000. Also on that date, Really acquired 30% of the ordinary share capital of Work when Work had retained earnings of $280,000. The summarised statement of financial position for the year-ended 31 December 20X9 is as follows:

	Really	Hard
Non-current assets	$000	$000
Property, plant and equipment	1,918	1,960
Investment in Hard	1,610	
Investment in Work	448	
	3,976	1,960
Current assets		
Inventory	760	1,280
Receivables	380	620
Cash	70	116
	5,186	3,976
Equity and reserves		
$1 ordinary shares	2,240	1,680
Retained earnings	2,464	1,204
	4,704	2,884
Current liabilities		
Payables	300	960
Taxation	182	132
	5,186	3976

Note: in the exam, all questions will be independent, and not based on a common scenario.

364 What is the amount for property, plant and equipment to be included in the consolidated statement of financial position?

    A $3,878,000

    B $5,558,000

    C $5,552,400

    D $3,872,400

365 What is the amount for retained earnings to be included in the consolidated statement of financial position?

    A $3,959,200

    B $3,451,800

    C $3,735,200

    D $3,740,800

366 Which of the following statements is most likely to indicate an investment by one entity in another which should be recognised and accounted for as an associate?

    A   Ownership of 100% of the ordinary shares of another entity

    B   Ownership of over 50% and less than 100% of the ordinary shares of another entity

    C   Ownership of between 20% and 50% of the ordinary shares of another entity

    D   Ownership of less than 20% of the ordinary shares in another entity

367 IFRS 10 Consolidated Financial Statements specify three necessary elements to determine whether or not one company controls another.

Which one of the following is not one of the three necessary elements to determine whether one entity has control of another?

    A   Power over the other entity

    B   Exposure or rights to variable returns from involvement in the other entity

    C   The ability to use power over the other entity to affect the amount of investor returns

    D   The ability to exercise significant influence over another entity

368 Which of the following would normally indicate that one entity has significant influence over the activities of another?

    A   Ability to appoint the majority of the board of directors of that other entity

    B   Ability to appoint at least one person to the board of directors of that other entity

    C   Ability to request that a director is appointed to the board of directors of that other entity

    D   Ability to submit requests regarding corporate policy to the board of directors of that other entity

369 Which of the following would normally indicate that one entity has control over the activities of another?

A   Ownership of some equity shares in another entity

B   Ownership of up to twenty per cent of the equity shares of another entity

C   Ownership of over fifty per cent of the equity shares of another entity

D   Ownership of between twenty per cent and fifty per cent of the equity shares of another entity

370 Which of the following would normally indicate that one entity has control of another?

A   Ownership of the majority of the equity share capital of that other entity

B   Ownership of between twenty per cent and fifty per cent of the equity share capital of that other entity

C   Ownership of less than twenty per cent of the equity shares of that other entity

D   Ownership of some of the shares of that other entity – the precise percentage of shares held is not relevant

371 Which of the following would normally indicate that one entity has significant influence over the activities of another entity?

A   Ownership of some equity shares in another entity

B   Ownership of up to twenty per cent of the equity shares of another entity

C   Ownership of over fifty per cent of the equity shares of another entity

D   Ownership of between twenty per cent and fifty per cent of the equity shares of another entity

372 Entity A acquired sixty per cent of the issued equity shares of entity B by exchanging three shares in entity A for every two shares acquired in entity B. At that date, entity B had issued equity capital of one hundred thousand shares. At the date of acquisition, the fair value of an equity share in entity A was $3.50 and the fair value of an equity share in entity B was $2.00. The nominal value per share of both entities was $1.00 per share.

What was the fair value of consideration paid by entity A to gain control of entity B?

A $80,000

B $90,000

C $180,000

D $315,000

373 Entity C acquired eighty per cent of the issued equity shares of entity D by paying cash of $3.00 per share plus exchanging three shares in entity C for every five shares acquired in entity D. At that date, entity D had issued equity capital of two hundred and fifty thousand shares. At the date of acquisition, the fair value of an equity share in entity C was $3.50 and the fair value of an equity share in entity D was $2.00. The nominal value per share of both entities was $1.00 per share.

What was the fair value of consideration paid by entity C to gain control of entity D?

$ [   ]

374 Entity X acquired sixty per cent of the issued equity shares of entity Z on 1 October 20X3. During the year ended 31 December 20X3, X and Z had sales revenue of $2 million and $1.5 million respectively. During the post-acquisition period, X made sales to Z of $0.1 million.

What is the group sales revenue figure for the year ended 31 December 20X3?

A $2.275 million

B $2.375 million

C $3.4 million

D $3.5 million

375 Entity T acquired eighty per cent of the issued equity shares of entity S on 1 July 20X6. The sales revenue for the year ended 31 March 20X7 for entity T and entity S was $5 million and $3 million respectively. During the post-acquisition period, S made sales to T of $0.5 million.

What is the group sales revenue figure for the year ended 31 March 20X7?

A $6.75 million

B $7.25 million

C $7.5 million

D $8.0 million

376 Entity F acquired eighty per cent of the issued equity shares of entity G on 1 July 20X6. The cost of sales for the year ended 31 March 20X7 for entity F and entity G were $10 million and $4 million respectively. During the post-acquisition period, F made sales to G of $1.6 million. The intra-group sales were made at a mark-up of twenty-five per cent. At the year end, one quarter of the goods sold by F to G remained within G's inventory.

What was the group cost of sales figure for the year ended 31 March 20X7?

A $12.480 million

B $12.320 million

C $11.480 million

D $11.320 million

377 On 1 June 20X5 Hightown acquired control of Southport. During the year ended 30 September 20X5, Hightown and Southport had cost of sales of $10 million and $6 million respectively. During the post-acquisition period, Hightown had sales to Southport of $1.8 million. These sales had been made at a mark-up of twenty per cent and at the year end, one third of the goods remained within Southport's inventory.

What was the group cost of sales figure for the year ended 30 September 20X5?

$ _____

378 On 1 July 20X4 Lion paid $20 million to acquire seventy per cent of the issued equity capital of Tiger. For the year ended 31 December 20X4, Tiger had earned profit after tax of $2 million. Tiger had retained earnings of $10 million at 1 January 20X4. At the date of acquisition, Tiger had issued equity capital of $8 million and the fair value of the non-controlling interest at that date was $6 million.

Based upon the available information, what was goodwill on acquisition of Tiger for inclusion in the Lion consolidated financial statements for the year ended 31 December 20X4?

$ _____

379 Pole acquired eighty per cent of the issued equity shares of Rod for $43 million on 1 March 20X8. Rod had retained earnings of $15 million at 1 July 20X7 and made a profit after tax of $6 million for the year ended 30 June 20X8. At the date of acquisition, Rod had issued share capital of $25 million and the fair value of the non-controlling interest was $10 million. On 1 March 20X8 the fair value of freehold land and buildings owned by Rod was $1 million in excess of their carrying amount.

Based upon the available information, what was goodwill on acquisition of Rod for inclusion in the Pole consolidated financial statements for the year ended 30 June 20X8?

A $4.0 million

B $8.0 million

C $16.0 million

D $20.0 million

380 Plank acquired sixty per cent of the issued equity share capital of Splinter on 1 January 20X2. On that date, Plank paid $3 cash per share acquired and also issued two shares (nominal value $1 per share) in exchange for each Splinter share acquired. At the date of acquisition, Splinter had ten million equity shares of $1 nominal value in issue, plus a share premium account balance of $10 million and had retained earnings of $50 million. The fair value of the non-controlling interest in Splinter at the date of acquisition was $14 million. The fair value of an equity share in Plank and Splinter were $4.50 and $1.50 respectively at 1 January 20X2.

What was goodwill on acquisition of Splinter for inclusion in the consolidated financial statements of Plank for the year ended 31 December 20X2?

$ _____

381 On 1 October 20X5, Luton acquired seventy-five per cent of the issued equity capital of Bedford. In exchange for gaining control of Bedford, Luton made immediate cash payment of $4.50 per share acquired and also issued one new share for each share acquired. At the date of acquisition, Bedford had issued share capital of fifteen million shares of $1 nominal value and a share premium account balance of $5 million. On 1 October 20X5, Bedford had retained earnings of $76.875 million and the fair value of the non-controlling interest in Bedford was $27 million. Bedford had a freehold factory that had a fair value of $2 million in excess of its carrying amount at the date of acquisition. The fair value of a $1 equity share of Luton at the date of acquisition was $5.00 per share.

What was goodwill on acquisition of Bedford for inclusion in the consolidated financial statements of Luton for the year ended 30 September 20X6?

A $35 million

B $37 million

C $39 million

D $40 million

382 On 1 January 20X6, Hyndland acquired ninety per cent of the issued equity capital of Shawfield. In exchange for gaining control of Shawfield, Hyndland made immediate cash payment of $3 per share acquired and also issued one new share of $0.5 nominal value per share for each share acquired. At the date of acquisition, Shawfield had issued share capital of 200,000 shares of $1 nominal value, a share premium account balance of $100,000 and retained earnings of $590,000. On 1 January 20X6, the fair value of the non-controlling interest in Shawfield was $75,000. In addition, at the date of acquisition, Shawfield had several items of property plant and equipment which together had a fair value of $90,000 and a carrying amount of $70,000. The fair value of a $0.5 equity share of Hyndland at 1 January 20X3 was $2.00 per share. There has been no impairment of goodwill.

What was goodwill on acquisition of Shawfield for inclusion in the consolidated financial statements of Hyndland for the year ended 30 September 20X6?

$ [   ]

383 On 1 July 20X5 Huyton acquired sixty per cent of the equity shares of Speke. For the year ended 31 December 20X5, Huyton made a profit after tax of $600,000 and Speke had a profit after tax of $400,000. During the post-acquisition period, Huyton sold goods to Speke which included a profit element of $20,000. At the year-end, one quarter of the goods sold by Huyton to Speke remained within the inventory of Speke.

What was the non-controlling interest share of the group profit after tax for the year ended 31 December 20X5?

A $75,000

B $80,000

C $120,000

D $160,000

384 Honey Co acquired 75% of Bee Co on 1 April 20X3, paying $2 for each ordinary share acquired. The fair value of the non-controlling interest at 1 April 20X3 was $300. Bee Co's individual financial statements as at 30 September 20X3 included:

Statement of financial position:	$
Ordinary share capital ($1 each)	1,000
Retained earnings	710
	———
	1,710
	———

Statement of profit or loss:	
Profit after tax for the year	250

Profit accrued evenly throughout the year.

What was goodwill on acquisition at 1 April 20X3?

A $715

B $90

C $517

D $215

385 Panther acquired 80% of the equity shares in Seal on 31 August 20X2. The statements of profit or loss for Panther and Seal for the year ended 31 December 20X2 were as follows:

	Panther	*Seal*
	$	$
Revenue	100,000	62,000
Cost of sales	25,000	16,000

During October 20X2, sales of $6,000 were made by Panther to Seal. None of these items remained in inventory at the year-end.

What is the consolidated revenue for Panther Group or the year ended 31 December 20X2?

$ [   ]

386 Tulip acquired 70% of the equity shares of Daffodil on 1 March 20X2. The following extracts are from the individual financial statements of profit and loss for each entity for the year ended 31 August 20X2:

	Tulip	*Daffodil*
	$	$
Revenue	61,000	23,000
Cost of sales	(42,700)	(13,800)
	———	———
Gross profit	18,300	9,200

What should be the consolidated gross profit for the year ended 31 August 20X2?

$ [   ]

387 Venus acquired 75% of Mercury's 100,000 $1 ordinary shares on 1 November 20X4. The consideration comprised $2 cash per share plus one share in Venus for every share acquired in Mercury.

Shares in Venus have a nominal value of $1 and a fair value of $1.75. The fair value of the non-controlling interest was $82,000 and the fair value of the net assets acquired was $215,500.

What should be recorded as goodwill on acquisition of Mercury in the consolidated Mercury Group financial statements?

$ [   ]

388 **Which of the following investments of Coffee should be equity accounted in the consolidated financial statements?**

(1)   40% of the non-voting preference share capital in Tea Co

(2)   18% of the ordinary share capital in Café Co with two of the five directors of Coffee Co on the board of Café Co

(3)   50% of the ordinary share capital of Choc Co, with five of the seven directors of Coffee Co on the board of Choc Co

A   (1) and (2)

B   (2) only

C   (1) and (3) only

D   (2) and (3) only

389 **State whether each of the following statements is true or false in relation to accounting for associates.**

	True	False
Equity accounting will always be used when an investing entity holds between 20% – 50% of the equity shares in another entity.		
Dividends received from an investment in associate will be presented as investment income in the consolidated financial statements.		

INTERPRETATION OF FINANCIAL STATEMENTS

The following data relate to questions 390 to 401. Barnstorm case-study.

Note: The following questions, based upon the financial statements of Barnstorm presented below are designed as a revision aid to test your knowledge of definitions and calculations of accounting ratios. You will not necessarily be required to state the ratio definition and calculate the ratio for two years in the real exam.

You should calculate all ratios to two decimal places.

The financial statements of Barnstorm for the year ended 31 July 20X4, with comparatives, are presented below.

Statement of profit or loss and other comprehensive income – year ended 31 July 20X4.

	20X4	20X3
	$000	$000
Revenue	1,391,820	1,159,850
Cost of sales	(1,050,825)	(753,450)
Gross profit	340,995	406,400
Operating expenses	(161,450)	(170,950)
Finance costs	(10,000)	(14,000)
Profit before tax	169,545	221,450
Tax	(50,800)	(66,300)
Profit for the year	118,745	155,150
Other comprehensive income:		
Revaluation surplus on land and buildings	10,000	
Total comprehensive income for the year	128,745	155,150

Statement of financial position at 31 July 20X4

	20X4	20X3
	$000	$000
Non-current assets		
Property, plant and equipment	559,590	341,400
Current assets		
Inventory	109,400	88,760
Receivables	419,455	206,550
Bank		95,400
	1,088,445	732,110

Equity and reserves		
$1 ordinary shares	140,000	100,000
Share premium	40,000	20,000
Revaluation reserve	10,000	
Retained earnings	406,165	287,420
	596,165	407,420
Non-current liabilities		
10% Bank loan 20X7	61,600	83,100
Current liabilities		
Payables	345,480	179,590
Bank overdraft	30,200	
Taxation	55,000	62,000
	1,088,445	732,110

Note: in the exam, all questions will be independent, and not based on a common scenario.

390 **Calculate the return on capital employed for the year ended 31 July 20X4, together with the comparative for the earlier year.**

20X4	
20X3	

391 **Calculate the gross profit margin for the year ended 31 July 20X4, together with the comparative for the earlier year.**

20X4	
20X3	

392 **Calculate the operating profit margin for the year ended 31 July 20X4, together with the comparative for the earlier year.**

20X4	
20X3	

393 **Calculate the asset turnover for the year ended 31 July 20X4, together with the comparative for the earlier year.**

20X4	
20X3	

394 Calculate the current ratio for the year ended 31 July 20X4, together with the comparative for the earlier year.

20X4	
20X3	

395 Calculate quick 'acid test' ratio for the year ended 31 July 20X4, together with the comparative for the earlier year.

20X4	
20X3	

396 Calculate the inventory holding period for the year ended 31 July 20X4, together with the comparative for the earlier year.

20X4	
20X3	

397 Calculate the trade receivables collection period for the year ended 31 July 20X4, together with the comparative for the earlier year.

20X4	
20X3	

398 Calculate the trade payables payment period for the year ended 31 July 20X4, together with the comparative for the earlier year.

20X4	
20X3	

399 Calculate the debt-equity ratio for the year ended 31 July 20X4, together with the comparative for the earlier year.

20X4	
20X3	

400 Calculate the gearing ratio for the year ended 31 July 20X4, together with the comparative for the earlier year.

20X4	
20X3	

401 Calculate interest cover for the year ended 31 July 20X4, together with the comparative for the earlier year.

20X4	
20X3	

402 W Co had sales of $20,000 and cost of sales of $15,400.

What W Co's gross profit margin?

A   77%

B   129%

C   43%

D   23%

403 The following extract relates to X Co for the years ended 30 June 20X5 and 20X6:

	20X5	20X6
Revenue	20,000	26,000
Cost of sales	(15,400)	(21,050)
Gross profit	4,600	4,950
Less expenses	(2,460)	(2,770)
Operating profit	2,140	2,180

What was the operating profit margin for 20X5 and 20X6?

	20X5	20X6
A	10.7%	8.38%
B	8.38%	10.7%
C	23.0%	19.0%
D	12.0%	10.0%

404 The following extract relates to Y Co for 20X5 and 20X6:

	20X5	20X6
	$	$
Statement of profit or loss extract		
Revenue	20,000	26,000
Statement of financial position extract		
Receivables	4,400	6,740
Cash	120	960

What is the receivables collection period for 20X5 and 20X6?

	20X5	20X6
A	80 days	95 days
B	82 days	108 days
C	75 days	111 days
D	95 days	80 days

405 The following extract of the statement of profit or loss relates to Z Co for the year ended 30 September 20X6:

	20X6
Statement of profit or loss extract	
Gross profit	15,175
Expenses	(2,460)
Profit before interest and tax	12,715
Finance cost	(5,000)
Profit before tax	7,715
Tax	(1,515)
Profit after tax	6,200

What is interest cover for the year?

A   2.54 times

B   3.03 times

C   1.54 times

D   1.24 times

406   Given a selling price of $700 and gross profit mark-up of 40%, what is the cost of an item?

A $280

B $420

C $500

D $980

407 A Co had sales of $220,000 and purchases of $160,000, together with opening inventory and closing inventory of $24,000 and $20,000 respectively.

What was inventory holding period in days (based on the average level of inventory for the period)?

A   44.5 days

B   22.2 days

C   53.4 days

D   49.0 days

408 What is the formula for calculating the inventory holding period in days?

A   Cost of goods sold divided by average inventories × 365

B   Sales divided by average inventories at cost × 365

C   Sales divided by average inventories at selling price × 365

D   Average inventories at cost divided by cost of goods sold × 365

409 B Co had the following details extracted from its statement of financial position:

	$000
Inventory	3,800
Receivables	2,000
Bank overdraft	200
Payables	2,000

What was the current ratio based upon the available information?

A   1.72:1

B   2.90:1

C   2.64:1

D   3.00:1

410 **D Co's gearing ratio would rise if:**

A   a decrease in long-term loans is less than a decrease in shareholder's funds

B   a decrease in long-term loans is more than a decrease in shareholder's funds

C   interest rates rose

D   interest rates fell

411 R Co had the following details extracted from its statement of financial position:

	$000
Inventory	3,800
Receivables	2,000
Bank overdraft	200
Payables	2,000

Based upon the available information, what was the quick (acid test) ratio of R Co?

A   2.63 : 1

B   0.9 : 1

C   29.0 : 1

D   1 : 1

412 Extracts from the financial statements of Miller for the year ended 31 May 20X2 are shown below:

	$000
Revenue	475
Cost of sales	(342)
Gross profit	133
Expenses	(59)
Finance cost	(26)
Profit before tax	48

What was the interest cover ratio for the year ended 31 May 20X2?

A   2.85

B   1.85

C   5.12

D   0.35

413 The following extract relates to R Co 20X6 and 20X5:

	20X6 $	20X5 $
Statement of profit or loss extract		
Cost of sales	55,000	48,000
Statement of financial position extract		
Trade payables	4,400	5,300
Overdraft	120	960

Calculate the payables payment period of R Co for 20X6 and 20X5.

20X6	days
20X5	days

414 An increase in the gearing ratio could be caused by the issue of ordinary shares for cash during the year.

Is the statement above true or false?

A   True

B   False

415 A reduction in the unit purchase cost of raw materials whilst the unit selling price remains unchanged will increase the gross profit margin.

Is the statement above true or false?

A   True

B   False

416 The following extracts relate to T Co or 20X3 and 20X2:

	20X3	20X2
	$	$
Inventory	18,000	16,000
Trade receivables	17,500	21,050
Cash and equivalents	3,095	
	38,595	37,050
Current liabilities		
Trade payables	20,750	18,500
Bank overdraft		500
	20,750	19,000

Calculate the current ratio of T Co for 20X3 and 20X2.

20X3	
20X2	

417 An increase in return on capital could be caused by an increase in long-term loans taken out by the business during the year.

Is the statement above true or false?

A　True

B　False

418 The following extracts relate to MN Co for 20X8 and 20X7:

	20X8	20X7
Issued share capital	50,000	50,000
Share premium	5,500	5,500
Retained earnings	34,500	24,500
	90,000	80,000
Non-current liabilities		
10% Bank loan	4,500	5,600
Current liabilities		
Bank overdraft	3,000	500

Calculate the debt/equity ratio of MN Co for 20X8 and 20X7.

20X8	
20X7	

419 **Which one of the following is likely to increase the trade receivables collection period?**

A   Offering credit customers a significant discount for prompt payment within seven days of receipt of invoice

B   Application of effective credit control procedures

C   Poor application of credit control procedures by a business

D   An increasing volume of credit sales during an accounting period

420 **Which one of the following is likely to reduce the trade payables payment period?**

A   Offering credit customers a significant discount for prompt payment within seven days of receipt of invoice

B   Paying trade suppliers within seven days of receipt of invoice to obtain a discount

C   Buying proportionately more goods on a cash basis, rather than on a credit basis

D   Buying an increasing volume of credit purchases during an accounting period

421 **Which one of the following is likely to increase the inventory holding period?**

A   Building up inventory levels in preparation of a sales and marketing campaign later in the year

B   Scrapping of old and obsolete items of inventory

C   Only ordering goods from a reliable supplier upon receipt of a customer order

D   Implementation of effective goods requisitioning and ordering policies

422   You have been advised that a business has an inventory turnover of 8.49.

What is the average number of days that inventory is retained in the business prior to its sale?

```
┌─────────────────┐
│                 │
└─────────────────┘
```

423   During the year, A Co made a bonus issue of shares to its shareholders.

What is the impact of this upon the gearing ratio?

A   The gearing ratio will increase

B   The gearing ratio will decrease

C   There will be no change to the gearing ratio

D   It is not possible to determine the impact on the gearing ratio as there is insufficient information available

424 **Which of the following statements could explain why return on capital for an entity increased from 20% in 20X7 to 25% in 20X8?**

(1) The entity reduced long-term borrowings during 20X8.

(2) The entity managed to increase in profit margin during 20X8.

(3) The entity made an issue of shares for cash during 20X8 to finance capital expenditure.

A None of the above

B (2) and (3) only

C (1) and (3) only

D (1) and (2) only

425 During the year, B Co made a rights issue of shares to its shareholders.

What was the impact of this upon the gearing ratio?

A It is not possible to determine the impact on the gearing ratio as there is insufficient information available

B The gearing ratio increased

C The gearing ratio decreased

D The gearing ratio remained unchanged

426 In an attempt to increase sales revenue during the year, C Co offered extended credit terms to its major customers. Whilst many major customers took advantage of the extended credit period, C Co did not increase its volume of sales.

What impact did this have upon the current ratio?

A There was no change to the current ratio

B It is not possible to determine the impact on the current ratio as there is insufficient information available

C The current ratio increased

D The current ratio decreased

427 On 1 July 20X5, D Co raised $5 million from an issue of ordinary shares. D Co then immediately used this cash to repay a loan of $5 million, which was not due for repayment until 30 June 20X9.

What impact did this have upon the debt/equity ratio?

A It is not possible to determine the impact on the debt/equity ratio as there is insufficient information available

B The debt/equity ratio increased

C The debt/equity ratio decreased

D There will be no change to the debt/equity ratio

428 XYZ Co has the following working capital ratios:

	20X9	20X8
Current ratio	1.2:1	0.9:1
Receivables days	60 days	50 days
Payables days	45 days	35 days
Inventory turnover	36 days	45 days

Which of the following statements regarding XYZ Co is true?

A   XYZ Co is taking longer to pay suppliers in 20X9 than in 20X8

B   XYZ Co is suffering a worsening liquidity position in 20X9

C   XYZ Co is managing inventory less efficiently in 20X9 in comparison with 20X8.

D   XYZ Co is reiving cash from customers more quickly in 20X9 than in 20X8

429 **State whether each of the following statements is true or false.**

	True	*False*
A statement of cash flows prepared using the direct method produces a different figure for investing activities in comparison with that produced if the indirect method is used.		
A bonus issue of shares does not feature in a statement of cash flows.		
The amortisation charge for the year on intangible assets will appear as an item under 'Cash flows from operating activities' in a statement of cash flows.		
Loss on the sale of a non-current asset will appear as an item under 'Cash flows from investing activities' in a statement of cash flows.		

430 **Which one of the following statements is true?**

A   Analysis of financial performance should include both financial and non-financial information available.

B   An entity will always have a poor quick or acid test ratio if is highly geared.

C   The use of financial ratios to evaluate performance is not appropriate for sole traders.

D   Calculation of financial ratios for one accounting period only provides sufficient information to assess financial performance.

Section 2

MULTI-TASK QUESTIONS

1 ICE CO

Task 1

The following is an extract from the trial balance of Ice Co, an entity, as at 31 December 20X1:

	Dr $	Cr $
Revenue		600,000
Inventory valuation at 1 January 20X1	24,000	
Purchases and other expenses	240,000	
Carriage inwards	2,000	
Carriage outwards	3,000	
Administrative expenses	180,000	
Distribution costs	75,000	
Returns inwards	500	

Note: Inventory valuation at 31 December 20X1 was $30,000.

Required:

(a) **Into which heading in the statement of profit or loss should the following items be included?** **(1 mark)**

	Cost of sales	Distribution costs	Administration expenses
Carriage inwards			
Carriage outwards			

(b) **Based upon the information available, what was Ice Co's gross profit for the year ended 31 December 20X1?** **(2 marks)**

$ [   ]

(c) **Based upon the information available, identify the adjustments required to gross profit in order to calculate Ice Co's draft profit before tax.** **(2 marks)**

		Selected answer
(i)	Gross profit - $30,000 - $180,000 - $75,000	
(ii)	Gross profit - $500 - $2,000 - $180,000 - $75,000	
(iii)	Gross profit - $3,000 - $180,000 - $75,000	

Task 2

You are now advised that, on 1 April 20X1, Ice Co raised loan finance of $100,000 which will be repayable in a single instalment on 31 March 20X5. Interest is payable annually at the rate of 6% in arrears.

(a) **What expense should be included in Ice Co's statement of profit or loss in relation to the loan finance?** **(1 mark)**

$ [   ]

(b) **How should the loan be classified in the statement of financial position at 31 December 20X1?** **(1 mark)**

		Selected answer
(i)	An equity component	
(ii)	A non-current liability	
(iii)	A current liability	

Task 3

On 21 January 20X2, Ice Co received notification from a customer that they had suffered injury as a result of using one of its products which had been purchased in December 20X1. The customer made a claim for compensation amounting to $5,000 and Ice Co's legal advisors have advised that it is virtually certain that compensation will be required to settle the claim.

How should this matter be reflected in Ice Co's financial statements for the year ended 31 December 20X1? **(2 marks)**

		Selected answer
(i)	It should not be recognised or disclosed in the financial statements for the year ended 31 December 20X1	
(ii)	It should be disclosed only in the financial statements for the year ended 31 December 20X1	
(iii)	It should be recognised as a liability in the financial statements for the year ended 31 December 20X1	

Task 4

Ice Co is considering whether to undertake some work in relation to the freehold land and buildings that it owns.

(a) **State whether each of the following costs should be capitalised or treated as revenue expenditure.** **(4 marks)**

		Capital or revenue
(i)	Work to install additional, high-specification, electrical power cabling and circuits so that additional plant and equipment can become operational	
(ii)	Replacement of some loose and damaged roof tiles following a recent storm	
(iii)	Repainting the factory administration office	
(iv)	Modifications to the factory entrance to enable a large item of plant and equipment to be installed	

(b) You have now been provided with an additional extract from Ice Co's trial balance as at 31 December 20X1 as follows:

	$	$
Freehold land and building – cost (Land $70,000)	120,000	
Freehold building – accumulated dep'n at 1 Jan 20X1		20,000
Plant and equipment - cost	120,000	
Plant and equipment – accumulated dep'n at 1 Jan 20X1		15,000

The freehold building is depreciated on a straight-line basis over its estimated useful life of 50 years. The plant and equipment is depreciated on a reducing balance basis at the rate of 15%. There were no purchases or disposals of non-current assets during the year.

Calculate the depreciation charge for the year which was included as an expense within cost of sales. **(2 marks)**

Freehold building	$
Plant and equipment	$

(Total: 15 marks)

2 WILLOW CO

You have been asked to help prepare the financial statements of Willow Co for the year ended 30 June 20X1.

Task 1

You have discovered that several purchase invoices have not been recorded in the purchases day book. The total value of the invoices was $2,300 including sales tax charged at 15%.

(a) **Complete the following table to state the accounting entries required to record the invoices in the general ledger.** **(2 marks)**

	$	Credit / Debit
Bank and cash		
Payables' ledger control account		
Purchases		
Sales tax		
Suspense account		

(b) **Complete the following statement relating to the omitted purchases invoices. (1 mark)**

This accounting error will / will not* result in the totals of the trial balance failing to agree.

*Delete which does not apply

Task 2

An extract of Willow Co's trial balance as at 30 June 20X1 is shown below.

	Debit	Credit
	$000	$000
Equity share capital @ $1 each		72,000
Share premium		13,000
Revaluation surplus at 1 July 20X0		10,000
Retained earnings at 1 July 20X0		12,920
Dividends paid	3,000	

During the year ended 30 June 20X1, Willow Co made a '1 for 5' bonus issue.

Complete the following table to identify the accounting entries required to record the bonus issue. **(4 marks)**

	$000	Credit / Debit
Bank and cash		
Equity share capital		
Retained earnings		
Share premium		

Task 3

Inventory at 30 June 20X1 had been valued at cost at $9,420,000. However, upon further investigation, information relating to three specific items was established as follows:

Product	Quantity	Cost per unit	Selling price per unit	Selling expenses
		$	$	$
Standard	70	1,000	1,500	200
Super	50	1,500	1,800	350
Elite	40	2,000	2,500	650

(a) **State the correct total value of each product that should be included in the inventory valuation at 30 June 20X1 in accordance with IAS 2 *Inventories*.** **(3 marks)**

Standard	$
Super	$
Elite	$

(b) **What adjustment should be made to the inventory valuation stated at cost of $9,420,000 to ensure that it complies with the requirements of IAS 2 *Inventories*?**

(2 marks)

$	Decrease / Increase*

* Delete which does not apply

Task 4

During the year ended 30 June 20X1, Willow Co purchased a licence which enabled it sell a new product 'Supreme' for a five-year period commencing 1 July 20X0. The licence cost $2,000,000 and cannot be renewed at the end of the five-year term.

(a) **A licence is an example of which type of asset?** **(1 mark)**

Current / Intangible / Tangible*	* Delete which does not apply

(b) **State the amortisation charge for the year ended 30 June 20X1 and the carrying amount of the licence at that date.** **(2 marks)**

Amortisation charge	$
Carrying amount	$

(Total: 15 marks)

3 CLER CO

You are helping to prepare the financial statements of Cler Co for the year ended 31 December 20X7. Your initial focus is upon accounting for amounts due to the business.

Task 1

One specific receivable for $3,500 is four months old and is now considered to be irrecoverable.

(a) **State the accounting entries required to write-off this amount in the general ledger.** **(1 mark)**

	$	Credit / Debit
Allowance for receivables		
Irrecoverable debts		
Trade payables' ledger control account		
Trade receivables' ledger control account		

Additionally, it has been agreed with another credit customer who also supplies goods to Cler Co on credit that an amount of $4,750 will offset against their respective receivable and payable balances due to each other.

(b) **Complete the following statement** **(2 marks)**

For Cler Co to apply the contra entries in its general ledger, it must credit / debit* the trade payables' ledger control account and credit / debit* the trade receivables' ledger control account.

* Delete which does not apply

Finally, in relation to amounts due to the business, you have been asked to confirm the accounting entries required to record a sale transaction to a credit customer for goods with a list price of $2,000. The customer is entitled to 10% trade discount and was also offered 5% early settlement discount if payment is received within 10 days of the invoice date. The customer is expected to take advantage of the early settlement discount terms.

(c) **State the accounting entries required to record this transaction in the general ledger.** **(2 marks)**

	$	Credit / Debit
Discount received		
Revenue		
Trade payables' ledger control account		
Trade receivables' ledger control account		

Task 2

You are now dealing with the bank reconciliation as at 31 December 20X7 and a colleague has provided you with the following information:

	$
Cheques not yet presented	2,400
Cheque returned unpaid by customer's bank	1,000
Lodgments not yet cleared	3,400
Debit balance per bank statement	1,500

Based upon the information available to you, complete the bank reconciliation as at 31 December 20X7: **(4 marks)**

	$	
Debit balance per bank statement	1,500	
Cheques not yet presented		
	———	
Sub-total		
Lodgments not yet cleared		
	———	
Balance per cash book		Credit / Debit*
Cheque returned unpaid by customer's bank		
	———	
Updated balance per cash book		Credit / Debit*
	———	

* Delete as appropriate

Task 3

Inventories at the close of business on 31 December 20X7 were valued at cost of $190,871. Included in this amount was a product at a cost of $4,000 that, due to a change in legislation, no longer meets current safety standards. Cler Co could modify this product at a cost of $1,500 and plans to do so. The product could then be sold for $6,000.

(a) **At what valuation should inventory be stated in the financial statements at 31 December 20X7?** **(1 mark)**

$ _____

(b) **Complete the accounting policy disclosure note for inventory for inclusion in the financial statements for the year ended 31 December 20X7.** **(2 marks)**

Inventory is stated at the higher / lower* of cost and net realisable value / selling price* for each separate item or product.

* Delete as appropriate

(c) **Complete the following table to state whether each of the following items should be included as part of the cost of inventory.** **(3 marks)**

		Included / excluded
(i)	Selling and administration expenses	
(ii)	Transport costs from supplier to Cler Co premises	
(iii)	Storage costs	

(Total: 15 marks)

4 CARBON CO

You are helping to prepare the financial statements of Carbon Co for the year ended 31 December 20X5. Your initial focus is upon accounting for property plant and equipment.

Task 1

Carbon Co purchased land and buildings at a cost of $4,000,000 (of which the land accounted for $2,500,000) on 1 January 20X2. At that date, it was estimated that the buildings had an estimated useful life of 50 years.

Carbon Co has now decided to account for the freehold land and buildings at their fair value. At 31 December 20X5, the fair value of land and buildings was $6,000,000, of which land accounted for $4,000,000.

(a) **State whether each of the following statements relating to accounting for property, plant and equipment are true or false:** **(3 marks)**

		True / False
(i)	When an entity does revalue its land and buildings, it is compulsory to make an annual transfer of 'excess depreciation' from revaluation surplus to retained earnings	
(ii)	Any revaluation surplus arising on revaluation of property, plant and equipment is included in the statement of profit or loss in arriving at profit before tax	
(iii)	The revaluation surplus is accounted for as an adjustment to cash inflows from operating activities	

(b) **State the accounting entries required to account for the revaluation at 31 December 20X5.** **(3 marks)**

	$000	Credit / Debit
Freehold land and buildings		
Depreciation charge for the year		
Accumulated depreciation provision		
Revaluation surplus		

Task 2

At 1 January 20X5, Carbon Co had a credit balance on its income tax account of $2,300,000. For the year ended 31 December 20X5, Carbon Co estimated that its income tax liability to be $2,400,000. During 20X5, the income tax liability for the previous year was settled at $2,350,000.

What was the income tax charge in the statement of profit or loss for the year ended 31 December 20X5? **(1 mark)**

$

Task 3

An extract of Carbon Co's trial balance at 31 December 20X5 is presented below:

	$000
Issued share capital @ $1 shares	10,000
Retained earnings – 1 January 20X5	25,500

On 1 February 20X5, Carbon Co made a '1-for-four' rights issue at an issue price of $2.50 per share. The rights issue was fully subscribed and taken up by the shareholders.

(a) **How many shares were issued as a result of making the rights issue?** **(1 mark)**

(b) **What were the total proceeds raised as a result of making the rights issue?** **(1 mark)**

$

(c) **What was the balance on the share premium account as a result of making the rights issue?** **(1 mark)**

$

Task 4

You are preparing Carbon Co's statement of changes in equity for the year ended 31 December 20X5.

Identify whether or not each of the following items would be presented in the statement of changes in equity. **(3 marks)**

	Included / excluded
Depreciation charge for the year	
Share issue made in the year	
Proposed dividend due to be paid on 26 February 20X6	
Dividend paid on 28 October 20X5	

Task 5

Carbon Co's gross profit margin for the year ended 31 December 20X5 was 28%, in comparison with 24% for the preceding year.

Which one of the following statements could be a plausible reason for the increase in the gross profit margin during 20X5? **(2 marks)**

		Selected answer
(i)	Distribution costs reduced during 20X5	
(ii)	Carbon Co sold more goods during 20X5 due to a successful marketing campaign early in the year	
(iii)	There was a change in the sales mix during 20X5, with proportionately fewer of its low-margin goods being sold	

(Total: 15 marks)

5 MARCUS

You are helping to prepare the financial statements of Marcus for the year ended 30 April 20X5. There are a number of accounting issues to deal with before the financial statements can be finalised.

Task 1

During the year, problems were experienced with goods from a particular supplier. In total, goods which cost $300,000, inclusive of sales tax at 20%, were returned to the supplier.

State the accounting entries required to record the return of goods to the supplier. (2 marks)

	$000	Credit / Debit
Revenue		
Returns inwards		
Returns outwards		
Sales tax		
Trade payables' ledger control account		
Trade receivables'' ledger control account		

Task 2

During the year, Marcus withdrew goods from the business for his personal use. The goods cost $15,000 and had a sale value of $20,000.

State the accounting entries required to record withdrawal of goods from the business by Marcus for personal use. **(3 marks)**

	$000	Credit / Debit
Drawings		
Trade payables' ledger control account		
Purchases		
Revenue		

Task 3

During the year, Marcus introduced a system of trade discounts and early settlement discounts for his customers.

State whether each of the following statements is true or false. **(3 marks)**

		True / False
(i)	Trade discount allowed to customers should be included as an expense in the statement of profit or loss	
(ii)	Early settlement discount allowed to credit customers is deducted from the invoice value at the point of sale when the customer is not expected to take advantage of the early settlement discount terms offered	
(iii)	Early settlement discount earned from suppliers should be included in the statement of profit or loss	

Task 4

You are now dealing with accruals and prepayments required at 30 April 20X5. You have been advised that the insurance premium of $18,000 paid on 31 December 20X4 was to cover the twelve month period to 31 December 20X5. You have also identified that, following a long-running dispute with a customer, there will be legal fees to pay, amounting to $6,000.

Complete each of the following three statements in relation to the information contained in this Task. **(3 marks)**

Accounting for the insurance accrual / prepayment* will increase / reduce* the profit for the year ended 30 April 20X5.

Accounting for the legal fees accrual / prepayment* will increase / reduce* the profit for the year ended 30 April 20X5.

The net effect upon the profit for the year ended 30 April 20X5 as a result of accounting for the accrual and/or prepayment required for insurance and legal fees will be to increase / reduce* profit for the year by $1,500 / $3,000 / $6,000*.

* Delete as appropriate

Task 5

A colleague has produced the trial balance as at 30 April 20X5 which does not balance. He therefore opened a suspense account for the difference. He has identified several issues and is not sure whether or not they may contribute to reconciling and clearing the difference.

Identify whether each of the following items is relevant or not to reconcile and clear the suspense account (4 marks)

		Relevant / Not relevant
(i)	Sales returns listed as a debit balance in the trial balance	
(ii)	Discounts received were recorded in the cash received book and credited to the Discounts received account in the general ledger	
(iii)	The total of the purchases day book for March was debited to the Trade payables' ledger control account and credited to the Purchases account	
(iv)	The cost of a machine purchased during the year was debited to the Repairs account as $8,080 and credited to the Cash account as $8,800	

(Total: 15 marks)

6   FIREWORK CO

The following financial statements and supporting information relate to Firework Co, a limited liability entity:

Statement of profit or loss and other comprehensive income for the year ended 30 June 20X5

	$000
Revenue	113,250
Less: Cost of sales	77,500
	————
Gross profit	35,750
Less: Distribution costs	3,000
Less: Administration expenses	1,000
Less: Interest payable	750
	————
Profit before tax	31,000
Less: Income tax expense	6,000
	————
Profit for the year	25,000
Other comprehensive income:	
Revaluation of property, plant and equipment	2,000
	————
Total comprehensive income for the year	27,000
	————

Statement of financial position at 30 June 20X5:

	20X5 $000	20X4 $000
ASSETS		
Non-current assets		
Property, plant and equipment	110,000	93,000
Current assets		
Inventories	36,000	30,000
Trade receivables	40,000	35,000
Cash and equivalents	Nil	10,000
Total assets	186,000	168,000
EQUITY AND LIABILITIES		
Equity share capital	20,000	15,000
Share premium	8,000	3,000
Revaluation surplus	10,000	8,000
Retained earnings	96,000	85,000
Total equity	134,000	111,000
Non-current liabilities		
Bank loan	7,000	17,000
Current liabilities		
Trade payables	36,500	30,000
Income tax	6,500	10,000
Bank overdraft	2,000	Nil
Total equity and liabilities	186,000	168,000

+

The following information is relevant to the financial statements of Firework Co:

(i)   During the year ended 30 June 20X5, Firework Co disposed of several items of plant and equipment for sale proceeds of $8,000,000. The loss on disposal of $2,000,000 is included within cost of sales. The depreciation charge for the year was $15,000,000.

(ii)   Firework Co estimated that the income tax liability arising on the profit for the year ended 30 June 20X5 was $6,500,000.

Required:

Based upon the information available, complete the statement of cash flows for Firework Co for the year ended 30 June 20X5 in accordance with the requirements of IAS 7 *Statement of cash flows*.   **(Total: 15 marks)**

Firework Co – Statement of cash flows for the year ended 30 June 20X5

	$000	
Cash flows from operating activities		
Profit after tax / Profit before tax*		
Adjustments for:		
Depreciation charge		Add / Subtract*
Loss on sale of plant and equipment		Add / Subtract*
Interest payable		Add / Subtract*
Change in inventories		Add / Subtract*
Change in trade receivables		Add / Subtract*
Change in trade payables		Add / Subtract*
	————	
Cash generated from operations	N/A	
Interest paid		Add / Subtract*
Income taxes paid		Add / Subtract*
	————	
Cash flows from financing / investing* activities	N/A	
Cash purchase of property, plant and equipment		Add / Subtract*
Disposal proceeds of plant and equipment		Add / Subtract*
	————	
Cash flows from financing / investing* activities	N/A	
Repayment of bank loan		Add / Subtract*
Proceeds of share issue		Add / Subtract*
Dividend paid		Add / Subtract*
	————	
Decrease / Increase* in cash and cash equivalents for the year		
Cash and cash equivalents at start of year		Add / Subtract*
	————	
Cash and cash equivalents at end of year		Net cash / net overdraft*
	————	

Note: * = delete which does not apply

7 CRACKER CO

The following financial statements and supporting information relate to Cracker Co, a limited liability entity:

Statement of profit or loss and other comprehensive income for the year ended 31 March 20X1

	$000
Revenue	88,740
Less: Cost of sales	73,750
Gross profit	14,990
Less: Distribution costs	1,200
Less: Administration expenses	610
	13,180
Add: Profit on disposal of plant and equipment	300
Add: Investment income	320
Less: Interest payable	2,150
Profit before tax	11,650
Less: Income tax expense	2,900
Profit for the year	8,750

There were no items of other comprehensive income during the year.

Statement of financial position at 31 March 20X1:

	20X1	20X0
ASSETS	$000	$000
Non-current assets		
Property, plant and equipment	73,000	70,500
Current assets		
Inventories	27,500	25,500
Trade receivables	37,500	33,000
Cash and equivalents	4,250	1,250
Total assets	142,250	130,250

	20X1	20X0
EQUITY AND LIABILITIES	$000	$000
Equity share capital	11,000	10,000
Share premium	610	Nil
Retained earnings	74,790	66,040
Total equity	86,400	76,040
Non-current liabilities		
10% Debenture	23,500	20,000
Current liabilities		
Trade payables	29,450	31,900
Income tax	2,900	2,310
Total equity and liabilities	142,250	130,250

Notes:

The following information is relevant to the financial statements of Cracker Co:

(i)   During the year ended 31 March 20X1, Cracker Co disposed of some items of plant and equipment. The carrying amount of these items at the date of disposal was $800,000. The depreciation charge for the year was $500,000.

(ii)   Cracker Co estimated that the income tax liability arising on the profit for the year ended 31 March 20X1 was $2,900,000.

Required:

Based upon the information available, complete the statement of cash flows for Cracker Co for the year ended 31 March 20X1 in accordance with the requirements of IAS 7 *Statement of cash flows*.   **(Total: 15 marks)**

Cracker Co – Statement of cash flows for the year ended 31 March 20X1

	$000
Cash flows from operating activities	
Profit after tax / profit before tax*	
Adjustments for:	
Depreciation charge	Add / Subtract*
Gain /loss * on disposal of plant and equipment	Add / Subtract*
Investment income	Add / Subtract*
Interest payable	Add / Subtract*
Change in inventories	Add / Subtract*
Change in trade receivables	Add / Subtract*
Change in trade payables	Add / Subtract*
Cash generated from operations	N/A
Interest paid	Add / Subtract*
Income taxes paid	Add / Subtract*

Cash flows from investing activities	N/A	
Investment income		Add / Subtract*
Cash purchase of property, plant and equipment		Add / Subtract*
Disposal proceeds of plant and equipment	*Item 1*	Add / Subtract*
	_____	
Cash flows from financing activities	N/A	
Proceeds of loan raised		Add / Subtract*
Proceeds of share issue	*Item 2*	Add / Subtract*
	_____	
Net change in cash and cash equivalents for the year		Decrease / Increase*
Cash and cash equivalents at start of the year		Add / Subtract*
	_____	
Cash and cash equivalents at end of the year		
	_____	

Note: * = delete which does not apply

Item 1: Disposal proceeds of plant and equipment:

Choose the correct calculation of the disposal proceeds of plant and equipment (all figures in $000):

		Selected answer
(i)	$800 - $300	
(ii)	$800 + $300	
(iii)	$800	

Item 2: Proceeds of the share issue:

Choose the correct calculation of the proceeds of the share issue (all figures in $000):

		Selected answer
(i)	$11,000 - $10,000	
(ii)	$11,000 - $10,000 + $610	
(iii)	$!!,000 - $10,000 - $610	

8   SPARKLER CO

The following financial statements and supporting information relate to Sparkler Co, a limited liability entity:

Statement of profit or loss and other comprehensive income for the year ended 30 September 20X9

	$000
Revenue	94,800
Less: Cost of sales	71,100
Gross profit	23,700
Less: Distribution costs	2,500
Less: Administration expenses	1,000
Add: Profit on disposal of plant and equipment	500
Less: Interest payable	2,700
Profit before tax	18,000
Less: Income tax expense	3,500
Profit for the year	14,500
Other comprehensive income:	
Revaluation surplus on property, plant and equipment	3,000
Total comprehensive income for the year	17,500

Statement of financial position at 30 September 20X9:

	20X9	20X8
	$000	$000
ASSETS		
Non-current assets		
Property, plant and equipment	95,000	85,000
Current assets		
Inventories	30,750	36,000
Trade receivables	39,250	45,000
Cash and equivalents	3,000	Nil
Total assets	168,000	166,000

	20X9	20X8
EQUITY AND LIABILITIES	$000	$000
Equity share capital	30,000	24,000
Share premium	10,000	8,000
Revaluation surplus	3,000	Nil
Retained earnings	60,875	66,500
Total equity	103,875	98,500
Non-current liabilities		
10% Debenture	25,000	20,000
Current liabilities		
Bank overdraft	Nil	4,500
Trade payables	35,000	38,500
Income tax	3,500	4,000
Accrued interest	625	500
Total equity and liabilities	168,000	166,000

The following information is relevant to the financial statements of Sparkler Co during the year ended 30 September 20X9

(a)   Sparkler Co disposed of some items of plant and equipment for sale proceeds of $2,000,000. The carrying amount of the items disposed of was $1,500,000.

(b)   Sparkler Co purchased property plant and equipment at a cost of $21,000,000. In addition, land and buildings were revalued during the year.

(c)   Sparkler Co estimated that the income tax liability arising on the profit for the year was $3,500,000.

Required:

Based upon the information available, complete the statement of cash flows using the indirect method for Sparkler Co for the year ended 30 September 20X9 in accordance with the requirements of IAS 7 *Statement of cash flows*.   (Total: 15 marks)

Sparkler Co – Statement of cash flows for the year ended 30 September 20X9

	$000
Cash flows from operating activities	
Profit before tax / Total comprehensive income*	
Adjustments for:	
Depreciation charge	Add / Subtract*
Profit on sale of plant and equipment	Add / Subtract*
Interest payable	Add / Subtract*
Change in inventories	Add / Subtract*
Change in trade receivables	Add / Subtract*
Change in trade payables	Add / Subtract*

Cash generated from operations	N/A	
Interest paid	Item 1	Add / Subtract*
Income taxes paid		Add / Subtract*
	————	
Net cash from operating activities	N/A	
Cash flows from investing activities		
Cash purchase of property, plant and equipment		Add / Subtract*
Disposal proceeds of plant and equipment		Add / Subtract*
	————	
Net cash from investing activities	N/A	
Cash flows from financing activities		
Proceeds of loan raised		Add / Subtract*
Proceeds of share issue		Add / Subtract*
Dividend paid	Item 2	Add / Subtract*
	————	
Net cash from financing activities	N/A	
Net change in cash and equivalents for the year		Decrease / Increase*
Cash and cash equivalents b/fwd		Add / Subtract*
	————	
Cash and cash equivalents c/fwd		
	————	

Note: * = delete which does not apply

Item 1: Interest paid:

Choose the correct calculation of interest paid (all figures in $000):

		Selected answer
(i)	$2,700 - $625 - $500	
(ii)	$2,700 + $500 + $625	
(iii)	$2,700 + $500 - $625	

Item 2: Dividend paid:

Choose the correct calculation of dividend paid in the year:

		Selected answer
(i)	Retained earnings b/fwd + Profit after tax – Retained earnings c/fwd	
(ii)	Retained earnings b/fwd + Total comprehensive income – Retained earnings carried forward	
(iii)	Retained earnings b/fwd – Profit after tax + Retained earnings c/fwd	

9 OUTFLOW CO

The following financial statements and supporting information relate to Outflow Co, a limited liability entity:

Statement of profit or loss and other comprehensive income for the year ended 30 April 20X2

	$000
Revenue	34,760
Less: Cost of sales	(33,560)
	———
Gross profit	1,200
Less: Distribution and administration expenses	(4,500)
Less: interest payable	(1,000)
	———
Loss before tax	(4,300)
Income tax	500
	———
Loss for the year	(3,800)
Other comprehensive income:	
Revaluation surplus on property, plant and equipment	2,000
	———
Total comprehensive income for the year	(1,800)
	———

Statement of financial position at 30 April 20X2:

	20X2	20X1
	$000	$000
ASSETS		
Non-current assets		
Property, plant and equipment – carrying amount	110,000	100,000
Current assets		
Inventories	30,000	33,000
Trade receivables	48,750	52,000
Income tax recoverable	500	Nil
	———	———
Total assets	189,250	185,000
	———	———

EQUITY AND LIABILITIES	$000	$000
Equity share capital @ $1 each	44,000	40,000
Share premium	5,000	4,000
Revaluation surplus	22,000	20,000
Retained earnings	72,450	77,250
Total equity	143,450	141,250
Non-current liabilities		
Long-term bank loan	15,500	8,000
Current liabilities		
Bank overdraft	4,000	3,250
Trade payables	26,300	27,500
Income tax	Nil	5,000
Total equity and liabilities	189,250	185,000

The following information is relevant to the financial statements of Outflow Co for the year ended 30 April 20X2:

(a)   Outflow Co scrapped numerous items of plant and equipment during the year for nil proceeds. The items scrapped were originally purchased for $7,000,000 and they had a carrying amount of $1,000,000 at the date of disposal. The gain or loss on scrapping is included within cost of sales.

(b)   Outflow Co made a depreciation charge for the year of $11,000,000 and several buildings had been revalued during the year.

(c)   Outflow Co estimated that it would receive a tax refund of $500,000 as a result of making a loss before tax for the year ended 30 April 20X2.

Required:

Based upon the information available, complete the statement of cash flows using the indirect method for Outflow Co for the year ended 30 April 20X2 in accordance with the requirements of *IAS 7 Statement of cash flows*.   **(Total: 15 marks)**

Outflow Co – Statement of cash flows for the year ended 30 April 20X2

	$000
Cash flows from operating activities	
(Loss before tax) / Profit before tax*	( )
Adjustments for:	
Depreciation charge	Add/ Subtract*
Loss on scrapped assets	Add/ Subtract*
Interest payable	Add/ Subtract*
Change in inventories	Add/ Subtract*
Change in trade receivables	Add/ Subtract*
Change in trade payables	Add/ Subtract*

Cash generated from operations	N/A
Interest paid	Add/ Subtract*
Income taxes paid	Add/ Subtract*
Cash flows from investing activities	N/A
Cash purchase of property, plant and equipment	Item 1 Add/ Subtract*
Cash flows from financing activities	N/A
Proceeds of loan raised	Add/ Subtract*
Proceeds of share issue	Item 2 Add/ Subtract*
Dividend paid	Add/ Subtract*
Net change in cash and cash equivalents in the year	Decrease / Increase*
Cash and cash equivalents b/fwd	Net cash at bank / Net overdraft*
Cash and cash equivalents c/fwd	Net cash at bank / Net overdraft*

Note: * = delete which does not apply

Item 1: Additions to property, plant and equipment in the year:

Choose the correct calculation of the cash paid for property, plant and equipment additions in the year (all figures in $000):

		Selected answer
(i)	$110,000 + $2,000 - $100,000 + $11,000 + $1,000	
(ii)	$110,000 - $100,000 + $11,000	
(iii)	$110,000 - $2,000 - $100,000 + $1,000 + $11,000	

Item 2: Proceeds of the share issue:

Choose the correct calculation of the proceeds of the share issue (all figures in $000):

		Selected answer
(i)	$40,000 + 4,000 - $44,000	
(ii)	$44,000 + $5,000 - $40,000 - $4,000	
(iii)	$44,000 - $40,000	

10   PATTY AND SELMA

The statements of profit or loss for two entities, Patty and Selma, for the year ended 31 December 20X1 are presented below:

	Patty $000	Selma $000
Revenue	987	567
Cost of sales	564	336
Gross profit	423	231
Administrative expenses	223	123
Operating profit	200	108
Finance costs	50	30
Profit before tax	150	78
Taxation	40	24
Profit for the year	110	54

The following notes are relevant to the preparation of the consolidated financial statements:

(i)   Patty acquired a 70% interest in the equity shares of Selma on 1 May 20X1.

(ii)   During the post-acquisition period, Patty sold goods to Selma for $120,000 including mark-up on cost of 20%. One quarter of these goods remained in the inventory of Patty at the year end.

(iii)   All items of income and expense in Selma's statement of profit or loss account accrued evenly during the year.

Required:

Task 1

Complete the following consolidated statement of profit or loss for the Patty group the year ended 31 December 20X1.   (8 marks)

	$000	
Revenue		
Cost of sales	Item 1	Add/ Subtract*
	———	
Gross profit	N/A	
Administrative expenses		Add/ Subtract*
	———	
Operating profit	N/A	
Finance costs	Item 2	Add/ Subtract*
	———	
Profit before taxation	N/A	
Income tax expense		Add/ Subtract*
	———	
Profit after tax for the year	N/A	
	———	
Profit after tax attributable to:		
Owners of Patty	N/A	
Non-controlling interest	Item 3	
	———	
	N/A	
	———	

Note: * = delete which does not apply

Item 1 - Choose the correct calculation for cost of sales

	All figures are in $000	*Selected answer*
(i)	$564 + ($336 × 8/12) - $120 - $5	
(ii)	$564 + ($336 × 8/12) + $120 - $5	
(iii)	$564 + ($336 × 8/12) - $120 + $5	

Item 2 - Choose the correct calculation for finance costs

	All figures are in $000	*Selected answer*
(i)	$50 – ($30 × 8/12)	
(ii)	$50 + ($30 × 8/12)	
(iii)	$50 + $30	

Item 3 - Choose the correct formula to calculate the non-controlling interest share of the consolidated profit for the year

		Selected answer
(i)	(NCI% × Subsidiary profit before tax × 8/12) + NCI share of unrealised profit on inventory	
(ii)	(NCI% × Subsidiary profit after tax × 8/12) - NCI share of unrealised profit on inventory	
(iii)	NCI% × Subsidiary profit after tax × 8/12	

Task 2

State whether each of the following statements is true or false. **(3 marks)**

		True / False
(i)	Accounting for the acquisition of a subsidiary always includes recognition and accounting for a non-controlling interest	
(ii)	Accounting for the acquisition of a subsidiary can be achieved by using equity accounting	
(iii)	The share capital and share premium account balances of a subsidiary are not included in the consolidated statement of financial position	

Task 3

(a) **Using the individual entity financial statements, calculate the following ratios Patty and Selma for the year ended 31 December 20X1.** **(2 marks)**

(i) **Gross profit margin**

Patty	%

Selma	%

(ii) **Operating profit**

Patty	%

Selma	%

Note: Ratios should be calculated to one decimal place.

You have been advised that the gross profit margin of an entity, Quartz, was **higher** than that for Patty, and also that the net profit percentage of Quartz was **lower** than that for Patty.

(a) **What conclusion could you arrive at regarding the relative financial performance of the two entities?** **(2 marks)**

		Selected answer
(i)	Patty is relatively better at minimising distribution costs and administration expenses than Quartz	
(ii)	Quartz is relatively better at minimising distribution costs and administration expenses than Patty	
(iii)	It is not possible to arrive at a conclusion regarding which entity is relatively better at minimising distribution costs and administration expenses	

(Total: 15 marks)

11 PENTAGON AND SQUARE

You have been presented with the following information relating to the acquisition of Square by Pentagon:

(i) Pentagon acquired 75% of the ordinary shares of Square on 1 January 20X4 for a total consideration of $250,000, $150,000 of which comprised an immediate cash payment. The balance of the consideration paid consisted of a share exchange of four shares in Pentagon for every three shares of Square acquired. At the date of acquisition, the fair value of a Pentagon share was $2.50. The share issue has not yet been accounted for.

(ii) At the acquisition date, the retained earnings of Square were $120,000 and revaluation surplus was $10,000. The fair value of the non-controlling interest in Square at the date of acquisition was $75,000.

(iii) The fair values of the net assets of Square at the acquisition date approximated to their carrying amounts, with the exception of a plot of land. This land was recorded in the financial statements of Square at its cost of $100,000 but was estimated to have a fair value of $170,000. This land was still owned by Square at 31 December 20X4.

Extracts from the statements of financial position for Pentagon and Square as at 31 December 20X4 are presented below:

	Pentagon	Square
Equity and liabilities	$	$
Equity		
Share capital @ $1 each	80,000	40,000
Revaluation surplus	20,000	10,000
Retained earnings	335,000	279,000

Required:

Task 1

(a)   Calculate the fair value of consideration paid to acquire the shares in Square. **(1 mark)**

	$
Fair value of consideration paid:	N/A
Cash	
Shares issued	Add/ Subtract*
	_____
	_____

Note: * = delete which does not apply

(b)   State the accounting entries required by Pentagon to record the issue of shares used as part of the consideration to acquire control of Square.   **(2 marks)**

	$	*Credit / Debit*
Investment in Square		
Issued share capital		
Retained earnings		
Revaluation surplus		
Share premium		

(c)   Choose the correct formula to calculate goodwill arising upon acquisition of Square. **(1 mark)**

		Selected answer
(i)	Fair value of consideration paid Plus: Fair value of non-controlling interest at acquisition Plus: Fair value of net assets at acquisition date	
(ii)	Fair value of consideration paid Less: Fair value of non-controlling interest at acquisition Plus: Fair value of net assets at acquisition date	
(iii)	Fair value of consideration paid Plus: Fair value of non-controlling interest at acquisition Less: Fair value of net assets at acquisition date	

Task 2

In addition to the information provided above, the following information is also relevant to the preparation of the consolidated financial statements at 31 December 20X4.

Assets	Pentagon	Square
Non-current assets	$	$
Property, plant and equipment	205,000	179,000
Investment in Square	150,000	
Current assets		
Inventories	80,000	50,000
Trade and other receivables	60,000	99,000
Cash and cash equivalents		51,000
Current liabilities		
Bank overdraft	12,000	
Trade and other payables	48,000	50,000

During the year ended 31 December 20X4, Pentagon sold goods to Square for $30,000, including a gross profit margin of 30%. One-third of these goods were included in the inventories of Square at 31 December 20X4.

State the amounts that each of the following items should be included in the consolidated statement of financial position as at 31 December 20X4. **(6 marks)**

	$
Property, plant and equipment	
Inventories	
Trade and other receivables	
Cash and cash equivalents	

Task 3

Choose the correct calculation of the non-controlling interest to include in the consolidated statement of financial position as at 31 December 20X4. **(2 marks)**

	All figures are in $	Selected answer
(i)	(25% × $75,000) + (25% × ($279,000 − $120,000))	
(ii)	$75,000 + (25% × ($279,000 + $120,000))	
(iii)	$75,000 + (25% × ($279,000 − $120,000))	

Task 4

(a) **Using the individual financial statements, calculate the quick (acid test) ratio for Pentagon and Square as at 31 December 20X4.** **(2 marks)**

Pentagon	:1

Square	:1

Note: Ratios should be calculated to one decimal place.

(b)   **Complete the following statement relating to the quick (acid test) ratio.**   **(1 mark)**

The quick (acid test) ratio is a measure of gearing / liquidity / profitability*. A quick (acid test) ratio of 0.75:1 indicates that an entity has a higher /lower* value of current assets than current liabilities. For the purposes of this ratio, inventories are excluded / included* within the definition of current assets.

* Delete which does not apply

(Total: 15 marks)

12   PIKE AND SALMON

Pike acquired 75% of the issued share capital of Salmon on 1 January 20X6 for $8,720,000. In addition, Pike also invested in $1 million of Salmon's 5% loan notes at par value. An extract of the financial statements of Pike and Salmon as at 31 March 20X6 is presented below:

	Pike	Salmon
Equity and liabilities	*$000*	*$000*
Equity		
Share capital	9,200	4,800
Retained earnings	12,480	1,290
Total equity	21,680	6,090
Non-current liabilities		
5% loan notes 20X9	16,440	11,180
Current liabilities	2,640	1,410
	40,760	18,680

The following information is relevant to the preparation of the consolidated financial statements:

(i)   At acquisition, the fair value of land owned by Salmon exceeded its cost by $1,000,000. This land was still owned at 31 March 20X6.

(ii)   During the post-acquisition period, Salmon sold goods to Pike for $500,000, on which it earned a margin of ten per cent. Eighty per cent of the goods remained in Pike's inventory at the year end. At 31 March 20X6 Salmon was still owed half of the total amount invoiced to Pike for these goods.

(iii)   The fair value of the non-controlling interest in Salmon at the date of acquisition was $2,400,000.

(iv)   For the year ended 31 March 20X6, Salmon made a profit after tax of $240,000.

Task 1

(a) Choose the correct calculation of Salmon's retained earnings at the date of acquisition. **(2 marks)**

	All figures are in $000	Selected answer
(i)	$6,090 + $240 + (3/12 × $240)	
(ii)	$1,290 – $240 + (9/12 × $240)	
(iii)	$1,290 – $240 + (3/12 × $240)	

(b) Choose the correct calculation of the fair value of net assets of Salmon at the date of acquisition. **(2 marks)**

	All figures are in $000	Selected answer
(i)	$4,800 + $1,290 + $1,000	
(ii)	$4,800 - $1,230 + (3/12 × $240) + $1,000	
(iii)	$4,800 + $1,290 – (3/12 × $240) + $1,000	

(c) Choose the correct calculation of goodwill at acquisition. **(2 marks)**

	All figures are in $000	Selected answer
(i)	$9,720 + $2,400 - $7,030	
(ii)	$8,720 + $2,400 - $7,030	
(iii)	$8,720 + $2,400 - $6,030	

Task 2

(a) What amount should be included in the consolidated statement of financial position for the 5% Loan notes as at 31 March 20X6? **(2 marks)**

$ _____

(b) What amount should be included in the consolidated statement of financial position for retained earnings at 31 March 20X6? **(2 marks)**

$ _____

You have now been provided with the following additional information relating to Pike and Salmon as at 31 March 20X6:

	Pike $000	Salmon $000
Assets		
Investments at cost	9,720	
Non-current assets	26,280	13,670
Current assets	4,760	5,010
Total assets	40,760	18,680

Task 3

Complete the following table to state at what amount each of the following items should be included in the consolidated statement of financial position at 31 March 20X6. (5 marks)

		$000
(i)	Non-current assets	
(ii)	Current assets	
(iii)	Current liabilities	
(iv)	Non-controlling interest	

(Total 15 marks)

13   PLATE AND SAUCER

The statements of profit or loss for two entities, Plate and Saucer, for the year ended 31 December 20X4 are presented below:

	Plate	Saucer
	$000	$000
Revenue	1,500	700
Less: Cost of sales	775	370
Gross profit	725	330
Less: Administrative expenses	317	135
Operating profit	408	195
Add: Interest receivable	15	
Less: Finance costs	60	20
Profit before tax	363	175
Less: Income tax	96	45
Profit for the year	267	130

The following notes are relevant to the preparation of the consolidated financial statements:

(i)   Plate acquired 70% of the equity shares in Saucer on 1 January 20X1.

(ii)   During the year ended 31 December 20X4, Saucer sold goods to Plate for $150,000 making a mark-up on cost of 20%. One fifth of these goods remained in the inventory of Plate at the year end.

(iii)   On 1 October 20X4, Plate made a $1 million loan to Saucer. Interest is charged at 6% annually in arrears.

Required:

Task 1

Complete the following consolidated statement of profit or loss for the Plate group for the year ended 31 December 20X4. **(9 marks)**

	$000	
Revenue		
Cost of sales	Item 1	Add/ Subtract*
	———	
Gross profit	N/A	
Administrative expenses		Add/ Subtract*
	———	
Operating profit	N/A	
Interest receivable		Add/ Subtract*
Finance costs	Item 2	Add/ Subtract*
	———	
Profit before taxation	N/A	
Income tax expense		Add/ Subtract*
	———	
Profit after tax for the year	N/A	
	———	
Profit after tax attributable to:		
Owners of Plate	N/A	
Non-controlling interest	Item 3	
	———	
	N/A	
	———	

Note: * = delete which does not apply

Item 1 - Choose the correct calculation for cost of sales

	All figures are in $000	Selected answer
(i)	$775 + $370 + 150 - $5	
(ii)	$775 + $370 − $150 + $5	
(iii)	$775 + $370 - $150 - $5	

Item 2 - Choose the correct calculation for finance costs

	All figures are in $000	Selected answer
(i)	$60 − $20 + ($1,000 × 6% × 9/12)	
(ii)	$60 + $20 - ($1,000 × 6%)	
(iii)	$60 + $20 − ($1,000 × 6% × 3/12)	

Item 3 - Choose the correct formula to calculate the non-controlling interest share of the consolidated profit for the year

		Selected answer
(i)	(NCI% × Subsidiary profit after tax) – (NCI share of unrealised profit on inventory)	
(ii)	(NCI% × Subsidiary profit after tax) + NCI share of unrealised profit on inventory	
(iii)	(NCI% × Subsidiary profit before tax) - NCI share of unrealised profit on inventory	

Task 2

Plate is considering the purchase of a shareholding in another entity and, if purchased, this investment would meet the definition of an associate.

Select which one of the following is the correct accounting treatment for an associate in the consolidated statement of financial position. **(2 marks)**

		Selected answer
(i)	All assets and liabilities of the associate are cross-cast on a line-by-line basis with all other assets and liabilities of the group	
(ii)	The group share of the net assets of the associate are cross-cast on a line-by-line basis with all other assets and liabilities of the group	
(iii)	The net interest in the associate is included as a one-line entry as a non-current asset investment	

Task 3

(a) **Using the individual entity financial statements of Plate and Saucer, calculate the operating profit margin for each entity for the year ended 31 December 20X4.(2 marks)**

Plate	

Saucer	

Note: Ratios should be calculated to one decimal place.

(b) **State whether each of the following statements is true or false** **(2 marks)**

		True / False
(i)	The operating profit margin will be affected by a change in the value of closing inventory, if all other factors remain unchanged	
(ii)	The operating profit margin is not affected by interest and finance charges incurred during the accounting period	

(Total: 15 marks)

14   PORT AND STARBOARD

The statements of financial position for Port and Starboard as at 31 December 20X6 are presented below:

Assets	Port	Starboard
Non-current assets	$	$
Property, plant and equipment	350,000	265,000
Investments	300,000	–
Current assets		
Inventories	109,000	80,000
Trade and other receivables	79,000	95,000
Cash and cash equivalents	12,000	25,000
Total assets	850,000	465,000
Equity and liabilities		
Equity		
Share capital	80,000	60,000
Share premium	20,000	10,000
Retained earnings	295,000	250,000
Non-current liabilities		
7% Bank loan 20X9	300,000	85,000
Current liabilities		
Trade and other payables	155,000	60,000
Total equity and liabilities	850,000	465,000

The following notes are relevant to the preparation of the consolidated financial statements:

(i)   Port acquired 80% of the ordinary shares of Starboard for $300,000 on 1 January 20X2. At the acquisition date, the retained earnings of Starboard were $150,000. The fair value of the non-controlling interest in Starboard at the date of acquisition was $80,000.

(ii)   At the date of acquisition, the fair values of the net assets of Starboard approximated their carrying amounts, with the exception of a plot of land. This land was recorded in the financial statements of Starboard at its cost of $150,000 but was estimated to have a fair value of $180,000. This land was still owned by Starboard at 31 December 20X6.

(iii)   During the year ended 31 December 20X6, Port sold goods to Starboard for $50,000 making a gross profit margin on the sale of 25%. Sixty per cent of these goods had been sold by Starboard by 31 December 20X6. At the reporting date, Starboard still had a payable due to Port for $30,000, and this agreed with the receivable recorded in Port's accounting records.

Required

Task 1:

(a) Choose the correct calculation of goodwill upon acquisition of Starboard. (2 marks)

		Selected answer
(i)	$300,000 + $80,000 – ($60,000 + $150,000 + $30,000)	
(ii)	$300,000 + $80,000 – ($70,000 + $150,000 + $30,000)	
(iii)	$300,000 + $80,000 – ($70,000 + $150,000 - $30,000)	

(b) Identify which one of the following would be the correct classification for goodwill in the consolidated statement of financial position   (1 mark)

		Selected answer
(i)	A tangible non-current asset	
(ii)	A current asset	
(iii)	An intangible non-current asset	

Task 2

Complete the following table to state at what amount each of the following items should be included in the consolidated statement of financial position at 31 December 20X6. (5 marks)

		$000
(i)	Property, plant and equipment	
(ii)	Inventories	
(iii)	Trade receivables	
(iv)	Trade and other payables	
(v)	7% Bank loan 20X9	

Task 3

(a) What amount should be included in the consolidated statement of financial position for the non-controlling interest as at 31 December 20X6?   (2 marks)

$ _____

(b) What amount should be included in the consolidated statement of financial position for retained earnings as at 31 December 20X6?   (2 marks)

$ _____

Task 4

Port is considering making an investment in another entity, Astern, which would be accounted for as an associate.

Which TWO of the following factors would be relevant when accounting for an associate?

(1 mark)

		Selected answer
(i)	Control of Astern	
(ii)	Exercising significant influence over Astern	
(iii)	Owning the majority of the ordinary shares of Astern	
(iv)	Owning between 20% and 50% of the ordinary shares of Astern	
(v)	Accounting for goodwill	
(vi)	Accounting for the non-controlling interest in Astern	

Task 5

State whether each of the following statements is true or false.

(2 marks)

		True / False
(i)	If the gross profit margin of a business improves, then the current ratio will also improve	
(ii)	If a bonus issue of shares is made, this will have no impact upon the current ratio	

(Total 15 marks)

15   HIDE AND SEEK

The following statements of profit or loss relate to Hide and its subsidiary Seek for the year ended 30 June 20X6:

	Hide	Seek
	$000	$000
Revenue	200,000	100,000
Less: Cost of sales	110,000	50,000
Gross profit	90,000	50,000
Less: Distribution costs	20,000	10,000
Less: Administrative expenses	40,000	20,000
Profit before tax	30,000	20,000
Less: Taxation	10,500	6,000
Profit for the year	19,500	14,000

The following notes are relevant to the preparation of the consolidated financial statements for the year ended 30 June 20X6:

(i)   Hide acquired 3 million of the $1 equity shares of Seek on 1 April 20X6 when Seek had a total of 4 million equity shares in issue, paying $8 per share.

(ii)   At 1 July 20X5, the retained earnings of Seek were $9.5 million and the carrying amounts of the net assets of Seek approximated to their fair values, with the exception of land and buildings, which had a fair value of $2 million in excess of their carrying amount.

(iii)   The fair value of the non-controlling interest in Seek at the date of acquisition can be measured by reference to the fair value of a Seek share at 1 April 20X6 which was $4.

(iv)   During the post-acquisition period, Seek sold goods to Hide. The goods originally cost $10 million and they were sold to Hide at a mark-up of 25%. By 30 June 20X6, Hide had sold 60% of these goods.

(v)   The income and expenses of Seek accrued evenly throughout the accounting period.

Required:

Task 1

Calculate goodwill arising on acquisition of Seek by Hide. (3 marks)

	$000
Fair value of consideration paid:	
Cash paid	
	———
Fair value of the NCI at acquisition	
	———
Fair value of net assets at acquisition:	
Share capital	
Retained earnings	Item 1
Fair value adjustment	
	———
	———
Goodwill on acquisition	Item 2
	———

Item 1 - Choose the correct calculation of retained earnings at the date of acquisition

	All figures are in $000	Selected answer
(i)	$9,500 + (3/12 × $14,000)	
(ii)	$9,500 + $14,000	
(iii)	$9,500 + (9/12 × $14,000)	

Item 2 - Choose the correct calculation for goodwill

		Selected answer
(i)	Fair value of consideration paid plus fair value of non-controlling interest at acquisition date plus fair value of net assets at acquisition	
(ii)	Fair value of consideration paid plus fair value of non-controlling interest at acquisition date minus fair value of net assets at acquisition	
(iii)	Fair value of consideration paid minus fair value of non-controlling interest at acquisition date + fair value of net assets at acquisition	

Task 2

Prepare the consolidated statement of profit or loss for the Hide group for the year ended 30 June 20X6. **(10 marks)**

Consolidated statement of profit or loss for the year ended 30 June 20X6

	$000
Revenue	
Cost of sales	Item 1
	————
Gross profit	N/A
Distribution costs	
Administrative expenses	
	————
Profit before tax	N/A
Income tax expense	
	————
Profit after tax	N/A
	————
Profit attributable to:	
Owners of Hide	N/A
Non-controlling interest	Item 2
	————
	N/A
	————

Item 1 - Choose the correct calculation of cost of sales

	All figures are in $000	Selected answer
(i)	$110,000 + (3/12 × $50,000) – $12,500 - $1,500	
(ii)	$110,000 + (3/12 × $50,000) – $12,500 + $1,000	
(iii)	$110,000 + (3/12 × $50,000) + $12,500 + $1,500	

Item 2 - Choose the correct calculation for the non-controlling interest share of group profit after tax.

		Selected answer
(i)	Non-controlling interest share of Seek's profit for the year minus provision for unrealised profit on inventory	
(ii)	Non-controlling interest share of Seek's post-acquisition profit for the year, plus non-controlling interest share of provision for unrealised profit on inventory	
(iii)	Non-controlling interest share of Seek's post-acquisition profit for the year, minus non-controlling interest share of provision for unrealised profit on inventory	

Task 3

Based upon the individual financial statements of Hide and Seek, Hide has a lower gross profit margin than Seek.

Which one of the following statements could be a plausible explanation for this situation?

(2 marks)

		Selected answer
(i)	Seek has lower levels of inventory than Hide at the start and end of the reporting period	
(ii)	Seek is able to purchase cheaper materials and has a lower wastage rate of material than Hide	
(iii)	Seek has lower distribution costs and administrative expenses than Hide	

(Total: 15 marks)

16 PUSH AND SHOVE

Below are the summarised draft financial statements of Push and Shove:

Statement of profit or loss for the year ended 30 September 20X8 (extract)

	Push	Shove
	$000	$000
Revenue	85,000	42,000
Less: Cost of sales	63,000	32,000
Gross profit	22,000	10,000
Less: Distribution and admin expenses	12,000	4,500
Less: Finance costs	600	400
Profit before tax	9,400	5,100
Less: Income tax expense	2,162	1,000
Profit for the year	7,238	4,100

Statements of financial position as at 30 September 20X8

	Push $000	Shove $000
Assets		
Non-current assets		
Property, plant and equipment	40,600	22,600
Current assets	16,000	6,600
Total assets	56,600	29,200
Equity and liabilities		
Equity shares of $1 each	10,000	4,000
Retained earnings	35,400	16,500
	45,400	20,500
Non-current liabilities:		
10% loan notes	3,000	4,000
Current liabilities	8,200	4,700
Total equity and liabilities	56,600	29,200

The following information is relevant to the preparation of the consolidated financial statements of Push for the year ended 30 September 20X8:

(i)   On 1 October 20X7, Push acquired 60% of the equity share capital of Shove in a share exchange of five shares in Push for six shares in Shove. The issue of shares has not yet been recorded by Push. At the date of acquisition shares in Push had a fair value of $6 each.

(ii)   At the date of acquisition, the fair values of Shove's net assets were approximately equal to their carrying amounts.

(iii)   Push has a policy of accounting for any non-controlling interest at fair value. The fair value of a $1 share in Shove at the date of acquisition was $3.50. Consolidated goodwill was not impaired at 30 September 20X8.

(iv)   Sales by Shove to Push during the year ended 30 September 20X8 were $6 million. Shove made a mark-up on cost of 20% on these sales. One quarter of these goods remained in the inventory of Push at the year-end.

(v)   At 30 September 20X8, Shove had a receivable due from Push of $1 million. This agreed with the amount payable to Shove in Push's financial statements.

Required:

Task 1

(a) State the accounting entries required to account for the issue of shares by Push upon acquisition of Shove. **(2 marks)**

	$000	Credit / Debit
Revaluation surplus		
Issued share capital		
Investment in Shove		
Retained earnings		
Share premium		

(b) Calculate goodwill on acquisition of Shove **(3 marks)**

	$000
Fair value of consideration paid	(Item 1)
	———
Fair value of the NCI at acquisition	
	———
Fair value of net assets at acquisition:	
Share capital	
Retained earnings	(Item 2)
	———
	———
Goodwill on acquisition	(Item 3)
	———

Item 1 - Choose the correct calculation of the fair value of consideration paid

	All figures are in $000	Selected answer
(i)	4,000 × 60% × $6	
(ii)	4,000 × 60% × 5/6 × $1	
(iii)	4,000 × 60% × 5/6 × $6	

Item 2 - Choose the correct calculation for retained earnings of Shove at the date of acquisition.

	All figures are in $000	Selected answer
(i)	$16,500	
(ii)	$16,500 - $4,100	
(iii)	$35,400 - $4,100	

Item 3 - Choose the correct calculation for goodwill

		Selected answer
(i)	Fair value of consideration paid plus fair value of non-controlling interest at acquisition date plus fair value of net assets at acquisition	
(ii)	Fair value of consideration paid minus fair value of non-controlling interest at acquisition date + fair value of net assets at acquisition	
(iii)	Fair value of consideration paid plus fair value of non-controlling interest at acquisition date minus fair value of net assets at acquisition	

Task 2

Calculate the following figures for inclusion in the consolidated statement of financial position: **(3 marks)**

		$000
(i)	Non-current assets	
(ii)	Current assets	
(iii)	Current liabilities	

Task 3

Choose the correct calculation of each of the following items for inclusion in the consolidated statement of financial position: **(4 marks)**

(a) Non-controlling interest at the reporting date

	All figures are in $000	Selected answer
(i)	$(4,000 \times 40\% \times \$1) + (40\% \times (4,100 + 250))$	
(ii)	$(4,000 \times 40\% \times \$3.50) + (40\% \times (4,100 - 250))$	
(iii)	$(4,000 \times 40\% \times \$6) + (40\% \times (4,100 + 250))$	

(b) Retained earnings at the reporting date

	All figures are in $000	Selected answer
(i)	$\$35,400 - (60\% \times (4,100 + 250))$	
(ii)	$\$45,400 - (60\% \times (4,100 - 250))$	
(iii)	$\$35,400 + (60\% \times (4,100 - 250))$	

Task 4

Choose the correct calculation of each of the following items for inclusion in the consolidated statement of profit or loss: (3 marks)

(a) **Revenue**

	All figures are in $000	Selected answer
(i)	$85,000 + $42,000 - $6,000	
(ii)	$85,000 + (40% × ($42,000 - $6,000)	
(iii)	$85,000 + $42,000 + $6,000	

(b) **Cost of sales**

	All figures are in $000	Selected answer
(i)	$63,000 + $32,000 - $6,000 - $250	
(ii)	$63,000 + $32,000 - $6,000 + $250	
(iii)	$63,000 + (40% × ($32,000 - $6,000 + $250))	

(Total 15 marks)

Section 3

LONG-FORM QUESTIONS

Note: The questions in this section are not in the format you would expect to face in the computer-based assessment. However, they are a useful addition to your revision studies.

1   CARBON

Carbon is a limited liability entity. A trial balance for the year ended 31 December 20X5 is presented below.

	Dr $	Cr $
Revenue		450,000
Purchases	180,000	
Administrative expenses	140,000	
Distribution expenses	56,000	
Plant and machinery – cost	150,000	
Plant and machinery – accumulated depreciation at 1 January 20X5		30,000
Trade receivables	36,000	
Allowance for receivables – 1 January 20X5		2,500
Inventory – 1 January 20X5	33,000	
Share capital		10,000
Trade payables		32,000
Retained earnings – 1 January 20X5		25,500
8% Loan – repayable 31 December 20X9		50,000
Cash	5,000	
	———	———
	600,000	600,000
	———	———

The following notes are relevant to the preparation of the financial statements for the year ended 31 December 20X5:

(i)   The current year tax charge has been estimated at $5,000.

(ii)   It has been determined that trade receivables of $1,500 are irrecoverable. In addition, it was decided that the allowance for receivables should be increased by $1,000.

(iii)   Depreciation on plant and machinery is charged at 20% per annum on a reducing balance basis. Depreciation is charged to cost of sales.

(iv)   The loan was taken out on 1 October 20X5. No interest has been accrued.

(v)   Closing inventory has been correctly valued at $27,000.

(vi)   A customer bought goods on credit from Carbon for $1,000 on 5 December 20X5. The customer returned these goods on 28 December 20X5. No entries have been posted for this return.

(vii)   Carbon is being sued by a customer regarding the sale of goods that the customer believes to be defective. Legal advisers think that it is probable that Carbon will lose the case and that they will have to pay damages of $20,000 in 20X6. Legal expenses are charged to administrative expenses.

Required:

Prepare a statement of profit or loss of Carbon the year ended 31 December 20X5 and a statement of financial position as at 31 December 20X5.   (Total: 15 marks)

2   MARKUS

Markus has prepared a trial balance for his business at 30 April 20X3 which is presented below.

	Dr $	Cr $
Capital account – 1 May 20X2		30,000
Finance costs	300	
Bank		7,400
Administrative expenses	65,800	
Distribution expenses	31,200	
Plant and machinery – cost	72,000	
Plant and machinery – accumulated depreciation at 1 May 20X2		25,000
Trade receivables	20,000	
Allowance for receivables – 1 May 20X2		3,150
Revenue		230,000
Inventory – 1 May 20X2	18,750	
Drawings	18,000	
Trade payables		17,500
Purchases	90,000	
6% Loan – repayable 31 July 20X5		3,000
	———	———
	316,050	316,050
	———	———

The following notes are relevant to the preparation of the financial statements for the year ended 30 April 20X3:

(i)   Markus took goods which cost $5,000 for personal use during the year, but this has not been recorded.

(ii)   It has been determined that trade receivables of $600 are irrecoverable. In addition, it was decided that the allowance for receivables should be reduced by $500.

(iii)   Depreciation on plant and machinery is charged at 15% per annum on a reducing balance basis. Depreciation is charged to cost of sales.

(iv)   The loan was taken out on 1 August 20X2 and interest has not yet been paid or accrued.

(v)   Closing inventory had been valued at $17,500. It was subsequently discovered that some items of inventory which had cost $5,000 had a net realisable value of $3,750.

(vi) At 30 April 20X3, a prepayment for insurance paid in advance of $400 had not yet been accounted for. Insurance is classified as an administrative expense.

(vii) At 30 April 20X3, an accrual for freight and delivery expenses amounting to $350 had not yet been accounted for. Freight and delivery expenses are classified as distribution expenses.

Required:

Prepare a statement of profit or loss of Markus the year ended 30 April 20X3 and a statement of financial position as at 30 April 20X3.   **(Total: 15 marks)**

3   FIREWORK CO

The following financial statements and supporting information relate to Firework Co, a limited liability entity:

Statement of profit or loss and other comprehensive income for the year ended 30 June 20X5

	$000
Revenue	113,250
Cost of sales	(77,500)
Gross profit	35,750
Distribution costs	(3,000)
Administration expenses	(1,000)
Interest payable	(750)
Profit before tax	31,000
Income tax expense	(6,000)
Profit for the year	25,000
Other comprehensive income:	
Revaluation of property, plant and equipment	2,000
Total comprehensive income for the year	27,000

Statement of financial position at 30 June:

	20X5	20X4
	$000	$000
ASSETS		
Non-current assets		
Property, plant and equipment	110,000	93,000
Current assets		
Inventories	36,000	30,000
Trade receivables	40,000	35,000
Cash and equivalents	Nil	10,000
	―――――	―――――
Total assets	186,000	168,000
	―――――	―――――
EQUITY AND LIABILITIES		
Equity share capital	20,000	15,000
Share premium	8,000	3,000
Revaluation surplus	10,000	8,000
Retained earnings	96,000	85,000
	―――――	―――――
Total equity	134,000	111,000
Non-current liabilities		
Bank loan	7,000	17,000
Current liabilities		
Trade payables	36,500	30,000
Income tax	6,500	10,000
Bank overdraft	2,000	Nil
	―――――	―――――
Total equity and liabilities	186,000	168,000
	―――――	―――――

Notes:

The following information is relevant to the financial statements of Firework:

(i)   During the year ended 30 June 20X5, Firework Co disposed of several items of plant and equipment for sale proceeds of $8,000,000. The loss on disposal of $2,000,000 is included within cost of sales. The depreciation charge for the year was $15,000,000.

(ii)   Firework Co estimated that the income tax liability arising on the profit for the year ended 30 June 20X5 was $6,500,000.

Required:

Based upon the information available, complete the statement of cash flows for Firework Co for the year ended 30 June 20X5 in accordance with the requirements of IAS 7 *Statement of cash flows.*

(Total: 15 marks)

4   PEDANTIC

On 1 October 20X7, Pedantic acquired 60% of the equity share capital of Sophistic in a share exchange of two shares in Pedantic for three shares in Sophistic. The issue of shares has not yet been recorded by Pedantic. At the date of acquisition shares in Pedantic had a market value of $6 each. Below are the summarised draft financial statements of both entities.

Statement of profit or loss for the year ended 30 September 20X8

	Pedantic	Sophistic
	$000	$000
Revenue	85,000	42,000
Cost of sales	(63,000)	(32,000)
Gross profit	22,000	10,000
Distribution costs	(4,000)	(3,500)
Administrative expenses	(8,000)	(1,000)
Finance costs	(600)	(400)
Profit before tax	9,400	5,100
Income tax expense	(2,162)	(1,000)
	7,238	4,100
Profit for the year		

Statements of financial position as at 30 September 20X8

	Pedantic	Sophistic
	$000	$000
Assets		
Non-current assets		
Property, plant and equipment	40,600	12,600
Current assets	16,000	6,600
Total assets	56,600	19,200
Equity and liabilities		
Equity shares of $1 each	10,000	4,000
Retained earnings	35,400	6,500
	45,400	10,500
Non-current liabilities:		
10% loan notes	3,000	4,000
Current liabilities	8,200	4,700
Total equity and liabilities	56,600	19,200

The following information is relevant:

(i)   At the date of acquisition, the fair values of Sophistic's net assets were equal to their carrying amounts.

(ii)   Sales from Sophistic to Pedantic in the post-acquisition period were $6 million. Sophistic made a mark up on cost of 20% on these sales. One quarter of these goods remained in the inventory of Pedantic at the year-end.

(iii)   Other than where indicated, statement of profit or loss items are deemed to accrue evenly on a time basis.

(iv)   At 30 September 20X8, Sophistic had a receivable due from Pedantic of $1 million. This agreed with the amount payable to Sophistic in Pedantic's financial statements.

(v)   Pedantic has a policy of accounting for any non-controlling interest at fair value. The fair value of the non-controlling interest at the acquisition date was $5.9 million. Consolidated goodwill was not impaired at 30 September 20X8.

Required:

(a)   **Prepare the consolidated statement of profit or loss for Pedantic for the year ended 30 September 20X8.**   **(6 marks)**

(b)   **Prepare the consolidated statement of financial position for Pedantic as at 30 September 20X8.**   **(9 marks)**

(Total: 15 marks)

Section 4

ANSWERS TO OBJECTIVE TEST QUESTIONS

THE CONTEXT AND PURPOSE OF FINANCIAL REPORTING

1   D

The directors of a company run the company; however, they are not personally liable for its losses. A sole trader business is owned and operated by the proprietor (sole trader).

Partners are jointly and severally liable for any losses of the business.

A company is owned by the shareholders (members) and run by the directors/management team.

2   C

3   D

4   A

Management require very detailed information in order to make informed decisions with regard to operations (e.g. whether to shut down a particular product line or source new suppliers).

Other parties need far less detail:

- Investors are interested in profitability and the security of their investment.
- The government is interested in profits (for tax purposes) and sales performance (in order to assess how the economy is performing).
- Lenders are interested in whether a business is solvent and able to repay their debt.

5   A

Accounting involves recording transactions as they occur and then summarising them in the form of the financial statements.

Financial accounting describes the production of financial statements for external users.

6   C

7   C

Both financial and management accounts should be equally accurate and reliable.

8   A

9   C

10   A

Accounting standards provide guidance on common transactions. They cannot provide guidance on all types of transactions.

11   D

12   B

13   B

Tutorial note:

A sole trader may have employees. A sole trader is fully liable for the debts of the business. A sole trader may have more than one place of business, perhaps with the support of employees or managers acting on their behalf.

14   A

A limited liability company is a separate legal entity and can own assets and incur liabilities in its own name.

15   B

16   C

17   B

18   C and D

Issued share capital and revaluation surplus apply only to limited company financial statements.

19   B and C

Dividends paid and share premium account applies only to limited company financial statements.

20   C

21

	True	*False*
The Conceptual Framework is a financial reporting standard		Correct
The Conceptual Framework assists in harmonising global accounting practices.	Correct	
The Conceptual Framework assists national standard setters to develop national standards.	Correct	
The Conceptual Framework assists users of financial information to interpret financial statements.	Correct	

The Framework is not an accounting standard itself, although it is used as a reference document when new standards are developed.

22   D

All of the remaining answers include only part of the full definition of an asset.

23   A

Equity or capital of the business is represented by the next assets of the business.

THE QUALITATIVE CHARACTERISTICS OF FINANCIAL INFORMATION

24

	It is an enhancing qualitative characteristic	*It is not an enhancing qualitative characteristic*
Comparability		Correct
Timeliness		Correct
Faithful representation	Correct	
Understandability		Correct

25   D

If applicable, the going concern concept presumes, but does not guarantee, that a business will continue in operational existence for the foreseeable future.

Commercial substance should always be reflected in financial statements, even where this differs from legal form.

A revaluation surplus is not realised. However, it is credited in other comprehensive income in the statement of profit or loss and other comprehensive income and then included in the statement of changes in equity.

26

	An enhancing qualitative characteristic	*Not an enhancing qualitative characteristic*
Relevance		Correct
Comparability	Correct	
Faithful representation		Correct
Verifiability	Correct	

Tutorial note:

The remaining answers are fundamental qualitative characteristics of useful financial information.

27   D

28   D

If a business is a going concern, it is reasonable to assume that non-current assets will be used over their expected useful economic life. It is therefore appropriate to value a non-current asset at cost less accumulated depreciation, which represents the consumption of cost or value so far.

29   B

30   D

THE USE OF DOUBLE-ENTRY AND ACCOUNTING SYSTEMS

DOUBLE ENTRY BOOKKEEPING

31   B

The computer does not qualify as inventory drawings as it is for the use of Oscar's daughter in her role as administrator to the business.

The computer is being transferred from inventory to non-current assets by debiting the non-current assets account. It is no longer part of cost of sales and is removed from cost of sales by a credit.

32 B

> ***Tutorial note:***
>
> *Drawings, carriage inwards (an expense), prepayments, carriage outwards (expense) and opening inventory are all debit balances. Accruals, rental income and purchase returns are all credit balances.*

33 C

34 A

35 D

	$	$
Sales		256,800
Cost of sales		
Opening inventory	13,400	
Purchases	145,000	
Carriage in	2,300	
Closing inventory	(14,200)	(146,500)
Gross profit		110,300
Discount received		3,900
Expenses		(76,000)
Carriage out		(1,950)
Net profit		36,250

36 $3,150

Bank

	$		$
Balance b/f	1,780	Drawings (4 × $200)	800
Receipt after trade discount	570		
Receipt from customer	400		
Bankings from canteen receipts	1,200	**Balance c/f**	3,150
	3,950		3,950

Trade discounts are deducted at source by the seller and only the reduced amount will be payable by the customer. Therefore, the net amount of $570 must have been received during the month.

37   **$2,675**

Bank

	$		$
Returns of goods purchased for cash	50	Overdraft at start of month	1,340
Rental income	1,300	Payments to credit suppliers	990
Receipts from customers	4,400	Reimbursement of petty cash float	45
		Payment of electricity bill	700
		Balance c/f	**2,675**
	_____		_____
	5,750		5,750
	_____		_____

38   **C**

39   **A**

40   **C**

41   **D**

An invoice is raised by a business and issued to a customer. It contains more than the amount due to be paid for goods and services supplied. It will also include the quantity and description of goods, the date of supply and the nett amount, sales tax applied and gross amount due.

42

	True	False
Business assets will always equal business liabilities		Correct
Business assets will always exceed business liabilities		Correct
Business assets include proprietor's capital		Correct
Business liabilities include proprietor's capital		Correct

Tutorial note:

Statements A and B ignore proprietor's capital and therefore cannot be true. Statements C and D are false as proprietor's capital is neither a business asset nor a business liability.

43

	True	False
Business assets will always equal business liabilities		Correct
Business assets will always exceed business liabilities		Correct
Business assets include proprietor's capital	Correct	
Business liabilities include proprietor's capital		Correct

Tutorial note:

The journal records all transactions not already recorded in a book of prime entry. Bank and cash transactions are recorded in the cash book and petty cash book respectively. Credit sales transactions are recorded in the sales day book.

44 B

	Ledger Account:	$
Debit	Depreciation expense – motor vehicles	10,000
Credit	Accumulated depreciation – motor vehicles	10,000

45 C

	Ledger Account:	$
Debit	Irrecoverable debts and allowance for receivables expense	4,300
Credit	Trade receivables' ledger control	4,300

Remember that the allowance for receivables is only adjusted at the end of the accounting period, rather than regularly throughout the accounting period.

46 D

	Ledger Account:	$
Debit	Sales revenue	2,500
Credit	Disposal of machinery	2,500

47 A

	Ledger Account:	$
Debit	Trade payables' ledger control account	1,250
Credit	Trade receivables' ledger control account	1,250

The trade payables' and trade receivables' ledgers do not form part of the double-entry ledger system within the general ledger. They are memorandum accounts only.

48 C

	Ledger Account:	$
Debit	Depreciation expense account	3,500
Credit	Accumulated depreciation account – buildings	3,500

49 B

	Ledger Account:	$
Debit	Trade payables' ledger control account	250
Credit	Discount received – income	250

50 D

	Ledger Account:	$
Debit	Purchases	6,400
Credit	Trade payables' ledger control account	6,400

51 $500

	$
Revenue	22,000
Purchases	(19,200)
(note: the business does not hold inventory)	
Rent	(5,400)
Bank interest	(825)
Heat and light	(4,475)
Loss for the year	(7,900)

Therefore closing capital for the accounting period ended 30 April 20X3 = $12,500 – $7,900 – $4,100 = $500.

LEDGER ACCOUNTS, BOOKS OF PRIME ENTRY AND JOURNALS

52 C

	A book of prime entry	Not a book of prime entry
Sales day book	Correct	
Trial balance		Correct
The journal	Correct	
Accounts receivable ledger		Correct

53 **B**

$25 + $(7.25 + 12.75 + 15) = $60

Tutorial note:

The petty cash float can always be calculated by adding together the amount in petty cash at the end of the month plus the vouchers evidencing expenditure for the month.

54 **B**

55 **$3,004**

Receivables ledger control account

	$		$
Balance b/f	69,472		
Sales	697,104	Cash received	686,912
		Irrecoverable debts	1,697
		Sales returns (β)	**3,004**
		Balance c/f	74,963
	———		———
	766,576		766,576
	———		———

56 **$385**

	$
Opening float	150
Receipts	
Photocopier use	25
Bank	500
Payments	
Cheque cashed	(90)
Payments (β)	**385**
	———
Closing float	200
	———

57   B

Tutorial note:

A debit balance on a purchase ledger account means that the business is owed money by its supplier. This could be explained by the business mistakenly paying an invoice twice. (Alternatively, a business might pay the full invoice amount and then receive a credit note from the supplier following the return of faulty goods.)

58 $38,100

Payables ledger control account

	$		$
Bank	68,900	Balance b/f	34,500
Discounts received	1,200	Purchases (credit)	78,400
Purchase returns	4,700		
Balance c/f	38,100		
	———		———
	112,900		112,900
	———		———
		Balance b/f	38,100

59 $19,000

Receivables ledger control account

	$		$
Sales	250,000	Bank	225,000
Bank: cheque returned	3,500	Sales returns	2,500
		Irrecoverable debts	3,000
		Contra: trade payables	4,000
		Balance c/f	**19,000**
	———		———
	253,500		253,500
	———		———
Balance b/f	19,000		

60   C

Tutorial note:

The non-current asset register is not a book of prime entry. As the part-exchange value received is not a cash receipt, it will be recorded in the journal.

61   D

Mike has received cash (a debit entry) and the credit entry should be made to the trade payables control account to cancel out the debit entry recorded when the second payment was made in error.

62   A

	Ledger Account:	$
Debit	Trade receivables' ledger control account	12,000
Credit	Sales	10,000
Credit	Sales tax	2,000

63   B

	Ledger Account:	$
Debit	Purchases (100/115 × $1,541)	1,340
Debit	Sales tax (15/115 × $1,541)	201
Credit	Payables' ledger control account	1,541

Tutorial note:

The gross invoice value is credited to the payables ledger control account as that is the total liability due to the supplier. The debit entries comprise the net cost is accounted for as a purchase cost and the related sales tax element, which is recoverable.

64   A

Item B describes a purchase order.

Item C describes a supplier statement.

Item D describes a remittance advice.

65   B

The sales and purchases day books record credit sales and credit purchases respectively.

66 $70.00

	$
Balance of petty cash in hand	66.00
Add: Sundry purchases	22.00
Loan to sales manager	10.00
Purchase of staff drinks	19.00
Less: Sundry sales receipts	(47.00)
Imprest balance	70.00

RECORDING TRANSACTIONS AND EVENTS

SALES AND PURCHASES AND SALES TAX

67 $655.50

	$
Price	600.00
Less: trade discount (5% × $600)	(30.00)
	570.00
Add: sales tax at 15% (15% × $570)	85.50
	655.50

Tutorial note:

Sales tax is always charged on the selling price net of trade (bulk purchase) discount given.

68 $75,788

Sales tax

	$		$
		Balance b/f	23,778
Tax on purchases		Tax on sales	
$\frac{17.5\%}{117.5\%}$ × $590,790	87,990	17.5% × $800,000	140,000
Balance c/f	**75,788**		
	163,778		163,778
		Balance b/f	75,788

69 $962.50

Sales tax

	$		$
Tax on purchases (input tax)		Tax on sales (output tax)	4,112.50
($18,000 × 17.5%)	3,150.00	($27,612.5 × 17.5/117.5)	
Balance c/f	962.50		
	———		———
	4,112.50		4,112.50
	———		———
		Balance b/f	962.50

70   C

	$
Sales net of sales tax	90,000
Purchases net of sales tax	(72,000)
	———
	18,000
	———
Tax payable @ 10%	$1,800

As sales exceed purchases, the excess sales tax is payable to the tax authorities.

71 $5,300

Sales tax

	$		$
Tax on purchases	6,000	Balance b/f	3,400
Bank	2,600	Tax on sales	10,500
Balance c/f	5,300		
	———		———
	13,900		13,900
	———		———
		Balance b/f	5,300

Tax on sales (outputs) = 17.5% × $60,000 = $10,500

Tax on purchases (inputs) = (17.5/117.5) × $40,286 = $6,000

72   B

Sales revenue is recorded exclusive of sales tax in the statement of profit or loss.

73   B

The receivables account should be debited with the full amount payable, including the tax. The entry in the sales account should be for the sales value excluding sales tax. Sales tax payable to the tax authorities should be credited to the sales tax account (liability = credit balance).

74   A

The receivables account should be credited with the full amount of the sales return, including the tax. The Sales returns account should be debited with the value of the returns excluding the sales tax. The sales tax account should be debited with the amount of tax on the returns (since the tax is no longer payable).

75   C

The supplier is owed the full amount of the invoice, including the sales tax, so the credit entry in the supplier account must be $9,200. The non-current asset account is recorded at cost excluding the sales tax. The input tax is recoverable, so debit the sales tax account with $1,200.

76

	True	False
Sales tax is a form of indirect taxation	Correct	
If input tax exceeds output tax the difference is payable to the tax authorities		Correct
Sales tax is included in the reported sales and purchases of a sales tax registered business		Correct
Sales tax cannot be recovered on some purchases	Correct	

If input tax (tax on purchases) exceeds output tax (tax on sales), the difference is recoverable from the tax authorities.

Sales and purchases are reported net of sales tax.

Sales tax cannot be recovered on certain expenses (such as client entertaining) and purchases (such as cars).

77 $578,200

Trade payables

	$		$
Cash paid	542,300	Balance b/f	142,600
Discounts received	13,200		
Goods returned	27,500		
Balance c/f	137,800	Purchases (β)	578,200
	720,800		720,800

78 **$84,000**

Trade receivables

	$		$
Balance b/f	10,000	Receipts from sales	85,000
Sales (β)	**84,000**		
		Balance c/f	9,000
	———		———
	94,000		94,000
	———		———

79 **C**

Cash

	$		$
Balance b/f	300	Bankings	50,000
Proceeds of sale of car	5,000	Wages	12,000
Sales (β)	**81,100**	Drawings	24,000
		Balance c/f	400
	———		———
	86,400		86,400
	———		———

80 **A**

The balance on the sales tax account is calculated as:

Credit sales ($121,000/100 × 20) = $24,200

Credit purchases ($157,110/120 × 20) =   ($26,185)

                                                        ———

                                                        ($1,985)

                                                        ———

The sales tax on the credit purchases (input tax) exceeds the sales tax on sales (output tax), the balance on the account represents an amount due to Alan, therefore is an asset, a debit.

81 **A**

Carriage inwards is an expense incurred in bringing goods purchased into the business, and carriage outwards is an expense incurred in delivering goods to customers.

82 **C**

The receivables account should be credited with the full amount of the sales return, including the sales tax. The sales returns (returns inwards) should be debited with the value of the returns excluding the sales tax. The sales tax account should be debited with the amount of tax on the returns (as the output tax will no longer be payable).

83 $920.00

	$
Price	800.00
Less: trade discount (8% × $800)	(64.00)
	————
	736.00
Add: sales tax (25% × $736)	184.00
	————
	920.00
	————

84   C

Trade discount is always deducted when calculating the amount invoiced by the seller. In addition, as Smith was not expected to take account of the early settlement discount terms, the amount of revenue receivable is calculated after deduction of trade discount only at $950 ($1000 × 95%). When Smith subsequently pays early to be eligible for the discount, the accounting entries should reflect that fact and record settlement of the amount outstanding and also reduced revenue.

Debit Cash $912 ($950 × 96%), Debit Revenue $38 ($950 × 4%), and Credit Trade receivables $950.

85   B

Trade discount is always deducted when calculating the amount invoiced by the seller. In addition, as Jones is expected to take account of the early settlement discount terms, the amount of revenue receivable is calculated after deduction of both trade discount and early settlement discount, a total of $2,280 ($2,500 × 95% × 96%). When Jones subsequently pays early to be eligible for the discount, the accounting entries should reflect the receipt of cash and clearance of the trade receivable for the amount expected as follows:

Debit Cash $2,280 and Credit Trade receivables $2,280.

86   D

Trade discount is always deducted when calculating the amount invoiced by the seller. In addition, as Black is expected to take account of the early settlement discount terms, the amount of revenue receivable is calculated after deduction of both trade discount and early settlement discount, a total of $4,104 ($4,500 × 95% × 96%). When Black subsequently pays outside the settlement discount period, the full amount of the receivable $4,275 ($4,500 × 95%) is due. The additional cash received in excess of the receivable amount of $171 is therefore accounted for as a cash sale as follows:

Debit Cash $4,275, Credit Revenue $171 and Credit Trade receivables $4,104.

87   A

Trade discount is always deducted when calculating the amount invoiced by the seller. In addition, as White is not expected to take account of the early settlement discount terms, the amount of revenue receivable is calculated after deduction of trade discount only, a total of $3,515 ($3,700 × 95%). When White subsequently pays outside the settlement discount period as expected, the full amount of the receivable is due.

Debit Cash $3,515, and Credit Trade receivables $3,515.

88   B

Trade discount is always deducted and, in addition, as Green is expected to take account of the early settlement discount terms, the amount of revenue receivable is calculated after deduction of trade discount and early settlement discount, a total of $1,276.80 ($1,400 × 96% × 95%). When Green subsequently pays outside the settlement discount period, the full amount of $1,344 ($1,400 × 96%) is due and the additional amount received of $67.20 ($1,344.00 – $1,276.80) is accounted for as a cash sale.

Debit Cash $1,344, and Credit Trade receivables $1,276.80 and Credit Revenue $67.20.

INVENTORY

89 $500

The inventory should be valued at the lower of cost and NRV.
Cost is $500 and NRV is ($1,200 – $250) = $950. The correct valuation is therefore $500.

90   A

	$
Opening inventory + units purchased	440
Units sold	(290)
	———
Closing inventory (units)	150
	———
FIFO Closing inventory: 150 units @ $2.78	**$417**
	———

	$
AVCO Weighted average cost	$
100 units @ $2.52	252
140 units @ $2.56	358
200 units @ $2.78	556
——	——
440	1,166
——	——
Average cost per unit	1,166/440 = $2.65
Opening inventory + units purchased	440.00
AVCO Closing inventory: 150 units @ $2.65	**$397.50**
FIFO higher by ($417.00 – $397.50)	**$19.50**

Tutorial note:

The periodic weighted requires the total cost of the inventory to be divided by the total units in the period to determine the weighted average cost for the period. This weighted average figure will then be used to value the inventory.

The continuous weighted method requires the weighted average to be calculated every time there is a purchase.

91   B

If prices have fallen during the year, AVCO will give a higher value of closing inventory than FIFO, which values goods for resale at the latest prices.

Where the value of closing inventory is higher, profits are higher.

92 $56,640

The number of units held at the year-end is 1,180 (1,200 – 20).

The sale on 31 December provides evidence of a net realisable value $2 below cost. Therefore each unit should be valued at its net realisable value:

1,180 units × $48 = $56,640.

93

	True	False
Inventory should be valued at the lower of cost, net realisable value and replacement cost.		
When valuing work in progress, materials costs, labour costs and variable and fixed production overheads must be included.		Correct
Inventory items can be valued using either first in, first out (FIFO) or weighted average cost.		Correct
An entity's financial statements must disclose the accounting policies used in measuring inventories.		Correct

Tutorial note:

Inventory should be valued at the lower of cost and net realisable value. Replacement cost is irrelevant.

94   C

When inventory is included in purchases at cost and closing inventory at cost, the effect on profit is nil (the same amount is both a debit and a credit in the statement of profit or loss). In this case, only the credit is recorded (closing inventory). Therefore profit is overstated by the cost of the fabric.

The inventory valuation is not misstated, as it includes the fabric received on 29 June.

95   A

Tutorial note:

Inventory drawings are credited to purchases in order to remove them from cost of sales, as these goods have not been sold.

96   B

Opening inventory must be removed from the statement of financial position inventory account (a credit) and expensed to the statement of profit or loss as part of cost of sales (a debit).

Closing inventory must be debited on to the statement of financial position as an asset and removed from the cost of sales (a credit).

97 $39,900

	$
Value at 7 July 20X6	38,950
Sales since year end (100/125 × $6,500)	5,200
Purchase since year end	(4,250)
Value at 30 June 20X6	39,900

98 $155

	Items	Unit value	
		$	$
Opening inventory	6	15	90
January: purchases	10	19.80	198
	16	18	288
February: sales	(10)	18	(180)
	6	18	108
March: purchases	20	24.50	490
	26	23	598
March: sales	(5)	23	(115)
	21	23	483

Sales (15 × $30)		450
Cost of sales ($180 + $115)		(295)
		———
Gross profit		155
		———

99 $1,110

Date		Units	Unit value	Inventory value
			$	$
1 October	Opening inventory	60		720
8 October	Purchase 40 units at $15	40		600
14 October	Purchase 50 units at $18	50		900
		———		———
		150	14.80	2,220
21 October	Sold 75 units: cost	(75)	14.80	(1,110)
		———		———
31 October	Closing inventory	75	14.80	1,110
		———		———

100   A

The net realisable value of inventory items is the selling price less the 4% commission payable.

	NRV	Lower of cost or NRV
	$	$
Henry VII	2,784	2,280
Dissuasion	3,840	3,840
John Bunion	1,248	1,248
		———
		7,368
		———

101   D

The closing inventory of 12 items (15 − 5 + 10 − 8) comprise

	$
10 items at $3.50 each	35.00
2 items at $3 each	6.00
	———
Cost on a FIFO basis is	41.00
	———

102 B

> **Tutorial note:**
>
> *If the inventory was not included in the original valuation of closing inventory, closing inventory will be increased by $1,000 (the lower of cost and net realisable value). Since closing inventory is $1,000 higher, cost of sales is $1,000 lower and profit $1,000 higher.*

103 $4,700

	Net realisable value $	Lower of cost or NRV $	Units	Value $
Basic	8	6	200	1,200
Super	8	8	250	2,000
Luxury	10	10	150	1,500
Total value				4,700

104 A

When prices are rising, FIFO will give a higher valuation for closing inventory, because the closing inventory will consist of the most recently-purchased items. Higher closing inventory means lower cost of sales and higher profit.

105 C

In contrast, if continuous weighted average cost per unit is calculated, a new cost per unit is calculated each time a purchase is made.

106 A

In contrast, if periodic weighted average cost per unit is calculated, this would be done at the end of the accounting period.

107 $85.00

	Units	Unit cost $	Total cost $
2 Feb	10	5.00	50.00
5 Feb	(6)	5.00	(30.00)
	4		20.00
7 Feb	10	6.50	65.00
	14	6.07	85.00

108 $80.50

Total cost of purchases/total units) = ((10 × $5.00) + (10 × $6.50))/20 units = $5.75 per unit. Closing inventory valuation is therefore 14 units × $5.75 = $80.50.

109 $73.50

Total cost of purchases/total units) = ((4 × $4.00) + (10 × $5.00) + (10 × $6.00))/24 units = $5.25 per unit. Cost of sales is therefore 14 units × $5.25 = $73.50.

110 $71.70

	Units	Unit cost $	Total cost $
1 Apr	4	4.00	16.00
12 Apr	10	5.00	50.00
	14	66.00/14 = 4.71	66.00
15 Apr	(6)	4.71	(28.26)
	8		37.74
17 Apr	10	6.00	60.00
	18	97.74/18 = 5.43	97.74
25 Apr	(8)	5.43	(43.44)
	10		54.30

Cost of sales = $28.26 + $43.44 = $71.70.

TANGIBLE NON-CURRENT ASSETS

111 C

Asset register	$	Ledger accounts	$
Carrying amount per question	85,600	Carrying amount per question	130,000
Addition of land	30,000	Disposal at carrying amount	(14,400)
	115,600		115,600

112 A

			$
1.1.X4	Cost		235,000
	Depreciation at 30%		(70,500)
			————
y/e 31.12.X4	Carrying amount		164,500
	Depreciation at 30%		(49,350)
			————
y/e 31.12.X5	Carrying amount		115,150
	Depreciation at 30%		(34,545)
			————
y/e 31.12.X6	Carrying amount		80,605
			————
	Accumulated depreciation (70,500 + 49,350 + 34,545)		154,395

Therefore

(1) Uplift cost account to valuation   Dr Cost $65,000

(2) Remove depreciation to date   Dr Accumulated depreciation $154,395

(3) Send the balance to the revaluation surplus   Cr Revaluation surplus $219,395

113 D

A non-current asset register is a detailed schedule of non-current assets, and is not another name for non-current asset ledger accounts in the general ledger.

114 $192,600

			$
Depreciation on additions:	20% × $48,000 × 6/12	=	4,800
Depreciation on disposals:	20% × $84,000 × 9/12	=	12,600
Depreciation on other assets:	20% × (960,000 – 84,000)	=	175,200
			————
			192,600
			————

115 $50,600

	$
Cost of plant	48,000
Delivery	400
Modifications	2,200
	————
	50,600
	————

Tutorial note:

The warranty cost cannot be capitalised. This is a revenue expense which must be debited to the statement of profit or loss.

116 B

		$	$	$
Year 1	Cost less dep'n @ 20%	2,400.00	(480.00)	1,920.00
Year 2	Dep'n (20% × $1,920)		(384.00)	1,536.00
Year 3	Dep'n (20% × $1,536)		(307.20)	1,228.80
Year 4	Sale proceeds			1,200.00
				————
	Loss on disposal			(28.80)
				————

117 B

	$	$
Original balance		125,000
Carrying amount of assets sold:		
Proceeds	9,000	
Less: Profit	(2,000)	
	————	
		(7,000)
		————
Adjusted balance		118,000
		————

118 $86,000

	$
Purchase cost of machine	80,000
Installation	5,000
Pre-production safety testing	1,000
	————
	86,000
	————

A non-current asset should be measured initially at its cost. 'Cost' means the amounts incurred to acquire the asset and bring it into working condition for its intended use. These include the purchase cost, initial delivery and handling costs, installation costs and professional fees. Costs of testing whether the asset is working properly may be included, but staff training costs cannot be capitalised.

119 A

	$
Cost	5,000
Year 1 (20% × 5,000)	(1,000)
Year 2 (20% × 4,000)	(800)
Year 3 (20% × 3,200)	(640)
Carrying amount at time of disposal	2,560
Sale proceeds	2,200
Loss on disposal	360

120 $4.72 million

	$m
Non-current assets at cost	10.40
Accumulated depreciation	(0.12)
Carrying amount	10.28
Revaluation amount	15.00
Transfer to revaluation surplus	4.72

121 D

Painting and replacing windows are maintenance and repairs, and so are classified as 'revenue expenditure' and must be expensed through the statement of profit or loss. The purchase of a car for resale means that the car is an item of inventory for the business, not a non-current asset. Legal fees incurred in purchasing a building are included in the cost of the building, and so are part of the non-current asset cost, i.e. capital expenditure.

122 D

Disposals account

	$		$
Cost	12,000	Accumulated depreciation (3 yrs × 20% × $12,000)	7,200
Profit (β)	200	Proceeds (part exchange allowance)	5,000
	12,200		12,200

123 $510,000

	Cost	Accum dep'n	Carrying amount
	$000	$000	$000
Opening balance	860	397	
Disposal	(80)	(43)	
	———	———	
	780	354	
Purchase	180		
	———		
Depreciation (10%)		96	
		———	
	960	450	510
	———	———	

124 C

125 $15,790

Depreciation charge 1 Jan – 30 June: 3% of $380,000 × 6/12 = $5,700
Accumulated depreciation at date of revaluation = $120,000 + $5,700 = $125,700 – i.e. 11.03 years have passed.

Total estimated useful life is 33.33 years, with a remaining estimated useful life of 22.3 years. Thus depreciation for second half of year = $450,000 / 22.3 years × 6/12 = $10,090. The total depreciation charge for the year = $5,700 + $10,090 = $15,790.

126 D

Do not include the vehicle tax in the cost of the car. Road tax is a revenue expense item.

	$	Acc dep'n $	Proceeds $	Profit $
Cost of asset	10,000			
Depreciation 20X1 (25% × $10,000)	(2,500)	2,500		
Depreciation 20X2 (25% × ($10,000 – $2,500))	(1,875)	4,375		
Depreciation 20X3 (25% × ($10,000 – $4,375))	(1,406)	5,781		
Depreciation 20X4 (25% × ($10,000 – $5,781))	(1,055)	6,836		
	———		———	———
Carrying amount at time of disposal	3,164		5,000	1,836
	———		———	———

127 D

The reducing balance method charges more depreciation in earlier years than in later years. It is therefore appropriate to use for assets such as motor vehicles that lose a large part of their value in the earlier years of their life.

128 **$5,000 LOSS**

Annual depreciation = $(40,000 – 10,000)/6 years = $5,000.

The machine was used for four years before disposal, giving accumulated depreciation of 4 × $5,000 = $20,000.

When the machine was sold, its carrying amount was $40,000 – $20,000 = $20,000. It was sold for $15,000, giving a loss on disposal of $5,000 as follows:

	$
Disposal proceeds	15,000
Carrying amount at disposal date	20,000
	———
Loss on disposal	5,000
	———

129 **$3,610**

Initial depreciation charge p.a. $\dfrac{\$20,000 - \$500}{10\,\text{years}} = \$1,950$

Carrying amount at date of change $20,000 – $1,950 = $18,050

New depreciation charge (for y/e 30 June X9 onwards) $\dfrac{\$18,050}{5\,\text{yrs}} = \$3,610$

Note that the revision of estimations takes place in the year ended 30 June 20X9 before the depreciation for that year is charged.

130 **A**

The revaluation surplus balance as at 31 October 20X2 is being asked for. When revaluing an asset, it is the carrying amount of the asset which is revalued, rather than the cost, and as the question states there is no annual transfer of the excess depreciation, the balance on the revaluation surplus can be found as: $150,000 – $81,600 = $68,400.

As the revaluation takes place on 1 November 20X1, a whole year's depreciation is calculated on the revalued amount. The new charge will take the revalued amount of $150,000 and depreciate the asset over its remaining useful economic life.

By looking at the accumulated depreciation brought forward you can tell how old the original asset is:

Original depreciation charge: $102,000/50 years = $2,040 per annum and as $20,400 is accumulated depreciation brought forward, then the asset must have already been held for 10 years. Therefore, the remaining useful economic life is 50 years – 10 years = 40 years.

The new depreciation charge should be calculated as: $150,000/40 years = $3,750.

131 **$625 PROFIT**

The capitalised cost of the truck is $20,000 – the insurance cost is not capitalised but accounted for as an expense in profit or loss. The net cost of the truck is: $17,000 ($20,000 – $3,000) and the annual depreciation charge will be $2,125 ($17,000/8 years).

At the disposal date, the business had owned the truck for exactly five years – therefore accumulated depreciation to disposal date is $10,625, giving a net carrying amount of $9,375 ($20,000 – $10,625). As the trade-in allowance is $10,000, this will result in a profit on disposal of $625.

132 Option 1 – Optional and Option 2 – Statement of changes in equity

When an entity has revalued a non-current asset, it is **optional** to account for excess depreciation arising on the revaluation. When excess depreciation is accounted for, the accounting adjustment is reflected in **the statement of changes in equity**.

Tutorial note:

Note that when an entity does decide to account for excess depreciation, it must apply that accounting policy every year and cannot apply the policy in some years and not in others.

133 $900 LOSS

The cost of the asset is $15,000 – the cost of the maintenance agreement is not capitalised but accounted for as a payment in advance and charged to profit or loss as an expense over three years. The net cost of the asset is: $13,000 ($15,000 – $2,000) and will be depreciated at 20% per annum.

At the disposal date, the business had owned the asset for 3.5 years – therefore accumulated depreciation to disposal date is $9,100, giving a net carrying amount of $5,900 ($15,000 – $9,100). As the trade-in allowance was $5,000, this will result in a loss on disposal of $900.

INTANGIBLE ASSETS

134 C

135 A

Tutorial note:

When accounting for intangible assets using the revaluation model, movements in the carrying amount are accounted for in other comprehensive income and other components of equity.

136 B

Answer (A) is not precise enough – there must be an annual impairment review to ensure that the asset is not overstated in the financial statements.

137

	Capitalised	Not capitalised
Employment costs of staff conducting research activities		Correct
Cost of constructing a working model of a new product	Correct	
Materials and consumables costs associated with conducting scientific experiments		Correct
Licence purchased to permit production and sale of a product for ten years	Correct	

138 B

When accounting for intangible assets using the cost model, annual impairment charges are accounted for in the statement of profit or loss.

139

	Research expense	Intangible asset
Market research costs	Correct	
Patented product design costs		Correct
Product advertising	Correct	
Employee training costs	Correct	

140 A

Tutorial note:

An intangible asset may be internally generated (development costs per IAS 38) and may also be purchased – therefore answers B and D are incorrect. Answer C is incorrect as assets can normally be sold.

141

	Written off as an expense	Capitalised as an asset
Project 1 – It is applying a new technology to the production of heat resistant fabric. Upon completion, the fabric will be used in the production of uniforms for the emergency services. Geranium has sufficient resources and the intention to complete the project.		Correct
Project 2 – It is considering whether a particular substance can be used as an appetite suppressant. If this is the case, it is expected be sold worldwide in chemists and pharmacies.	Correct	
Project 3 – It is developing a material for use in kitchens which is self-cleaning and germ resistant. A competitor is currently developing a similar material and, for this reason, Geranium is unsure whether its project will be completed.	Correct	

The costs of a development project are capitalised only if:

- The project is separately identifiable.
- Expenditure can be reliably measured.
- It is commercially viable.
- It is technically feasible.
- It is projected to be profitable.
- Resources are available to complete it.

Project 2 falls short of these criteria: it does not appear that the appetite suppressant properties of the substance have yet been confirmed and therefore it is not yet commercially viable.

Project 3 may not be completed and therefore does not meet all six criteria.

The costs of projects 2 and 3 should be expensed to the statement of profit or loss and other comprehensive income.

142 $147,292

	$
Project A	34,000
Project B	78,870
Project C ($290,000 + $19,800) × 4/36	34,422
	———
	147,292

Project A is a research project and all costs should be written off to the statement of profit or loss and other comprehensive income as incurred. Project B is a development project. Costs can only be capitalised when the capitalisation criteria are met. Those costs incurred before this was the case cannot be reinstated as an asset.

Project C is a development project which has resulted in capitalised expenditure. This asset must be amortised over the 36 months of sales of the product. Amortisation for the current year should be 4 months (1 September to 31 December 20X5).

143

	True
Research costs should be expenses to the statement of profit or loss.	Correct
All types of goodwill can be capitalised.	
Capitalised development costs that no longer meet the criteria specified by IAS 38 must be written off to the statement of profit or loss.	Correct
Capitalised development costs are amortised from the date the assets is available to use or sell.	Correct
Research costs written off can be re-capitalised when the developed asset is feasible.	
Only purchased intangibles can be capitalised.	

ACCRUALS AND PREPAYMENTS

144 $453,600

Rental income (property 1 and 2)

	$		$
Balance b/f	5,400	Balance b/f	12,300
Statement of profit or loss		Cash received	
rental income (β)	**453,600**	(280,000 +160,000)	440,000
Balance c/f	6,700	Balance c/f	13,400
	————		————
	465,700		465,700
	————		————
Balance b/f	13,400	Balance b/f	6,700
	————		————

145 $858,600

Rental income

	$		$
Balance b/f	42,300	Balance b/f	102,600
Statement of profit or loss (β)	**858,600**	Cash received	838,600
Balance c/f	88,700	Balance c/f	48,400
	————		————
	989,600		989,600
	————		————

146 A

		$
Statement of profit or loss	9/12 × $10,800	8,100
	3/12 × $12,000	3,000
		———
		11,100
		———
Statement of financial position prepayment	9/12 × $12,000	9,000

147 D

Statement of profit or loss (5/12 × $24,000) + (7/12 × $30,000) = $27,500

Statement of financial position $7,500 paid on 1 January therefore amount prepaid by tenant is: 2/3 × $7,500 = $5,000. For Vine this is prepaid/deferred income, i.e. income received in advance – a liability.

148 A

Charge to P&L = $1,800 × 7/12 = $1,050. Prepayment $1,800 × 5/12 = $750

149 $385

Motor expenses

	$		$
Balance b/f (insurance)	80	Balance b/f (fuel)	95
Cash paid – petrol	95		
– other bills	245	**Statement of profit or loss (β)**	**385**
Balance c/f (petrol)	120	Balance c/f (insurance)	60
	———		———
	540		540
	———		———

The insurance prepayment covers 4 months as at the start of September. Therefore there must be a prepayment of 3 months at the end of September.

150 ACCRUAL $560 and P&L EXPENSE $3,320

The accrual for May and June 20X3 is assumed to be 2/3 × $840 = $560.

Electricity expenses

	$		$
Bank	600	Opening balance b/f	300
Bank (720+900+840)	2,460		
Closing balance c/f	560	Statement of profit or loss	3,320
	———		———
	3,620		3,620
	———		———

151 **$12,600**

The premium for the year 1 July 20X2 to 30 June 20X3 was $13,200 × 1/1.1 = $12,000

Statement of profit or loss charge:

6 months at $12,000 plus 6 months at $13,200 = $6,000 + $6,600 = $12,600

152 **B**

The charge in the statement of profit or loss will be the amount of interest incurred from 1 January (when the loan was taken out) to 30 September (the year end) i.e. 9/12 × 12% × $100,000 = $9,000. This represents three interest payments.

However, as only two interest payments were made (1 April and 1 July) the third payment due to be made on 1 October, which relates to the three months to 30 September, will be accrued: 3/12 × 12% × $100,000 = $3,000.

153 **C**

	$
Prepayment brought forward at the start of the year	10,000
Payment during the year	36,000
	———
	46,000
Less: Prepayment carried forward at the year end	
(7 months, therefore $36,000 × 7/12)	(21,000)
	———
Charge for insurance in the statement of profit or loss	25,000
	———

154 **B**

Accrued income is income not yet received for a service already provided (income received in arrears). The correct double entry to record accrued income is:

Dr Accrued income (statement of financial position), Cr Income (statement of profit or loss) which will increase profit.

155 **B and C**

The meter rental charge covers the period 1 Oct – 31 Dec and has been paid before the year end. Therefore, there is a prepayment of two months rental as follows: ($60 × 2/3) = $40.

The usage charge is paid in arrears and has been paid up to 30 Sept – therefore an accrual of one month is required as follows: ($135 × 1/3) = $45.

IRRECOVERABLE DEBTS AND ALLOWANCES FOR RECEIVABLES

156 B

Receivables ledger control account

	$		$
Balance b/f (W)	13,150	Cash	115,500
Sales	125,000	Irrecoverable debts	7,100
		Balance c/f	15,550
	———		———
	138,150		138,150
	———		———

	b/f	c/f
	$	$
Gross receivables	13,150	15,550
Allowance	(1,150)	(2,100)
	———	———
Net receivables	12,000	13,450
	———	———

157 D

Receivables' ledger control account

	$		$
Balance b/f	34,500	Cash received	247,790
Credit sales (β)	278,090	Contra	1,200
		Irrecoverable debts	18,600
		Balance c/f	45,000
	———		———
	312,590		312,590
	———		———
Balance b/f	45,000		

Total sale = Credit sales + Cash sales

= $278,090 + $24,000 = $302,090

Note:

Discounts received are relevant to the payables ledger control account.

The double-entry for the increase in allowance for receivables is:

Dr Irrecoverable debts expense   12,500

Cr Allowance for receivables   12,500

158 B

Receivables' ledger control account

	$		$
Balance b/f	84,700	Contra with payables ledger control account	5,000
Credit sales	644,000	Irrecoverable debts	4,300
		Cash received from credit customers	625,780
		Balance c/f	93,620
	———		———
	728,700		728,700
	———		———

The double entry for a contra is Dr payables ledger control account (payables) and Cr receivables ledger control account (receivables).

Discounts received are relevant to payables not receivables. Cash sales should not feature in the receivables ledger control account.

The correct double entry for the increase in the allowance for receivables is Dr irrecoverable debts expense and Cr allowance for receivables.

159 A

	$	Allowance $	Expense $
Receivables balance (draft)	58,200		
Irrecoverable debts	(8,900)		8,900
	———		
	49,300		
Specific allowance: Carroll	(1,350)	1,350	
Juffs	(750)	750	
Mary	(1,416)	1,416	
	———	———	
Allowance c/f		3,516	
Allowance b/f		5,650	
		———	
Decrease in allowance		2,134	(2,134)

Total expense = $8,900 – $2,134 = $6,766

160 B

The write off of debts will reduce the gross receivables balance by $72,000 to $766,000.

The allowance is to be adjusted to $60,000 (hence an adjustment of $12,000).

The net balance is therefore $766,000 less $60,000, i.e. $706,000.

161 A

Year-end receivables	5% × $7,000,000	=	$350,000
Year-end allowance for receivables	4% × $350,000	=	$14,000
Allowance at start of year	100/120 × $14,000	=	$11,667
Increase in allowance		=	$2,333

Irrecoverable debts expense

	$		$
Write off of irrecoverable debts	3,200	Recovery of irrecoverable debts	450
Increase in allowance	2,333	Statement of profit or loss (β)	5,083
	─────		─────
	5,533		5,533
	─────		─────

162 B

Trade receivables

	$		$
Balance b/f	10,000	Receipts	90,000
Sales	100,000	Contra with payables	800
Irrecoverable debts recovered	1,000	Balance c/f	20,200
	─────		─────
	111,000		111,000
	─────		─────

163 C

When a debt is written off as irrecoverable, the transaction is recorded as:

Dr Irrecoverable debts account (expense) and Cr Receivables ledger control account.

Any subsequent change to the allowance for receivables should be dealt with as a separate matter.

164 A

Receivables

	$		$
Balance b/f	37,500	Contra with payables	15,750
Sales (credit)	357,500	Irrecoverable debts written off	10,500
		Bank (β)	329,750
		Balance c/f	39,000
	─────		─────
	395,000		395,000
	─────		─────

Cash sales do not affect receivables. Discounts received affect payables, not receivables.

The allowance for receivables does not affect the amount of receivables, but specific irrecoverable debts written off do affect receivables.

165 A

Receivables (5% of $2 million) = $100,000.

Required specific allowance for receivables = $4,000.

Current allowance for receivables = $4,000 × ¾ = $3,000.

Increase in allowance = $1,000. An increase in the allowance for receivables reduces profits.

166 A

	$
Irrecoverable debts written off (800 + 550)	1,350
Irrecoverable debt recovered	(350)
Reduction in allowance for receivables	(200)
Charge to statement of profit or loss	800

167 B

The allowance for receivables will reduce the carrying amount of receivables. An increase in an allowance for receivables will therefore reduce net current assets.

168 A

	$	$
Receivables balance	230,000	
Write off irrecoverable debts	(11,429)	11,429
Specific allowances – Emily		450
– Lulu		980
	218,571	
Total allowance at end of year		12,859
Allowance b/f		(11,700)
Increase in allowance = Dr to statement of profit or loss		1,159

169 D

Tutorial note:

In comparison with making cash sales, the provision of credit will not improve the cash flow position of the business, rather it may result in a deterioration of cash flow. This is particularly true as some customers will be late in paying and others will not pay at all.

170 C

Tutorial note:

An aged receivables analysis is a list of how much each credit customer owes and how old their debt is. It enables the credit control function to identify which customers to chase, and also helps in the calculation of the allowance for receivables at the year-end. Separate information should be maintained of credit approval of customers, together with agreed limits.

171 $6,966

Adjust the receivables control account for the specific allowance

	$	$
Balance on the receivables control account:	425,700	
Less: irrecoverable debts	(8,466)	8,466
	417,234	
Specific allowance required	(2,400)	2,400
Irrecoverable debt recovered		(2,000)
		8,866

The question states that the allowance for receivables at 1 April 20X3 was $1,900. The receivables expense for the year ended 31 March 20X4 is therefore $8,866 − $1,900 = $6,966.

PROVISIONS AND CONTINGENCIES

172

	Provision required	Provision not required
A retail outlet has a policy of providing refunds over and above the statutory requirement to do so. This policy is well publicised and customers have made use of this facility in the past.	Correct	
A customer has made a legal claim against an entity, claiming that faulty goods sold to them caused damage to their property. The entity's lawyers have advised that the claim will possibly succeed and, if it does, compensation of $10,000 will be payable.		Correct

Tutorial note:

Based upon the stated and publicised policy it would appear probable that customers who return goods in accordance with the policy will expect to receive a refund – this requires a provision. The outcome of the legal claim has been assessed as only possible (rather than probable) that there will be an outflow of economic benefits. This does not require a provision, only a disclosure note of the contingent liability.

173 A

174 A

Warranties meet the criteria required to create a provision; a provision should be made for the best estimate of the obligation. The likelihood of a liability arising for Quidditch as a result of the guarantee is assessed as possible. A provision cannot be recognised in the financial statements unless the likelihood is probable.

175 C

A is incorrect – a contingent asset is only recognised and accounted for if it is virtually certain to arise.

B is incorrect as only contingent assets which are regarded as probable are disclosed in the financial statements.

D is incorrect as a contingent liability which is regarded as probable must be recognised and accounted for in the financial statements.

176 D

A is incorrect – a contingent asset is only recognised and accounted for if it is virtually certain to arise.

B is incorrect as contingent assets can be recognised if they are virtually certain.

C is incorrect as a contingent liability which is regarded as remote can be ignored when preparing the financial statements.

For the same reason, D is correct as contingent liabilities which are regarded as remote can be ignored when preparing the financial statements.

177 B

(1) is incorrect – a provision may be classified as a non-current liability when the probable outflow of economic benefits is expected to occur more than twelve months from the reporting date.

(2) is correct as normally a liability can be precisely quantified whereas quantification of a provision requires estimation and judgement.

(3) is correct – there is a future probable outflow of economic benefits, but the exact amount and/or date of the outflow is still to be confirmed.

178 C

Tutorial note:

IAS 37 requires that a provision should be recognised when it is probable that there will be a future outflow of economic benefits as a result of a past event.

Based upon the licence terms, damage has already been caused which will cost $5 million to rectify in 20X7 or later. This should be recognised and classified as a non-current liability. If damage has not yet been caused, there is not yet an obligation to rectify it. Therefore at 31 August 20X4 no provision can be made for expected future damage.

179 D

IAS 37 requires that a provision should be recognised when it is probable that there will be a future outflow of economic benefits as a result of a past event. Therefore, a provision to settle customer claims should be recognised. As it is only probable that the counter-claim against Bottler will succeed, it cannot be recognised in the statement of financial position – it is disclosed in a note to the financial statements.

180 C

An increase in the provision from $10,000 to $13,000 requires that a charge is made in profit or loss and that the provision balance within current liabilities is increased by the same amount.

181 B

Tutorial note:

IAS 37 requires that a provision should be recognised when it is probable that there will be a future outflow of economic benefits as a result of a past event. Contingent liabilities that are regarded as possible, rather than probable, should be the subject of a disclosure note in the financial statements.

CAPITAL STRUCTURE AND FINANCE COSTS

182

	True	False
A rights issue capitalises the entity's reserves, which can be a disadvantage, as this can reduce the amount of reserves available for future dividends.		Correct
A rights issue is offered to the entity's existing shareholders and is usually at a discounted price compared to the nominal value of a share.		Correct

Statement 1 referring to capitalisation of reserves applies to a bonus issue and is therefore incorrect. A rights issue does not 'capitalise entity reserves', as a rights issue but raises cash resources at an issue price less that market value. A rights issue is being offered to existing shareholders and does bring in cash but at a discounted price compared to the market value of a share. Statement 2 refers to a discounted price compared to nominal value – this is incorrect.

183

	Selection
Cash	Correct
Retained earnings	
Finance cost	
Equity	
Long-term debt	Correct

On issue of redeemable preference shares, the two items effected would be cash, as cash is coming in from the issue of shares and secondly, long-term debt. This is because, although legally they are shares, in substance redeemable preference shares are more like debt (as they have fixed return and are repayable/redeemable at a future date).

184 D

Opening retained earnings + profit – prior year final dividend = closing retained earnings

Opening retained earnings = $79,285 – $12,200 – $320,568

Opening retained earnings = $253,483

185 $15,000

	$
Net profit for the year	36,000
Dividend	(21,000)
Added to retained earnings	15,000

You should recognise that it is the profit for the period less any dividend paid that is added to the retained earnings balance. Accounting for the revaluation does not affect retained earnings for the year – this is accounted for through other comprehensive income and revaluation surplus within other components of equity.

186 B

187 A and D

188 C

Tutorial note:

A rights issue is an issue of shares for cash. It is usually made at less than full market price to encourage current shareholders to take up the share issue.

189 C

A bonus issue of shares is a free issue of shares to current shareholders on a pro-rata basis in relation to their current shareholding.

190 B

	True	False
Dividends paid by an entity are excluded from the statement of changes in equity		Correct
Dividends received by an entity are included in the statement of changes in equity.		Correct
Dividends received by an entity are excluded from the statement of changes in equity.	Correct	
Dividends paid by an entity are included in the statement of changes in equity.	Correct	

Dividends received are accounted for in the statement of profit or loss as income. Dividends paid are accounted for in the statement of changes in equity.

191 C

Tutorial note:

Dividends are paid from retained earnings. They must be accounted for as an expense in the statement of profit or loss.

192 D

Debit / Credit	Ledger Account:	$
Debit	Bank (20,000 × $1.75)	35,000
Credit	Share capital ($20,000 × $1)	20,000
Share premium	Share premium ($20,000 × $0.75)	15,000

193 B

The accounting entries would be:

Dr Share premium $31,250

Cr Share capital (250,000/4) = 62,500 × $0.50 = $31,250

194 D

Redeemable preference shares have the characteristics of a liability as they will be redeemed at some future date which will require an outflow of economic benefits. They should be classified as a liability, rather than equity.

195 B

A limited company may choose to (or not) revalue its land and buildings. A limited company may (or may not) make a share issue at a premium. When a share issue is made, the company must receive at least the nominal value of the shares issued, although often it will receive a premium in excess of the nominal value.

PREPARING A TRIAL BALANCE

FROM TRIAL BALANCE TO FINANCIAL STATEMENTS

196 $4,500

	$	$
Property, plant and equipment	209,000	
Inventory	4,600	
Receivables and payables	5,900	6,300
Bank overdraft		790
Loan		50,000
Capital		100,000
Drawings	23,000	
Sales		330,000
Purchases	168,200	
Sales returns	7,000	
Sundry expenses	73,890	
Discounts received (β)		4,500
	491,590	491,590

197 D

	True	False
The trial balance provides a check that no errors exist in the accounting records of a business.		Correct
The trial balance is one of the financial statements prepared annually by an entity for its shareholders.		Correct

When a trial balance agrees, this does not confirm that no errors have been made in the accounting records. Only those errors resulting from accounting entries without an equal debits and credits will be highlighted by the trial balance. An entity will prepare the statement of profit or loss and other comprehensive income, the statement of financial position, the statement of cash flows and the statement of changes in equity. The trial balance is not one of the financial statements prepared by an entity for its shareholders.

198 C

All three items are limitations of a trial balance.

Figures in the trial balance are not necessarily the final figures to be reported in the financial statements; they are subject to year-end adjustments.

Errors of commission (where an entry has been posted to the wrong account) are not identified by the trial balance since an equal debit and credit entry are still posted.

Although a trial balance can identify if double entry has broken down, it does not indicate in which accounts wrong entries were made.

199 $23,690

	$	$
Sales		120,000
Opening inventory	2,600	
Purchases	78,900	
Closing inventory	(1,900)	(79,600)
	_____	_____
Gross profit		40,400
Rental expense (3,400 – 200)	3,200	
Sundry expenses	13,900	
Bank interest	(270)	
Decrease in allowance	(120)	(16,710)
	_____	_____
Net profit		23,690
		_____

200 B

	Increase	Decrease	
	$	$	$
Closing inventory	45,700		
Depreciation (20% × $470,800)		94,160	
Irrecoverable debt		230	
Deferred income		6,700	
	———	———	
	45,700	101,090	
Decrease in net assets	———	———	55,390

201 C

	Dr	Cr
	$	$
Premises/Acc Dep'n	500,000	120,000
Inventory	23,000	
Share capital		200,000
Retained earnings		105,000
Receivables	43,500	
Carriage in	1,500	
Allowance for receivables		3,400
Bank overdraft		1,010
Payables		35,900
Sales		500,080
Purchases	359,700	
Sales returns	10,300	
Sundry expenses	14,000	
Suspense	13,390	
	———	———
	965,390	965,390
	———	———

202 B

Depreciation charge	= Closing cost × percentage depreciation rate
	= **$5,000** (10% × $50,000)
Closing accumulated depreciation	= Accumulated depreciation b/f + charge for the year
	= $15,000 + $5,000
	= $20,000
Carrying amount	= Closing cost less closing accumulated depreciation
Carrying amount	=$50,000 – $20,000
	= **$30,000**

203 C

	Charge for the year $				Closing $
Rent	24,000	Rent accrual			**2,000**
		(12 × $2,000)	Due	24,000	
		Paid		22,000	
				────	
		Accrual		2,000	
				────	
Insurance	28,000	Insurance prepayment			**2,000**
		Paid		30,000	
		Due		28,000	
				────	
		Prepayment		2,000	
				────	

The rental charge in the statement of profit or loss will be $24,000 ($2,000 × 12 months). Only $22,000 has been paid, therefore an accrual of $2,000 will appear in the statement of financial position. The insurance charge will be according to the notes given after the trial balance totalling $28,000. The amount paid is $30,000, thus a prepayment of $2,000 will appear in the statement of financial position.

Note: In the trial balance the amount paid will be shown.

204 A

		$
Irrecoverable debts	1,600 + 3,000	4,600
Decrease in allowance for receivables (W1)		(440)
		────
Total irrecoverable debt expense		4,160
		────
Receivables	(29,600 – 3,000 irrecoverable debt)	26,600
Less: Closing allowance for receivables		(2,660)
		────
Net closing receivables		23,940
(W1) – movement in allowance for receivables		
Closing allowance for receivables		2,660
Opening allowance for receivables		3,100
		────
Decrease in allowance for receivables		440
		────

205 D

Depreciation charge	= (Closing cost – accumulated depreciation b/f) × percentage depreciation rate
	= ($50,000 – $21,875) × 25%
	= $7,031
Closing accumulated depreciation	= Accumulated depreciation b/f + charge for the year
	= $21,875 + $7,031
	= $28,906
Carrying amount	= Closing cost less closing accumulated depreciation
Carrying amount	= $50,000 – $28,906
Carrying amount	= $21,094

206

	Selection
A casting error of $300 made when totalling the sales day book	
A transposition error made when posting the total of cash payments into the general ledger	
Discount received was included in the trial balance as a debit balance	Correct
A cheque paid to a supplier recorded was debited to cash and correctly recognised in trade payables	Correct

CONTROL ACCOUNT RECONCILIATIONS

207 C

208 B

	PLCA $		Payables' ledger $
Draft balance	768,420	Draft balance	781,200
Reverse incorrect debit entry	28,400		
Discounts received – correct entry	(15,620)		
	————		————
Revised balance	781,200		781,200
	————		————

Items A and D would explain the discrepancy if the balance on the control account was $12,780 greater than the balance on the payables' ledger.

Item C would explain the balance on the payables' ledger being $25,560 greater than the balance on the control account.

209 A

Payables' ledger control account

	$		$
Contras against debit balances in receivables ledger	48,000	Balance b/f	318,600
Cash paid to suppliers	1,367,000	Purchases	1,268,600
Purchase returns	41,200		
Discounts received	8,200		
Balance c/f	122,800		
	1,587,200		1,587,200

210 D

	Payables' ledger $	Supplier statement $
Per question	230	3,980
Cheque (1)		(270)
Goods returned (2)		(180)
Contra (3)		(3,200)
Revised balance	230	330

Difference $100 (330 – 230)

211 A

The control account has been debited by $10 more than it should have been. The account should be credited. This error would have had no effect on the receivables ledger and so part of the difference has been explained.

212 B

	Lord's records $
Per question	14,500
Unrecorded discount	(150)
Revised balance = supplier statement	14,350

Lord believes that he owes $150 more than the supplier has stated. Items A, C and D would result in q different outcome.

213 D

Items A and B will result in an error in the control account. Item C will result in an error in the total of individual customer account balances. Item D will not affect either of the totals, although there are errors in the individual accounts of the two customers affected, with one account balance too high and the other too low by the same amount.

214 D

	SLCA
	$
Draft balance per question	37,642
Correction of misposted contra	(1,802)
	———
Revised balance = receivables ledger balance	35,840
	———

The balance on the control account exceeds the total of the individual account balances by $1,802. Items A, B and C would all have the effect of making the total of the individual account balances higher by $1,802. Item D, however, by recording a credit item as a debit item in the control account, has made the control account debit balance too high by $901 × 2 = $1,802.

215 B

	$		$
Balance per ledger account	260	Balance per supplier's statement	1,350
Cash discount disallowed	80	Less: Goods returned	(270)
		Less: Cash in transit	(830)
Adjusted ledger account balance	———		———
	340	Revised balance	250
	———		———

Unreconciled difference = ($340 – $250) = $90

216 D

The purchase day book has been undercast by $500 (i.e. the total is $500 lower than it should be). As a result of this, the purchases account has been debited and the payables ledger control account (total payables) credited with $500 too little.

The sales day book has been overcast by $700. As a result, the sales account has been credited and the receivables ledger control account (total receivables) has been debited with $700 too much.

As a result of these errors, the control account balances need to be adjusted, and profit reduced by ($500 + $700) $1,200, by reducing sales and increasing purchases.

Neither error affects the entries in the accounts of individual customers and suppliers.

217 A

As a result of the error, total payables are understated by $259,440 – $254,940 = $4,500. To correct the error, increase the balance in the payables ledger control account by crediting the control account.

The error has affected the control account only, and not the entries in the individual supplier account for Figgins in the purchase ledger, so the total of suppliers' balances is unaffected.

218 B

Error (1) Total sales and total receivables have been recorded $370 too much. Credit the receivables ledger control account by $370.

Error (2) Total receivables has been recorded ($940 – $490) $450 too little. Credit the receivables ledger control account by $450.

As a result of these two errors, total receivables have been under-credited by $820 ($450 + $370).

The errors have not affected the accounts of individual customers.

219 $367,300

	$
Trade payables b'fwd 1 May 20X4	130,000
Purchases for the year – bal fig	**367,300**
Cash paid	(340,000)
Contra with trade receivables' ledger	(3,800)
Discount received	(3,500)
Trade payables c'fwd 30 April 20X5	150,000

BANK RECONCILIATIONS

220 D

	$		$
Cash book balance per question (credit)	(1,350)	Balance per bank statement (β)	(1,707)
Standing order not recorded	(300)	Unpresented cheques	(56)
		Uncleared lodgements	128
		Bank error	(15)
Revised cash book balance	(1,650)	Revised balance = cash book	(1,650)

On the bank statement the overdrawn balance is shown as a debit (i.e. from the bank's perspective they are owed money).

221 B

Note that the draft ledger account balance shows an overdraft, however the bank statement shows a positive balance:

	Bank statement $	Ledger account $
Balance per question	250	(190)
Unpresented cheques	(150)	
Misposting of cash receipt		260
Bank interest		30
	――――	――――
	100	100
	――――	――――

222

	True	False
When preparing a bank reconciliation, unpresented cheques must be deducted from a balance of cash at bank shown in the bank statement.	Correct	
A cheque from a customer paid into the bank but dishonoured must be corrected by making a debit entry in the cash book.		Correct
An error by the bank must be corrected by an entry in the cash book.		Correct
An overdraft is a debit balance in the bank statement.	Correct	

Item 1 – unpresented cheques are those issued by a business but not yet banked by the recipient. They should be deducted from the balance shown on the bank statement in order to reflect the true bank balance.

Item 2 – a dishonoured cheque is recorded by crediting the cash book. The cheque would previously have been debited to cash when received. The credit is the reversal of that entry.

Item 3 – a bank error should be corrected by amendment to the balance per the bank statement.

Item 4 – from the bank's perspective an overdraft means that they are owed money by the customer. Hence it is shown as a debit (an asset to the bank) in the bank statement.

223 B

	$
Balance per bank statement (overdrawn)	(38,640)
Add: Lodgement not credited	19,270
	(19,370)
Less: Unpresented cheques	(14,260)
Balance per cash book	(33,630)

224 B

	$
Balance per bank statement	(200)
Unpresented cheques	(1,250)
Error	97
Uncleared lodgements	890
Revised balance = revised cash book balance	(463)

225 B

	$		$
Cash book balance	(8,970)	Bank statement balance (β)	(11,200)
Bank charges	(550)	Unpresented cheques	(3,275)
		Uncleared lodgements	5,380
		Bank error	(425)
Revised cash book balance	(9,520)	Revised cash book balance	(9,520)

226 B

Cash

	$		$
Original balance (β)	11,960	Dishonoured cheque	300
Error: receipt recorded as payment (2 × $195)	390	Bank charges	50
		Balance c/f (= revised bank balance)	12,000
	12,350		12,350

	$
Bank statement balance	13,400
Unpresented cheques	(1,400)
Revised balance	12,000

227 D

	$
Balance per bank statement	(715)
Less: Unpresented cheques	(824)
Add: Outstanding lodgements	337
	(1,202)
Less: Bank error	(25)
Statement of financial position/cash book overdraft	(1,227)

228 D

Cash

	$		$
Reversal of standing order (entered twice)	125	Draft balance	5,675
Revised balance	6,450	Dishonoured cheque	900
	6,575		6,575

The dishonoured cheque for $450 should have been credited to the bank balance. Instead it was debited. The bank balance is therefore too high by $900.

229 B

Cash book

	$		$
Cash sales	1,450	Balance b/f	485
Cash receipts	2,400	Payments to suppliers (95% × $1,800)	1,710
		Dishonoured cheques	250
		Balance c/f	1,405
	3,850		3,850

230 B

	$
Balance per bank statement	(800)
Unpresented cheque	(80)
	─────
Revised bank balance	(880)
	─────

The dishonoured cheque requires adjustment in the cash book. After this adjustment, the cash book balance will equal the revised bank balance.

231 B

Cash

	$		$
Draft balance	2,490		
		Bank charges	50
		Dishonoured cheque	140
		Revised balance	2,300
	─────		─────
	2,490		2,490
	─────		─────

232 A

Cash

	$		$
		Draft balance	1,240
		Bank charges	75
Revised balance	1,315		
	─────		─────
	1,315		1,315
	─────		─────

	$
Balance per bank statement (β)	(1,005)
Unpresented cheques	(450)
Uncleared lodgements	140
	─────
Revised balance = cash book balance	(1,315)
	─────

233 C

An unrecorded difference is a transaction that is reflected in the bank statement but has not yet been entered into the cash book – usually because the accountant is not aware of the transaction until advised by the bank.

Examples include direct debits, standing orders, bank charges, bank interest, dishonoured cheques and direct credits. Uncleared lodgements and unpresented cheques are examples of timing differences – amounts which have been entered into the cash book but have not yet cleared the bank.

234 A

	$
Adjusted cash book balance per bank reconciliation	1,060
Outstanding lodgements	(5,000)
Unpresented cheques	2,800
	———
Balance overdrawn at the bank	(1,140)
	———

In the books of the bank and on the bank statement, an overdraft will appear as a debit balance.

CORRECTION OF ERRORS AND SUSPENSE ACCOUNTS

235 A

Suspense account

	$		$
Imbalance on TB (362,350 – 347,800)	14,550		
Disposals (2)	9,000		
Allowance for receivables (3)	2,600	Balance c/f	26,150
	———		———
	26,150		26,150
	———		———
Balance b/f	26,150		

The suspense account is only affected where the initial debit and credit were unequal:

(1)   An incorrect entry into the sales day book means that the subtotal of the day book is wrong and both sides of the double entry have been made for the wrong amount. This does not affect the suspense account.

(2)   An unequal entry has occurred:

		$
Entry was:	Dr Cash	9,000
	(Cr Suspense	9,000)
To correct:	Dr Suspense	9,000
	Cr Disposals	9,000

(Do not worry about the other journals required to record the disposal – they have not been recorded at all and so do not affect the suspense account.)

(3)   An unequal entry has occurred:

Entry was:	Dr Irrecoverable debt expense	1,300
	Dr Allowance for receivables	1,300
	(Cr Suspense	2,600)
To correct:	Dr Suspense	2,600
	Cr Allowance for receivables	2,600

236   C

If the sales day book is undercast, then the debit and credit entries to the accounts are equal (although for the wrong amount).

Discounts received should be credited to the discounts received account. The credit entry has simply been made to the wrong account. It is assumed that the debit entry is correct and therefore an equal debit and credit entry have been made.

The omission of an opening accrual or prepayment will always result in an imbalance on the trial balance.

The undercasting of the debit side of the cash account will result in an incorrect balance for cash being extracted and shown on the trial balance. This will cause total debit balances to be unequal to total credit balances.

237   A

An extraction error arises when the balance on a particular account is not listed correctly in the trial balance. Therefore the trial balance does not balance.

An error of commission arises where an equal debit and credit have been recorded but one entry has been made to the wrong account.

An error of omission arises where a transaction has been completely omitted from the accounting records.

An error of original entry arises where an equal debit and credit have been made but for the wrong amount.

238   D

The suspense account initially has a credit balance in order to make the total debits equal to the total credits.

Where an opening accrual has been omitted, it should be recorded and the opposite entry made to the suspense account:

Dr Suspense account	$7,568
Cr Rental expense	$7,568

Suspense account

	$		$
Opening accrual	7,568	Per trial balance	7,568

Tutorial note:

Carriage inwards should be a debit in the trial balance of $3,784. If the account balance is wrongly shown as a credit, the total credits in the trial balance will exceed the total debits by 2 × $3,784.

Discounts received

Correct entry		*Actual entry*	
Dr Payables ledger control account	$3,784	Cr Payables ledger control account	$3,784
Cr Discounts received.	$3,784	Cr Discounts received	$3,784
		(Dr Suspense account	$7,568)

The actual entry made was a double credit. This will result in a debit balance arising on the suspense account.

Sales day book

If the sales day book is undercast, the entries to the sales and receivables ledger control accounts will be equal, but for the wrong amount. This will not result in an imbalance on the trial balance.

239 C

The correct entry for sales commission is:

Dr Sales commission and Cr Cash

As the debit was made to the wages and salaries account in error, the amount need to be removed from that account and transferred to commission paid account.

Personal accounts are not maintained for the directors of an entity.

Where repairs are carried out by an entity's own staff using items of inventory, the correct journal to transfer the relevant costs to the repairs account is:

Dr Repairs and Cr Wages/purchases

If rent received is credited to the wrong account, no suspense account entry arises. The correction journal will involve debiting the account wrongly credited and crediting the rent receivable account.

240 B

(1) A debit and credit are made for an equal amount (albeit to the wrong account in the case of the debit), and therefore the suspense account is not affected.

(2) The undercasting of the debit side of the wages account will result in an incorrect balance being extracted. This will result in an imbalance on the trial balance and the creation of a suspense account.

(3) The correct entry for discounts received is:

Dr Payables ledger control account, and Cr Discounts received

The error made will therefore result in a double debit (correctly to the payables ledger control account, and incorrectly to purchases). When double entry recording of transactions breaks down, a suspense account will be created.

(4) An equal debit and credit entry are made and therefore the suspense account is not affected.

241 C

Should do		Did do		To correct	
Dr Cash	13,000	Dr Cash	13,000	Dr Suspense	26,000
Cr Sales revenue	13,000	Dr Purchases	13,000	Cr Purchases	13,000
		(Cr Suspense	26,000)	Cr Sales revenue	13,000
Dr Plant and machinery	18,000	(Dr Suspense	18,000)	Dr Plant and machinery	18,000
Cr Cash	18,000	Cr Cash	18,000	Cr Suspense	18,000

242 B

(1) Double entry has been maintained (an equal debit and credit entry have been made). Therefore there is no effect on the suspense account.

To correct: Dr Plant account $43,200, and Cr Cash $43,200

In addition, depreciation should have been charged at 10% × $48,000, i.e. $4,800.

To record extra depreciation: Dr Depreciation expense $4,320

Cr Accumulated depreciation $4,320

(2) This transaction has been omitted completely from the accounts therefore it has no effect on the suspense account.

To correct: Dr Bank charges $440, and Cr Cash $440

(3) A debit entry has been made, but no credit entry. A suspense account entry will therefore be required to correct this error:

Should do		Did do		To correct	
Dr Payables ledger account	$800	Dr Payables ledger account	$800	Dr Suspense	$800
Cr Sundry payables (amount due to Director)	$800	(Cr suspense	$800)	Cr Sundry payables	$800

(4) The balance on the cash book will be $10,000 too high as a result of the understatement. Therefore the trial balance will not balance and a suspense account will arise.

To correct: Dr Suspense $10,000, and Cr Cash $10,000

243 D

Correction journals only affect profit if one side is posted to an statement of profit or loss account and the other to a statement of financial position account. For this purpose, a suspense account is a statement of financial position account:

		Increase	*Decrease*	
		$	$	$
Draft profit				630,000
(1)	Extra depreciation		4,320	
(2)	Bank charges		440	
(3)	No effect			
(4)	No effect			
			———	(4,760)
				625,240

244 C

Should do		*Did do*		*To correct*	
Dr Purchases	$4,000	Dr Purchases	$4,700	Dr Suspense	$700
Dr Sales tax	$700	Dr Sales tax	$700	Cr Purchases	$700
Cr PLCA	$4,700	Cr PLCA	$4,700		
		(Cr Suspense	$700)		

Purchases (and sales) are recorded net of sales tax. Payables (and receivables) are recorded gross of sales tax.

245 C

Profit is only affected when one (but not both) side of the correction journal is posted to the statement of profit or loss. Both entries in the journal to record cash drawings are to statement of financial position accounts. The expense of $420 has already been recorded when the allowance was made during the year.

To correct the misclassification, interest receivable will be reduced and rental income increased by the same amount. Therefore there is no effect on profit. Both entries in the journal to record the receipt are to statement of financial position accounts.

246 A

Suspense account			
	$		$
Balance per TB	500	Misrecording of decrease in allowance for receivables	840
Sales account undercast	150		
Balance c/f	190		–
	840		840

The misposting of rent received to the rent payable account does not affect the suspense account as double entry was maintained, despite the error.

247   C

An error of principle breaks the 'rules' of an accounting principle or concept, for example incorrectly treating revenue expenditure as capital expenditure. The purchase of a non-current asset should be debited to a non-current asset account, not to the purchases account.

248   B

Should do		Did do		To correct	
(1) Dr Motor expense	$4,600	Cr Cash	$4,600	Dr Motor expense	$4,600
Cr Cash	$4,600	Cr MV cost	$4,600	Dr MV cost	$4,600
		(Dr Suspense	$9,200)	Cr Suspense	$9,200
(2) Dr Cash	$360	Dr Cash	$360	Dr Green's account	$360
Cr Brown's account	$360	Cr Green's account	$360	Cr Brown's account	$360
(3) Dr Rent expense	$9,500	Dr Rent expense	$5,900	Dr Rent expense	$3,600
Cr Cash	$9,500	Cr Cash	$9,500	Cr Suspense	$3,600
		(Dr Suspense	$3,600)		
(4) Dr Payables control	$325	Dr Payables control	$325	Dr Purchases	$325
Cr Discount received	$325	Cr Purchases	$325	Cr Discounts received	$325
(5) Dr Cash	$100	–		Dr Cash	$100
Cr Sales	$100			Cr Sales	$100

249   B

Accounting for an expense should reduce profit. By crediting $40 to the Bank interest receivable account, when bank charges should have been debited to an expense account, has the effect of increasing profit by $40, rather than the proper outcome of reducing profit by $40. As a result of this error, profit has been overstated by 2 × $40 = $80.

250   A

Should do	Did do	To correct
(1) Dr Gas expense $420	Dr Gas expense $240	Dr Gas expense $180
Cr Cash $420	Cr Cash $420	Cr Suspense $180
	(Dr Suspense $180)	
(2) Dr Stationery $50	Cr Discounts received $50	Dr Stationery $50
Cr Cash $50	Cr Cash $50	Dr Discounts received $50
	(Dr Suspense $100)	Cr Suspense $100
(3) Dr Bank $70	Dr Bank $70	Dr Suspense $70
Cr Interest $70	(Cr Suspense $70)	Cr Interest $70

Suspense account

	$		$
Balance b/f (β)	210	Error (1)	180
Error (3)	70	Error (2)	100
	——		——
	280		280
	——		——

251 D

The error has been to debit the customer (receivable) account and credit the supplier (payable) account, instead of debiting the supplier account and crediting the customer account. As a result receivables are over-stated by 2 × $270 = $540, and payables are over-stated by $540. The error should be corrected, but sales and purchases are unaffected, so profit is unaffected. Total assets (receivables) and total liabilities (payables) are both $540 too high, so that net assets are unchanged.

252 D

Tutorial note:

The key to answering these types of questions correctly is to consider each option individually and establish if the error will cause a suspense account to be created. This will only occur if there has been a one-sided entry or both sides of a journal have been posted to the same side of the ledger.

In option A, there is a debit and a credit entry in the transaction so even though these are incorrect entries they will not cause the trial balance to be out of balance.

In option B, the sales day book total is posted to the Sales account and the Receivables account, so even though the total is incorrect, there will still be a journal that balances and this will not cause the trial balance to be out of balance.

In option C, Discounts received should be debited to the Payables ledger control account, which has happened, and should be credited to Discounts received. They have been incorrectly credited to Purchases, but as the transaction has a debit and credit entry of equal value it will not cause the trial balance to be out of balance.

Finally, in option D, purchases from the purchase day book should have been debited to Purchases and credited to Payables ledger control account. The credit entry has been dealt with correctly but instead of debiting purchases the entry has been made to credit sales. This journal entry has two credits and does not balance so the trial balance will not balance leading to a suspense account being required.

253 $1,160 Dr

The correct answer is calculated as follows:

	$
Balance b/f	1,820 Cr
(1) Sundry income	(180) Dr
(2) Sales ledger	(2,800) Dr
	———
Balance c/f	(1,160) Dr
	———

Transaction (1) requires an entry to the suspense account as too little sundry income has been recorded in the ledger account. The correcting journal entry is to Dr Suspense and Cr Sundry income with the difference of $180.

In Transaction (2) there has been a one-sided entry, so to correct it a post to Dr Suspense Cr Sales with $2,800 is required.

Transaction (3) does not require an entry to the suspense account as the incorrect total of the day book will be posted into the ledger accounts and will not cause the trial balance to be out of balance.

254 $1,860 Dr

The correct answer is calculated as follows:

	$
Balance b/f	1,250 Dr
(1) Purchase ledger control	160 Dr
(2) Receivables	450 Dr
	———
Balance c/f	1,860 Dr
	———

Transaction (1) – an addition error in a general ledger account will cause an imbalance. As a closing liability balance has been undercast this will have caused a credit entry to the suspense and will need correction by debiting the suspense account and crediting the purchase ledger control account with $160.

Transaction (2) – Again, an imbalance has occurred as there has been a one sided transaction. The only entry has been to debit cash and therefore the credit has been made to the suspense account. In order to clear this off the suspense account, the adjustment would be to debit the suspense account and credit receivables.

Transaction (3) – Does not require an entry to the suspense account as the incorrect total from the purchase returns day book has been posted into the ledger accounts and therefore will not need adjusting through the suspense account as no imbalance has occurred. The correction journal would be to debit purchase ledger control account and credit purchase returns.

255 C

	Current assets $	Current liabilities $
A – cash received and deferred income recognised	5,000	5,000
B – reduction in bank balance to pay premium	(5,000)	
B – insurance prepayment (3/6 × $5,000)	2,500	
C – Loan cash received	12,000	
C – interest accrual (5% × $12,000 × 6/12)		300
Current assets and current liabilities	14,500	5,300

Note that the liability to repay the loan is a non-current liability.

256 $72,200

Answer: $57,400 + $15,500 – ((($15,500 – $1,500)/10) × 6/12) = $72,200

PREPARING BASIC FINANCIAL STATEMENTS

STATEMENT OF FINANCIAL POSITION AND STATEMENT OF PROFIT OR LOSS AND OTHER COMPREHENSIVE INCOME

257 A

Opening net assets + capital injections + profit – drawings = closing net assets

Opening net assets + $9,800 + $8,000 – $4,200 = $19,000

Opening net assets = Opening capital = $5,400

258 B

	$	$
Sales (β)		25,600
Cost of sales		
Opening inventory	1,500	
Purchases	12,950	
Inventory drawings	(75)	
Closing inventory	(900)	
		(13,475)
Gross profit		12,125

259 B

The profit or loss charge would be $500 underprovision b/fwd plus the charge for the current year of $8,000 = $8,500. The liability outstanding would be $8,000.

260 D

Capital = net assets

If a supplier is paid by cheque, assets reduce as do liabilities, therefore there is no change to net assets.

If raw materials or non-current assets are purchased on credit, assets increase as do liabilities; again there is no change to net assets.

If wages are paid in cash, assets decrease (the other effect is to reduce profits which in turn reduces capital).

261 B

The loan was included as a current liability, but should be treated as a non-current liability. Correcting the error will reduce total current liabilities, and this will increase net current assets (= current assets minus current liabilities).

262 B

Profit is the increase in net assets between the beginning and end of the period, plus drawings taken out of the business, minus new equity introduced in the period (which is not profit).

263 C

The separate business entity concept means that accounting information should only relate to the business, not the owner of the business. Therefore goods taken by the owner must be treated as drawings and removed from the inventory of the business.

264 D

Current assets	$	Current liabilities	$
Receivables	23,800	Overdraft	3,250
Allowances for receivables	(1,500)	Payables	31,050
Inventory	12,560	Rent accrual	1,200
Petty cash	150	Loan	25,000
	———		———
	35,010		60,500
	———		———

The bank statement shows a debit balance, indicating an overdraft (from the bank's perspective, they are owed money by Andrew).

The first instalment of the loan (25%) is due within 12 months and so shown as a current liability.

265 A

		Assets	=	Liabilities	+	Capital

Assets   =   Liabilities   +   Capital

At start of week:

15,700   =   11,200   +   4,500(β)

1 May

+300   + 300   + 1,400

+1,400

3 May

−750   − 750

4 May

−400   − 400

7 May

+1,200   + 1,200

−600   − 600

At end of week:

16,850   =   11,500   +   5,350

266 $70,000

Only the revaluation surplus arising in the year is included within other comprehensive income. The depreciation charge and the gain on disposal are accounted for in profit or loss.

267 $18,000

The development expenditure should be capitalised and should not, therefore be written off as an expense. The remaining items totalling $18,000 should be charged as an expense for the year.

268 $900

The original annual depreciation charge = $80,000/50 years = $1,600. The property has been depreciated for $16,000/$1,600 = 10 years, leaving a remaining estimated useful life of 40 years. The revised annual depreciation charge is ($100,000/40 years) = $2,500. The amount of the excess depreciation transfer is: $2,500 − $1,600 = $900.

269 D

Debit or Credit	Account	$
Debit	Non-current asset – property	40,000
Debit	Accumulated depreciation	40,000
Credit	Revaluation surplus	80,000

270 C

	Cost of sales	Administrative expense	Distribution costs
	$	$	$
Opening inventory	12,500		
Closing inventory	(17,900)		
Purchases	199,000		
Distribution costs			35,600
Administrative expenses		78,800	
Audit fee		15,200	
Carriage in	3,500		
Carriage out			7,700
Depreciation (70:30:0)	28,000	12,000	
	225,100	106,000	43,300

271 B

The first statement is false: the nominal value of the ordinary shares is 50c and therefore there are 200,000 in issue. The ordinary dividend paid is:

200,000 × 3c = $6,000

The second statement is true. A preference dividend is accounted for when it falls due and therefore the part of the dividend not yet paid must be accrued at the year end.

272 C

Share premium

	$		$
		Balance b/f	30,000
Bonus issue (W2)	12,500	Rights issue (W1)	90,000
Balance c/f	107,500		
	120,000		120,000

(W1)	**Rights issue**	Existing number of shares	400,000
		New shares	100,000
	At $1.15 each	Dr Cash	$115,000
		Cr Share capital	$25,000
		Cr Share premium	$90,000
(W2)	**Bonus issue**	Existing shares	500,000
		New shares	50,000
		Dr Share premium	$12,500
		Cr Share capital	$12,500

273

	Selection
Statement of profit or loss and other comprehensive income	
Statement of financial position	
Statement of cash flows	Correct
Statement of changes in equity	Correct

Only dividend income is shown in the statement of profit or loss and other comprehensive income. Only dividends payable in respect of preference shares are shown in the statement of financial position.

The statement of cash flows includes all dividends paid. The statement of changes in equity includes dividends paid and dividends payable.

274 C

The tax charge is disclosed in the statement of profit or loss and other comprehensive income.

A revaluation surplus is not realised. However, in accordance with IAS 1 (revised) it is included in the statement of profit or loss and other comprehensive income and also shown in the statement of changes in equity.

275 D

Dividends are not shown in an entity's statement of profit or loss and other comprehensive income. Instead they are presented in the statement of changes to equity.

Unpaid ordinary dividends are only accrued at the year-end if they have been declared prior to the year end. In practise this is very rare.

276

	True	False
An entity may make a rights issue if it wished to raise more equity capital.	Correct	
A rights issue might increase the share premium account whereas a bonus issue is likely to reduce it.	Correct	
A rights issue will always increase the number of shareholders in an entity whereas a bonus issue will not.		Correct
A bonus issue will result in an increase in the market value of each share		Correct

A rights issue involves the issue of new shares for cash and therefore more equity capital will be raised.

The rights issue price will probably be above nominal value and therefore the share premium account will be increased by the amount of the premium. A bonus issue does not involve cash; when recording the transaction, the debit entry is normally made to the share premium account, therefore reducing it.

Both a rights and a bonus issue involve the potential issue of shares to existing shareholders. Therefore neither will increase the number of shareholders in an entity.

A bonus issue will result in more shares in issue without affecting the value of the entity as a whole. Therefore each share will be worth less, not more.

277   C

An overprovision from a previous year (i.e. credit balance) reduces the tax charge in the current year in the statement of profit or loss.

Tax payable is the full amount of the estimation of the charge for the year.

278

	Current	Non-current
A sale has been made on credit to a customer. They have agreed to terms stating that payment is due in 12 months' time.	Correct	
A bank overdraft facility of $30,000 is available under an agreement with the bank which extends 2 years.	Correct	
Albatros Co purchases a small number of shares in another entity which it intends to trade.	Correct	
A bank loan has been taken out with a repayment date 5 years hence.		Correct

The credit sale is part of the entity's normal operating cycle and is therefore classified as a current asset. The bank overdraft is repayable on demand and therefore classified as a current liability. The shares have been purchased to sell and so are classified as a current asset investment.

279   D

	Share capital $	Share premium $	Revaluation surplus $	Retained earnings $	Total $
Share issue	2,000	3,000			5,000
Revaluation			230,000		230,000
Profit					
(178,000 – 45,000 – 5,600)				127,400	127,400
Dividends – ordinary				(12,000)	(12,000)
– preference				(8,000)	(8,000)
Total change	2,000	3,000	230,000	107,400	342,400

280 D

Preference shares do not generally carry voting rights. Preference dividends are fixed amounts, normally expressed as a percentage of their nominal value. Preference dividends are paid out in preference to ordinary dividends.

281 A

Accounting standards require that the commercial substance of a transaction is recorded rather than its legal form. Redeemable preference shares are repayable at a specified future date and therefore have the qualities of debt. They are therefore accounted for as liabilities.

282 B

Paid up share capital is the amount of the nominal value which have been paid currently. Issued share capital is the share capital which has actually been issued to shareholders. Authorised share capital is the nominal value of the maximum number of shares that an entity can have in issue at any one time.

283

	Selection
It is the cheapest way for an entity to raise finance through the issuing of shares	
It makes the shares in the entity more marketable	Correct
The total reserves of the entity will increase	
Issued share capital is brought more into line with assets employed in the entity	Correct

A bonus share issue does not raise finance for an entity, as the shares are issued for no consideration (i.e. for free). Each share becomes worth less (as there are more shares in issue but the value of the entity as a whole remains the same), and so more marketable.

The reserves decreases when there is a bonus issue. The double entry is to debit the reserves and credit the share capital. Share capital increases (at the expense of other reserves) and so may seem more appropriate when compared to net assets.

284 B

Loan notes can be issued at a discount to their nominal value (unlike shares). Interest is always paid based on the nominal value. Interest accrued $8,000 (12% × $400,000 × 2/12).

285 D

Transfers between revenue reserves, as mentioned in A and B, have no effect on the overall total of revenue reserves; issuing shares at a premium increases capital reserves; the paying of dividends must be from revenue reserves, so these will decrease.

286

	Choice: A, B or C
Excess depreciation on revaluation	C
Increase in carrying amount of the property	B
Depreciation charge	A

Tutorial note:

Excess depreciation is accounted for in the statement of changes in equity. It is not accounted for in the statement of profit or loss and other comprehensive income.

287 D

288 B

When the charge in the statement of profit or loss is less than the year-end liability, this will be caused by an adjustment relating to an overprovision in an earlier year. If there had been an underprovision, the shortfall would need to be charged in the current year, thus increasing the income tax charge in the statement of profit or loss.

289 C

IFRS 15 Revenue from Contracts with Customers requires that revenue should recognised only when performance obligations have been complied with. As both transactions relate to the sale of goods, they would appear to be obligations satisfied at a point in time.

Clooney has complied with the obligation to deliver the food processor on 28 August and transfers to control to Pitt on that date. Revenue can therefore be recognised on this transaction.

Similarly, it would appear the obligations to Damon were fulfilled on 26 August 20X7 when Damon collected the goods: control was transferred on that date. A receivable should be recognised for any amount due but not yet received on both transactions.

290 $16,000

The revenue relating to the course fees relate to goods and services to be provided in 20X9. Therefore, sales revenue on the study materials and lectures should not be recognised in the financial statements for the year ended 20 December 20X8. Revenue can be recognised in 20X9 as and when the separate performance obligations are fulfilled.

The course materials sold to students is a completed transaction as at 31 December 20X8 and sales revenue can be recognised on this transaction at a total amount of $16,000 (40 × $400). There is no further obligation other than to deliver the study material, which was complied with prior to 31 December 20X8.

291 $nil

Although customer orders have been received along with deposits, Vostok has not yet done anything to earn the revenue by 31 July 20X2. The deposits received should be accounted for as deferred income and treated as a current liability, rather than being recognised as revenue. It is only when the computer games have been despatched that Vostok will be able to regard the obligation as discharged and consequently recognise revenue.

292 $14,500

	$
Customers for a full year ((12 – 1) × $1,200)	13,200
Terminated contract to 31 August (5/12 × $1,200)	500
New contracts from 1 December (2 × 4/12 × $1,200)	800
Revenue for the year ended 31 March 20X6	14,500

Note that, for revenue recognition in this situation, it is irrelevant when the cash is received for the services provided. Revenue can be recognised only when it has been earned – in the case of service provision, this will occur when services are provided over a period of time.

293 $437.50

	$
Total revenue from the servicing agreement	2,250
Therefore, revenue per annum is $2,250/3	750
Revenue for period 1 September X7 – 31 Mar X8 is:	**437.50**
7/12 × $750	

Provision of a service is normally regarded as giving rise to obligations that are satisfied over a period of time.

294 C

	P & L	Liability	Asset
	$	$	$
Balance b/fwd 1 Jan 20X8		(2,350)	
Cash paid – March 20X8		2,050	
Release overprovision to P/L	(300)	300	
Repayment due	(2,120)		2,120
	(2,420)	Nil	**2,120**

295 A

	P & L	Liability	Asset
	$	$	$
Balance b/fwd 1 July 20X5		(16,940)	
Cash paid		17,500	
Charge overprovision to P/L	560	(560)	
Repayment due	(4,500)		4,500
	_____	_____	_____
	(3,940)	Nil	**4,500**
	_____	_____	_____

DISCLOSURE NOTES

296 C

> **Tutorial note:**
>
> *IAS 38 requires that development costs should only be capitalised when the directors are satisfied that those costs will be recovered at some future date.*

If the directors are not satisfied on this point, such costs cannot be capitalised, – they must be written off as incurred.

297 B

Statement A is inappropriate as there are strict criteria for application of the valuation model to be applied, rather than arbitrary judgement of the directors. Normally intangible assets should be accounted for using a consistent valuation model. In addition, there is no indication of the amortisation rate or expected useful lives of the intangible assets.

Statement C is inappropriate as any increases in carrying amount should be accounted for in other comprehensive income and other components of equity. In addition, the valuation model will only be relevant intangible assets are traded on an active market.

298 C

Statement A is inappropriate as it implies that land is also depreciated over fifty years. Land should not be depreciated as it does not have a finite useful life.

Statement B is inappropriate as assets which have a finite useful life should be subject to depreciation to spread the cost over the estimated useful life to the business.

299 B

Statement A is inappropriate as compares the total cost of inventory with its total realisable value. This is likely to result in inventory being overvalued. Statement C would also result in an overvaluation of inventory.

300 B

The statement is false as, although non-adjusting events are not accounted for in the financial statements, if material, they must be disclosed in the notes to the financial statements.

301 D

302

	Disclosed	*Not disclosed*
Reconciliation of carrying amounts of non-current assets at the beginning and end of period.	Correct	
Useful lives of assets or depreciation rates used.	Correct	
Increases in asset values as a result of revaluations in the period.	Correct	
Depreciation expense for the period.	Correct	

Here is an example of a non-current asset disclosure note, which should demonstrate why items (1),(3) and (4) are all correct in this question as they would be disclosed within this note:

	Land and buildings	*Plant & equipment*
Asset	$	$
Balance b/fwd	X	X
Revaluation	X	X
Additions	X	X
Disposals	(X)	(X)
Balance c/fwd	X	X
Accumulated depreciation		
Balance b/fwd	X	X
Charge for year	X	X
Disposals	(X)	(X)
Balance c/fwd	X	X
CA at start of year (b/fwd)	X	X
CA at year end (c/fwd)	X	X

Don't forget that disclosures can be numerical and narrative. Hence Item (2) which is an example of a narrative note that would also be included, describing, in this example note, what the useful life or depreciation rates for land and buildings and plant and equipment would be.

303

	Selection
Revenue	Correct
Closing inventory	
Finance costs	Correct
Dividends paid	
Tax expense	Correct
Depreciation charge for the year	

Item (2) is disclosed on the statement of financial position. Item (4) is disclosed in the statement of changes in equity. Item (6) is disclosed in the notes to the financial statements, rather than on the face of the statement of profit or loss.

304 C

Disclosure requirements may be monetary (e.g. the depreciation charge for the year) or narrative (e.g. a statement of accounting policies).

305 FALSE

Disclosure is required of either the estimated useful lives, or the depreciation rates used. In effect, disclosure of the depreciation rates used provides information regarding the estimated useful lives of the assets, and vice versa.

306 D

307 FALSE

In addition to stating the balance at the beginning and at the end of the year, the entity also needs to provide a reconciliation of the movement in the provision during the year.

308 D

There should be disclosure of depreciation and amortisation charges made during the year. In addition, in relation to revaluation of property, plant and equipment, the date of the valuation should be disclose, together with a statement of whether or not the valuer was a person independent of the entity.

309 B

EVENTS AFTER THE REPORTING PERIOD

310

	Adjusting	*Non-adjusting*
A flood on 3 October 20X8 that destroyed a relatively small quantity of inventory which had cost $1,700.		Correct
A credit customer with a balance outstanding at 30 September 20X8 was declared insolvent on 20 December 20X8.	Correct	
Inventory valued at a cost of $800 at 30 September 20X8 was sold for $650 on 11 November 20X8.	Correct	
A dividend on ordinary shares of 4c per share was declared on 1 December 20X8.		Correct

The flood on 3 October does not provide additional information of conditions that existed at the year end and therefore is non-adjusting. The credit customer's insolvency is confirmed before the financial statements were approved and provides evidence of irrecoverability of the amount outstanding at 30 September and is therefore an adjusting event. The sale of inventory in November provides evidence of its net realisable value for the inventory valuation at 30 September 20X8 and is therefore an adjusting event. The declaration of the ordinary dividend is a non-adjusting event.

311 D

Details of adjusting events are not disclosed by note; instead, if material, the event is accounted for in the financial statements. The sale of inventory after the reporting date at a price lower than that at which it is valued in the statement of financial position is an adjusting event. A fall in the market value of property, plant and equipment after the reporting date is a non-adjusting event. It should therefore be disclosed if material. Statement (4) is a definition of an event after the reporting date.

312 B

Events 1, 2 and 4 occur between the reporting date and date of approval of the financial statements and each provides additional information of the situation as at the reporting date. Each of these is an adjusting event. Event 1 would initially be classed as a non-adjusting event as it occurred after the reporting date and does not provide additional information of the situation at that date. However, is it threatens the ability of Brakes Co to continue as a going concern, it is regarded as an adjusting event.

Event 3 is specifically identified in IAS 10 as non-adjusting.

313 A

314 B

Tutorial note:

IAS 10 specifically precludes adjusting for a dividend that was proposed before the year end and paid after the year end.

REVENUE FROM CONTRACTS WITH CUSTOMERS

315 $8,000

Rep Co has the obligation to arrange the sale and to collect the cash from the customer. Its obligations are therefore discharged on 28 September. Revenue of $8,000 (10% × $80,000) can be recognised in the year ended and 30 September 20X4. Note that as $80,000 was received from the customer, the balance of $72,000 ($80,000 – $8,000 commission earned) should be accounted for as a liability until it is paid to Zip Co.

316 $880

Loc Co should only recognise revenue when a performance obligation has been satisfied. The obligations to deliver and install the machine are satisfied at a point in time and were completed on 1 October 20X5, so revenue of $850 ($750 + $100) can be recognised. Revenue relating to the supply of the service support agreement is recognised over a period of time and, at the reporting date, three months of support service has been provided to the customer, so $30 ($120 × 3/12) can also be recognised as revenue in the year ended 31 December 20X5. Total revenue recognised on this transaction in the year is therefore $880.

317 C

Revenue on the contract with Far Co has been recognised appropriately. Revenue on the contract with Res Co should be only for commission earned, not the full contract price. Revenue on the contract with Cap Co should be spread evenly over the time period for the supply of the service, and only nine months of service has been provided, not a full year. Revenue on the contract with Ber Co should be $50,000, the cost of sales and gross profit would both be $25,000.

318 B

Contracts do not need to be in writing, although many business entities may prefer to have written contracts so that there is certainty as to what has been agreed with customers.

319

	True	*False*
On any reasonable basis		Correct
At a point in time	Correct	
Annually		Correct
Over a period of time	Correct	

Revenue should be recognised when an obligation has been discharged, either at a point in time (usually for the sale of goods) or over a period of time (usually for provision of a service).

STATEMENTS OF CASH FLOWS

320 D

	$
Issue of shares (560,000 – 220,000)	340,000
Issue of loan notes	300,000
	640,000

Interest paid is included within the 'operating activities' heading of the cash flow statement.

321 $13,000 INFLOW

Interest received = $13,000. Interest and dividends paid are normally shown within cash from operating activities. An alternative presentation may place dividends paid within cash from financing activities.

322 C

Bonus issues do not involve the transfer of cash, whereas rights issues result in a cash inflow. The revaluation of non-current assets does not involve the transfer of cash.

323

	Selection
Depreciation should be deducted, not added	
Increase in inventories should be added, not deducted	
Decrease in receivables should be added, not deducted	Correct
Increase in payables should be added, not deducted	Correct

Depreciation is a non-cash expense and should therefore be added back to profit. An increase in assets (inventory and receivables) means that less cash is available (as it has been used to fund assets), hence an increase in assets is shown as a deduction in the cash flow statement. An increase in liabilities (payables) means that more cash is available (i.e. it has not been used to pay liabilities), hence an increase in liabilities is shown as an addition in the cash flow statement.

324 D

The carrying amount of non-current assets is shown in the statement of financial position.

Depreciation charged on non-current assets and any profit or loss on disposal is shown in the statement of profit or loss and other comprehensive income. Revaluation surpluses relating to non-current assets are shown in the statement of changes in equity.

In relation to non-current assets, the indirect statement of cash flows will include:

(a)   depreciation

(b)   profit or loss on disposal

(c)   proceeds of the disposal of non-current assets

(d)   payments to acquire non-current assets.

325 D

	$	$
Cash generated from operations (β)	419,254	
Tax and dividends paid	(87,566)	
	———	
Net cash from operating activities (β)		331,688
Purchase of property, plant and equipment	(47,999)	
Proceeds from sale of property, plant and equipment	13,100	
	———	
Net cash from investing activities		(34,899)
Redemption of loans	(300,000)	
	———	
Net cash from financing activities		(300,000)
		———
Decrease in cash and cash equivalents		(3,211)
		———

326 A

	$000
Profit for the year (β)	**1,175**
Add back depreciation	100
Less: Increase in receivables & inventory	(575)
	———
Cash flow from operating activities	700
Add: Cash from issue of shares	1,000
Less: Repayment of debentures	(750)
Less: Purchase of non-current assets	(200)
	———
Increase in cash	750
	———

327 B

Non-current assets at carrying amount

	$		$
Balance b/f	50,000	Disposals (4,000 – 1,500)	2,500
Additions (β)	7,500	Depreciation	9,000
		Balance c//f	46,000
	———		———
	57,500		57,500
	———		———

328 C

	$
Profit	8,000
Add: depreciation (not a cash expense)	12,000
Less: purchase of new non-current assets	(25,000)
	———
Reduction in bank balance	(5,000)
	———

329 D

	$
Profit for the year	18,750
Depreciation	1,250
Non-current asset purchases	(8,000)
Decrease in inventories	1,800
Increase in receivables	(1,000)
Increase in payables	350
	———
Increase in cash and cash equivalents	13,150
	———

330 D

Items added include the depreciation charge for the period, any losses on disposals of non-current assets, reductions in inventories and receivables (including prepayments) and any increase in trade payables (including accruals).

331 D

	True	False
The direct method of calculating net cash from operating activities leads to a different figure from that produced by the indirect method, but this is balanced elsewhere in the statement of cash flows.		Correct
An entity making high profits must necessarily have a net cash inflow from operating activities.		Correct
Profits and losses on disposals of non-current assets appear as items under investing activities in the statement of cash flows.		Correct

Statement (1) is incorrect: net cash flow from operating activities is the same, whichever method of presentation is used. Statement (2) is incorrect. Companies with high profits can be cash-negative, due to high spending on new non-current assets and/or a large build-up of working capital. Statement (3) is incorrect. Profits and losses on non-current asset disposals are shown as an adjustment to net profit before tax.

332 D

New purchases (additions) are given in the question as $2,000. The assets disposed of had a cost of $3,000 and accumulated depreciation at the time of disposal of $1,500. Their carrying amount at disposal was therefore $1,500. The profit on disposal was $500, so the cash received from the disposal was $2,000.

333 A

Major non-cash transactions are not highlighted within the statement of cash flows (although they are disclosed elsewhere in a set of accounts). These are of interest to the users of accounts as they may have an impact on future cash flows.

334 D

	$
Cash sales	212,500
Less:	
Cash purchases	(4,600)
Cash expenses	(11,200)
Cash paid to credit suppliers (W1)	(121,780)
Cash paid as wages and salaries (W2)	(33,800)
Cash generated from operations	41,120

(W1)

Payables

	$		$
		Balance b/f	12,300
Cash paid (β)	121,780	Purchases	123,780
Balance c/f	14,300		
	———		———
	136,080		136,080
	———		———

(W2)

Wages and salaries

	$		$
		Balance b/f	1,500
Cash paid (β)	33,800	Statement of profit or loss and other comprehensive income expense	34,600
Balance c/f	2,300		
	———		———
	36,100		36,100
	———		———

335   C

	$000
Retained profit for the year ($82,000 – $72,000)	10,000
Add back:	
Dividends payable (current year's)	1,600
Tax payable (current year's estimate)	15,000
Loan note interest payable (10% × $40,000)	4,000
	———
Operating profit	30,600
	———

The additional $10,000 loan notes were issued at the beginning of the year. Therefore, the total loan notes at the start of the year will be $40,000. The loan notes interest for the year will be $4,000 (i.e. 10% × $40,000).

336 $75,000 OUTFLOW

	$
Cash purchase of non-current assets	(140,000)
Disposal proceeds of non-current assets ($50,000 – $3,000)	47,000
Disposal proceeds of investments	18,000
	———
Net cash outflow from investing activities	(75,000)
	———

337 $10,000 INFLOW

	$
Proceeds of issue of share capital	60,000
Repayment of bank loan ($150 – $100)	(50,000)
Net cash inflow from financing activities	10,000

338 $1,395 OUTFLOW

	$000
Balance b/fwd	2,500
Revaluation in year ($1,700 – $1,200)	500
Depreciation charge for the year	(75)
Disposal removed at carrying amount	(120)
Cash paid for additions (bal fig)	1,395
Balance c/fwd	4,200

339

	Selection
Payments made to suppliers	Correct
Increase or decrease in receivables	
Receipts from customers	Correct
Increase or decrease in inventories	
Increase or decrease in payables	
Finance costs paid	Correct

Items (2) (4) and (5) are relevant only under the indirect method of preparation of the statement of cash flows. Item (6) is included within operating activities under both the direct and indirect method of preparation.

340 TRUE

Using the direct or indirect method to prepare a statement of cash flows, there are no differences in the presentation of 'cash flows from investing activities' and 'cash flows from financing activities'. Only the presentation of 'cash flows from operating activities' will differ.

341 FALSE

The depreciation charge for the year is disclosed as an adjustment to reported profit for the year within 'cash flows from operating activities' using the indirect method, rather than the direct method.

INCOMPLETE RECORDS

342 D

	$	$	%
Sales (100/70 × $756,000)		**1,080,000**	100
Cost of sales			
Opening Inventory	77,000		
Purchases	763,000		
Closing Inventory	(84,000)		
	————	(756,000)	70
		324,000	30

343 A

	$	$	%
Sales		650,000	100
Cost of sales			
Opening inventory	380,000		
Purchases	480,000		
Lost inventory (β)	**(185,000)**		
Closing inventory	(220,000)		
	————	(455,000)	70
Gross profit		195,000	30

344 B

	$	$	%
Sales (174,825 – 1,146)		173,679	125%
Cost of goods sold			
Opening inventory	12,274		
Purchases (136,527 – 1,084)	135,443		
Closing inventory (β)	**(8,774)**		
	————		
$173,679 × 100/125		(138,943)	100%
Gross profit		34,736	25%

345 D

	$	$	%
Sales		630,000	140
Cost of sales			
Opening Inventory	24,300		
Purchases (β)	458,450		
Closing Inventory	(32,750)		
	————		
100/140 × $630,000		(450,000)	100
		————	
		180,000	40

Payables ledger control account

	$		$
		Balance b/f	29,780
Cash paid to suppliers (β)	**453,630**	Purchases (cash and credit)	458,450
Balance c/f	34,600		
	————		————
	488,230		488,230
	————		————

346 C

	$
Inventory at 6 January 20X6	32,780
Sales at cost (β)	6,020
Purchases	(4,200)
	————
Inventory at 31 December 20X5	34,600

Profit on sales: $8,600 – $6,020 = $2,580

Gross margin: $\dfrac{2,580}{8,600} = 30\%$

347 D

Cash

	$		$
Balance b/f	620		
Receipts from customers (β)	16,660	Payments	16,780
		Balance c/f	500
	————		————
	17,280		17,280
	————		————

Receivables

	$		$
Balance b/f	6,340		
Sales (β)	15,520	Cash receipts	16,660
		Balance c/f	5,200
	_____		_____
	21,860		21,860
	_____		_____

Gross profit: 25/125 × $15,520 = $3,104

348 B

	$	$
Sales		148,000
Opening inventory	34,000	
Purchases	100,000	
	_____	
	134,000	
Closing inventory (β)	**(26,000)**	
	_____	
Cost of sales (148,000 – 40,000)		108,000
		_____
Gross profit		40,000
		_____

349 C

You might need to answer this by testing each answer in turn.

$$\frac{\text{Gross profit}}{\text{Cost of sales}} \quad \frac{28,800}{72,000} = 40\%$$

	$
Sales	100,800
Cost of sales	(72,000)
	_____
Gross profit	28,800
	_____

350 C

	$	$	%
Sales		480,000	150
Cost of sales			
Opening inventory	36,420		
Purchases (β)	324,260		
Closing inventory	(40,680)		
	————		
100/150 × $480,000		(320,000)	100
		————	
		180,000	50

PLCA

	$		$
		Balance b/f	29,590
Cash paid (β)	**319,975**	Purchases	324,260
Balance c/f	33,875		
	————		————
	353,850		353,850
	————		————

351 B

Closing net assets	=	Opening net assets	+	Capital injections	–	Loss for the period	–	Drawings
($56,000 – $18,750)		($40,000 – $14,600)						($6,800 + $250)
$37,250	=	$25,400	+	$20,000	–	(β) **$1,100**	–	$7,050

352 D

As the inventory is insured, its cost (not selling price) is recoverable from the insurer. Therefore this amount is shown as a current asset.

The cost should also be taken out of cost of sales as these goods have not been sold.

PREPARING SIMPLE CONSOLIDATED FINANCIAL STATEMENTS

353 **A**

	$
Cost of investment	1,400,000
FV of NCI @ acquisition	525,000
Less fair value of net assets at acquisition –	
(600,000 × 0.50) + $50,000	(350,000)
	1,575,000

354 **C**

	$
Reserves of Tom	400,000
Post-acquisition reserves of Jerry –	
($20,000 × 80%)	16,000
	416,000

355 **C**

	$
Cost of investment	750,000
FV of NCI @ acquisition	150,000
Less fair value of net assets at acquisition –	
$20,000 + $10,000	(30,000)
Goodwill	870,000

356 **B**

	$
FV of NCI @ acquisition	25,000
Post-acquisition reserves of Barlow	2,000
(15,000 – 10,000) × 40%	
	27,000

357 A

	$
FV of NCI @ acquisition	50,000
Post-acquisition reserves of Barlow	5,250
(75,000 – 60,000) × 35%	
	———
	55,250
	———

358 A

Receivables = 540 + 160 – 40 =	$660,000
Payables = 320 + 180 – 40 =	$460,000

359 B

	$	
Sales value	1,044	120%
Cost value	870	100%
	———	———
Profit	174	20%
	———	———

Workings:

Mark-up means profit is based on cost, therefore cost represents 100%. If profit is 20%, the sales value must be worth 120%.

Total profit is $174 and 60% is still in stock = $104.40

360 $4,400,000

Non-current assets = $1,800,000 + $2,200,000 + fair value adj 400,000 = $4,400,000

361 C

	$m	
Sales value	24	100%
Cost value	18	75%
	———	———
Total profit	6	25%
	———	———

Workings:

Profit is $6m and half of the amount is still in inventory i.e. $3m

362 A

Profit attributable to non-controlling interest should be $6,000,000 × 20% = $1,200,000

The PURP adjustment does not affect the NCI as the parent is selling to the subsidiary.

363   D

Sales = 120 + 48 − 24 (intra-group) = $144m

Cost of sales = 84 + 40 − 24 + 3 (PURP) = $103m

364   A

Non-current assets = $1,918,000 + $1,960,000 = $3,878,000

365   B

	$
Reserves of Really	2,464,000
Post-acquisition reserves –	
($1,204,000 + $112,000)) × 75%	987,000
	3,451,000

366   C

Ownership of more than 50% of the ordinary shares of another entity indicates a control relationship – such investments should be accounted for as a subsidiary. Ownership of less than 20% of the ordinary shares of another entity is not normally enough to indicate either significant influence or control relationships: such a shareholding should be accounted for as a trade investment.

367   D

The ability to exercise significant influence relates to an investment classified as an associate.

368   B

The ability of one entity to exercise significant influence over another is normally indicated by the ability to appoint at least one director to the board of that entity. If an entity was able to appoint the majority of the board of directors that would normally be regarded as having control of that other entity.

369   C

The ability of one entity to exercise control over another is normally indicated by the ability to appoint the majority of the board of directors of that other entity. Significant influence over another is normally indicated by the ability to appoint at least one director to the board of that entity.

370   A

The ability of one entity to exercise control over another is normally indicated by ownership of the majority of equity shares in that other entity.

371 D

The ability of one entity to exercise significant influence over another is normally indicated by ownership of between twenty per cent and fifty per cent of the equity shares of that other entity.

372 D

	$000
100,000 × 60% × 3/2 × $3.50	315

373 $1,020,000

	$000
250,000 × 80% × $3.00 cash	600
250,000 × 80% × 3/5 × $3.50	420
	————
	1,020
	————

374 A

	$000
S2m + ($1.5m × 3/12) – $0.1m	2,275

375 A

	$000
S5m + ($3m × 9/12) – $0.5m	6,750

376 C

	$000
10m + (9/12 × 4m)	13,000
Less: post-acq'n intra-group sales	(1,600)
Add: PURP re closing inventory	80
(1.6m × 25/125 × 1/4)	————
	11,480
	————

377 $10,300

	$000
10m + (4/12 × 6m)	12,000
Less: post-acq'n intra-group sales	(1,800)
Add: PURP re closing inventory	100
(1.8m × 20/120 × 1/3)	————
	10,300
	————

378 **$7,000**

		$000
Consideration paid		20,000
FV of NCI at acquisition		6,000
FV of net assets acquired:		
Equity share capital	8,000	
Retained earnings to I Jan X4	10,000	
Retained earnings to acquisition (6/12 × 2,000,000)	1,000	
	–––––––	(19,000)
Goodwill on acquisition		7,000

379 **B**

		$000
Consideration paid		43,000
FV of NCI at acquisition		10,000
FV of net assets acquired:		
Equity share capital	25,000	
Retained earnings at I July X7	15,000	
Retained earnings to acquisition (8/12 × 6,000,000)	4,000	
Fair value adjustment	1,000	
	–––––––	(45,000)
Goodwill on acquisition		8,000

380 **$16,000**

		$000
Cash paid (10m × 60% × $3)		18,000
Shares (10m × 60% ×2/1 × $4.50)		54,000
FV of NCI at acquisition		14,000
FV of net assets acquired:		
Equity share capital	10,000	
Share premium	10,000	
Retained earnings	50,000	
	–––––––	(70,000)
Goodwill on acquisition		16,000

381 A

		$000
Cash paid (15m × 75% × $4.50)		50,625
Shares (15m × 75% × 1 × $5.00)		56,250
FV of NCI at acquisition		27,000
FV of net assets acquired:		
Equity share capital	15,000	
Share premium	5,000	
Retained earnings	76,875	
FV adjustment	2,000	
		(98,875)
Goodwill on acquisition		35,000

382 $65,000

		$000
Cash paid (200 × 90% × $3)		540
Shares issued (200 × 90% × 1 × $2)		360
FV of NCI at acquisition		75
FV of net assets acquired:		
Equity share capital	200	
Share premium	100	
Retained earnings	590	
FV adjustment ($90 – $70)	20	
		(910)
Goodwill on acquisition		65

383 B

	$000
NCI share of group profit after tax	
(400 × 6/12 × 40%)	80

Note: Huyton made the intra-group sales and therefore bears all of the PURP adjustment. Only the post-acquisition element of Speke's profit after tax is taken into account.

384 D

	$
Ordinary share capital	1,000
Retained earnings	585
($710- (6/12 × $250)	1,585
Goodwill is calculated as:	$
Consideration transferred (75% × 1000) × $2 = $1,500	1,500
FV of NCI	300
	1,800
Less FV of NA at acquisition	(1,585)
Goodwill	215

The financial statement extracts are given at the year-end date of 30 September 20X3. Therefore, the net assets at the acquisition date (1 April 20X3) must be calculated by deducting the amount of retained earnings that was earned in the 6 months since the acquisition.

385 $114,667

The interest in Seal Co was acquired on 31 August 2012, which means that during the year ended 31 December 2012, Seal Co had only been a subsidiary for 4 months of the year, therefore only the post-acquisition results of the subsidiary should be consolidated.

Intra-group sales should also be eliminated, and as all these were made in October, they are all in the post-acquisition period and need to be cancelled. This means the consolidated revenue for Panther Group would be calculated as:

$100,000 + (4/12 × $62,000) – $6,000 = $114,667.

386 $22,900

The 70% holding was acquired on 1 March 20X2, which means that during the year ended 31 August 2012, Daffodil Co had only been a subsidiary for 6 months of the year. Only post-acquisition results of the subsidiary should be consolidated. This means the consolidated gross profit would be reported as:

Tulip $18,300 + Daffodil ($9,200 × 6/12) $4,600 = $22,900.

387 $147,750

	$
Fair value of consideration transferred:	
Cash paid 75% × 100,000 = 75,000 acquired × $2	150,000
Shares issued in Venus 75% × 100,000 = 75,000 × 1/1 × $1.75	131,250
	281,250
Plus: Fair value of the non-controlling interest at acquisition	82,000
	363,250
Less: Fair value of net assets at acquisition	(215,500)
Goodwill	147,750

388 B

An associate is often identified when between 20% and 50% of the equity shares of another entity are held as this is presumed to give significant influence over that entity. However, for an associate to exist, it is not a case of just a matter of the percentage of equity shares held, it also depends on whether the investing entity can exercise significant influence, which can be evidenced through the number of directors who can be appointed on the board and who participate in decision making. The investment in statement 3 is not equity accounted as the entity has appointed the majority of the board of directors, giving it control.

389

	True	False
Equity accounting will always be used when an investing entity holds between 20% – 50% of the equity shares in another entity.		Correct
Dividends received from an investment in associate will be presented as investment income in the consolidated financial statements.		Correct

Statement (1) is incorrect. Firstly, if an investing entity holds 30% in another entity and has no other investments, consolidated accounts would not be produced and therefore equity accounting would not be used. Secondly, despite an investing entity having a 20% holding in another entity, significant influence may not exist. i.e. another entity may hold the remaining 80% of the shares and hence equity accounting would not be used in the investing entity books.

Statement (2) is incorrect. In the consolidated accounts, the basic principle of equity accounting is that the group's share of the associate's profit after tax is included, not the dividend income which would be shown in the investing entity's own statement of profit or loss.

INTERPRETATION OF FINANCIAL STATEMENTS

390 27.30% and 48.00%

ROCE: ((Operating profit/capital employed) × 100), where operating profit is defined as profit before interest and before tax. Capital employed is defined as shareholders' funds plus long-term loans.

20X4: ((340,995 − 161,450) /(596,165 + 61,600) × 100) = 27.30%

20X3: ((406,400 − 170,950/(407,420 + 83,100) × 100) = 48.00%

391 24.5% and 25.04%

Gross profit margin: ((Gross profit/Revenue) × 100)

20X4: ((340,995/1,391,820) × 100) = 24.50%

20X3: ((406,400/1,159,850) × 100) = 35.04%

392 12.9% and 20.30%

Operating profit margin: ((Operating profit/Revenue) × 100), where operating profit is defined as profit before interest and before tax.

20X4: (((340,995 − 161,450)/1,391,820) × 100) = 12.90%

20X3: (((406,400 − 170,950)/1,159,850) × 100) = 20.30%

393 2.12 and 2.36

Asset turnover: (Revenue/Capital employed)

20X4: (1,391,820/(596,165 + 61,600)) = 2.12

20X3: (1,159,850/(407,420 + 83,100)) = 2.36

394 1.23 and 1.62

Current ratio: (Current assets/Current liabilities)

20X4: ((528,855/430,680) = 1.23

20X3: ((390,710/241,590) = 1.62

395 0.97 and 1.25

Quick 'acid test' ratio: ((Current assets − inventory)/Current liabilities)

20X4: ((528,855 − 109,400)/430,680) = 0.97

20X3: ((390,710 − 88,760)/241,590) = 1.25

396 38 days and 43 days

Inventory holding period: ((Inventory/Cost of sales) × 365)

20X4 ((109,400/1,050,825) × 365) = 38 days

20X3 ((88,760/753,450) × 365) = 43 days

397 110 days and 65 days

Trade receivables collection period: ((Trade receivables/Credit sales) × 365)

20X4 ((419,455/1,391,820) × 365) = 110 days

20X3 ((206,550/1,159,850) × 365) = 65 days

398 120 days and 87 days

Trade payables payment period: ((Trade payables/Cost of sales) × 365)

20X4 ((345.480/1,050,825) × 365) = 120 days

20X3 ((179,590/753,450) × 365) = 87 days

399 10.33% and 20.40%

Debt-equity ratio: (Long-term loans/Shareholders' funds) × 100)

20X4 ((61,600/596,165) × 100) = 10.33%

20X3 ((83,100/407,420) × 100) = 20.40%

400 9.37% and 16.94%

Gearing ratio: (Long-term loans/(Shareholders' funds + long-term loans) × 100)

20X4: (((61,600/(596,165 + 61,600)) × 100) = 9.37%

20X3 (((83,100/(407,420 + 83,100) × 100) = 16.94%

401 17.95 times and 16.82 times

Interest cover: ((Operating profit/Interest payable) × 100)

20X4 (((340,995 − 161,450)/10,000) × 100) = 17.95 times

20X3 (((406,400 − 170,950)/14,000) × 100) = 16.82 times

402 D

(4,600/20,000) × 100 = 23%

403 A

20X5 (2,140/20,000) × 100 = 10.7%

20X6 (2,180/26,000) × 100 = 8.38%

404 A

20X5 (4,400/20,000) × 365 = 80 days

20X6 (6,740/26,000) × 365 = 95 days

405 A

12,715/5,000 = 2.54 times

406 C

		$
Selling price (SP)	140	700
Cost of sales (COS)	100	???
Gross profit	40	???

Cost of sales × 140/100 = 700 Cost of sales = 700/1.4 = $500

407 D

Inventory turnover is found by dividing cost of goods sold by average inventory.

Average inventory is

$$\left(\frac{24,000 + 20,000}{2}\right) = \$22,000$$

$$\text{Inventory turnover} = \frac{\text{Cost of sales}}{\text{Average inventory}}$$

	$
Opening inventory	24,000
Purchases	160,000
	184,000
Less: Closing inventory	(20,000)
Cost of goods sold	164,000

Inventory holding period is therefore 22,000/164,000 × 365 = 49 days.

408 D

You need only know the correct formula here.

409 C

The current ratio is current assets divided by current liabilities: 5,800/2,200 = 2.64:1.

410 A

The gearing ratio is the proportion of long-term loans to shareholders' funds, thus it follows that if a decrease in long-term loans is less than a decrease in the shareholders' funds, the gearing ratio will rise.

411 B

The quick ratio is: current assets less inventory divided by current liabilities, that is 2,000:2,200 = 0.9:1.

412 A

The formula to calculate interest cover is: Profit before interest and tax/Finance cost. The complication in this question is that the profit before interest and tax is not given in the information and so must be calculated. Profit before interest and tax (133 − 59)/26 = 2.85

413 29 days and 40 days

20X6: 4,400/52,000 × 365 = 29 days

20X5: 5,300/48,000 × 365 = 40 days

414 False

An issue of ordinary shares will reduce the gearing ratio.

415 True

The gross profit margin will increase if unit purchase or production costs fall whilst unit selling price remains unchanged.

416 1.86 and 1.95

20X3: 38,595/20,750 = 1.86

20X2: 37,050/19,000 = 1.95

417 False

Return on capital employed = Profit before interest and tax/Capital employed. An increase in long-term loans would increase capital employed which, in turn, would reduce return on capital employed.

418 5.0% and 7.0%

20X8: 4,500/90,000 = 5.0%

20X7: 5,600/80,000 = 7.0%

Note that this ratio excludes current liabilities.

419 C

If a significant discount is offered to credit customers, they are likely to take advantage of this, which will reduce the trade receivables collection period. Similarly, application of effective credit controls is likely to reduce the trade receivables collection period. The period taken to pay trade payables will not affect the trade receivables collection period. As an isolated factor, an increase in the volume of credit sales will not affect the trade receivables collection period.

420 B

Prompt payment of suppliers' invoices will reduce the trade payables payment period. Buying proportionately more, or proportionately fewer, goods on credit will not affect calculation of the trade payables payment period. Offering a discount to credit customers will not affect the trade payables payment period.

421 A

Option A would result in increased inventory levels, and therefore increase the inventory holding period. All other answers are likely to lead to a reduction in the inventory holding period.

422 43 days

365/8.49 = 43 days

423 C

The effect of a bonus issue of shares would be to increase issued share capital and reduce either share premium or retained earnings. There would be no change to either shareholders' funds or to long-term loans – the gearing ratio would remain unchanged.

424 D

An issue of shares would increase capital employed and would therefore lead to a reduction in the return on capital employed ratio. A reduction in long-term borrowings would reduce capital employed, and consequently increase the return on capital employed ratio. Similarly, an improved profit margin would increase profit, and therefore lead to an increase in the ratio.

425 C

A rights issue of shares will result in B Co receiving cash in exchange for the issue of shares, which will either reduce an overdraft or increase cash and bank balances. This will increase equity, and the gearing ratio will decrease.

426 C

If credit customers take advantage of extended credit periods, this will increase trade receivables. If all other factors remain unchanged, there will be an increase in current assets and, consequently, in the current ratio.

427 C

An issue of ordinary shares will increase equity, and the repayment of a non-current liability loan will decrease +-liabilities. These two factors will combine to reduce the debt/equity ratio.

428 A

There is an increase in payables days from 35 days in 20X8 to 45 days in 20X9.

429

	True	False
A statement of cash flows prepared using the direct method produces a different figure for investing activities in comparison with that produced if the indirect method is used.		Correct
A bonus issue of shares does not feature in a statement of cash flows.	Correct	
The amortisation charge for the year on intangible assets will appear as an item under 'Cash flows from operating activities' in a statement of cash flows.	Correct	
Loss on the sale of a non-current asset will appear as an item under 'Cash flows from investing activities' in a statement of cash flows.		Correct

430 A

Section 5

ANSWERS TO MULTI-TASK QUESTIONS

1 ICE CO

Key answer tips

This question tests your knowledge of accounts preparation for a corporate entity.

It examines several different syllabus areas, and you therefore need to have a sound understanding of the syllabus as a whole. As each of the tasks is independent, you can attempt them in any order. Apply good exam technique to deal first with the topics you feel most confident about.

The question includes classification of expenses, deciding upon whether a provision or disclosure is required and whether or not to capitalise several items of expenditure.

Task 1

(a) **Into which heading in the statement of profit or loss should the following items be included?** **(1 mark)**

	Cost of sales	Distribution costs	Administration expenses
Carriage inwards	Correct		
Carriage outwards		Correct	

Tutorial note

The cost of inventory includes all costs incurred in bringing it to its location and condition. This will include carriage inwards costs, and they should be included as part of cost of sales. Carriage outwards relate to the delivery of finished goods to customers and are not, therefore, part of cost of sales.

(b) Based upon the information available, what was Ice Co's gross profit for the year ended 31 December 20X1? **(2 marks)**

$363,500

	$
Workings:	
Revenue ($600,000 – $500 returns inwards)	599,500
Less: Cost of sales:	
Opening inventory	24,000
Purchases and other expenses	240,000
Carriage inwards	2,000
Less: Closing inventory	(30,000) 236,000
Gross profit	363,500

Tutorial note

Remember that 'returns inwards' relates to returns made by customers of goods previously sold to them by the business. Consequently, the value of any returns inwards must be deducted from revenue in the statement of profit or loss. Returns inwards are not an expense item

(c) Based upon the information available, identify the adjustments required to gross profit in order to calculate Ice Co's draft profit before tax. **(2 marks)**

		Selected answer
(i)	Gross profit - $30,000 - $180,000 - $75,000	
(ii)	Gross profit - $500 - $2,000 - $180,000 - $75,000	
(iii)	Gross profit - $3,000 - $180,000 - $75,000	Correct

Task 2

(a) What expense should be included in Ice Co's statement of profit or loss in relation to the loan finance? **(1 mark)**

$4,500 $100,000 × 6% × 9/12

(b) How should the loan be classified in the statement of financial position at 31 December 20X1? **(1 mark)**

		Selected answer
(i)	An equity component	
(ii)	A non-current liability	Correct
(iii)	A current liability	

Task 3

How should this matter be reflected in Ice Co's financial statements for the year ended 31 December 20X1? **(2 marks)**

		Selected answer
(i)	It should not be recognised or disclosed in the financial statements for the year ended 31 December 20X1	
(ii)	It should be disclosed only in the financial statements for the year ended 31 December 20X1	
(iii)	It should be recognised as a liability in the financial statements for the year ended 31 December 20X1	Correct

Task 4

(a) **State whether each of the following costs should be capitalised or treated as revenue expenditure.** **(4 marks)**

		Capital or revenue
(i)	Work to install additional, high-specification, electrical power cabling and circuits so that additional plant and equipment can become operational	Capital
(ii)	Replacement of some loose and damaged roof tiles following a recent storm	Revenue
(iii)	Repainting the factory administration office	Revenue
(iv)	Modifications to the factory entrance to enable a large item of plant and equipment to be installed	Capital

(b) **Calculate the depreciation charge for the year which was included as an expense within cost of sales.** **(2 marks)**

Freehold building	$1,000	$50,000 × 2%
Plant and equipment	$15,750	($120,000 − $95,000) × 15%

(Total: 15 marks)

Marking scheme	
	Marks
Task 1 – P&L account preparation	5
Task 2 – Accounting for loan liability and finance	2
Task 3 – Accounting treatment of injury claim	2
Task 4 – Property, plant and equipment	6
	—
Total	**15**
	—

2   WILLOW CO

Key answer tips

This question tests your knowledge of accounts preparation for a corporate entity. It examines your knowledge of double-entry bookkeeping, along with technical knowledge of accounting for inventories and intangible assets. Ensure that you are able to state definitions and apply those definitions when performing relevant calculations.

Each of the tasks is independent and can be attempted in any order. If you do attempt questions out of order, ensure that you remember check that you have answered all questions required. Apply good exam technique to deal first with the topics about which you feel most confident.

Task 1

(a)   Complete the following table to state the accounting entries required to record the invoices in the general ledger.   **(2 marks)**

	$	Credit / Debit
Bank and cash		
Payables' ledger control account	2,300	Credit
Purchases ($2.300 × 100/115)	2,000	Debit
Sales tax ($2.300 × 15/115)	300	Debit
Suspense account		

(b)   Complete the following statement relating to the omitted purchases invoices. **(1 mark)**

This accounting error **will not** result in the totals of the trial balance failing to agree.

Note: as the invoices have been omitted completely from the general ledger, the trial balance will still agree.

Task 2

Complete the following table to identify the accounting entries required to record the bonus issue.   **(4 marks)**

	$000	Credit / Debit
Bank and cash		
Equity share capital ($72,000 × 1/6)	12,000	Credit
Retained earnings		
Share premium	12,000	Debit

Tutorial note

The trail balance is dated at the year-end – i.e. after the share issue has been made. Therefore, the total of 72,000 needs to be reduced by 12,000 (1/6 × 72,000) = 60,000. Consequently, when the '1 for 5' bonus issue is made, 12,000 shares will be issued. As no cash is raised from the share issue, the debit entry can be made to the share premium account (it is a non-distributable reserve). If there was no share premium account, the debit entry could be made against retained earnings.

Task 3

(a) State the correct total value of each product that should be included in the inventory valuation at 30 June 20X1 in accordance with IAS 2 Inventories. **(3 marks)**

Standard	$70,000	70 × $1,000 i.e. cost
Super	$72,500	50 × ($1,800 - $350) i.e. NRV
Elite	$74,000	40 × ($2,500 - $650) i.e. NRV

Inventory is measured at the lower of cost and net realisable value for each separate product or item.

(b) What adjustment should be made to the inventory valuation stated at cost of $9,420,000 to ensure that it complies with the requirements of IAS 2 Inventories?

(2 marks)

| $8,500 | Decrease | ($75,000 - $72,500) + ($80,000 - $74,000) |

Reduce the Super and Elite products to net realisable value as this is lower than cost.

Task 4

(a) A licence is an example of which type of asset? **(1 mark)**

| Intangible |

(b) State the amortisation charge for the year ended 30 June 20X1 and the carrying amount of the licence at that date. **(2 marks)**

| Amortisation charge | $400,000 | $2,000,000 / 5 yrs |
| Carrying amount | $1,600,000 | $2,000,000 - $400,000 |

(Total: 15 marks)

Marking scheme	
	Marks
Task 1 – Purchase invoices and trial balance	3
Task 2 – Bonus issue	4
Task 3 – Inventory valuation	5
Task 4 – Intangible asset	3
Total	15

3   CLER CO

Key answer tips

This question tests your knowledge of accounts preparation for a corporate entity. It tests your knowledge of double-entry bookkeeping, including performing a bank reconciliation. Part of this question relates to accounting for inventories and you need to ensure that you have a sound understanding of accounting and disclosure requirements relating to inventories. Apply good exam technique to ensure that you answer all parts of the multi-task question.

Task 1

(a)   **State the accounting entries required to write-off this amount in the general ledger.**

(1 mark)

	$	Credit / Debit
Allowance for receivables		
Irrecoverable debts	3,500	Debit
Trade payables' ledger control account		
Trade receivables' ledger control account	3,500	Credit

(b)   **Complete the following statement**   **(2 marks)**

For Cler Co to apply the contra entries in its general ledger, it must **debit** the trade payables' ledger control account and **credit** the trade receivables' ledger control account.

(c)   **State the accounting entries required to record this transaction in the general ledger.**   **(2 marks)**

	$	Credit / Debit
Discount received		
Revenue	1,710	Credit
Trade payables' ledger control account		
Trade receivables' ledger control account	1,710	Debit

Workings:

		$
List price of goods less: 10% trade discount	$2,000 × 90%	1,800
Less: early settlement discount	5% × $1,800	(90)
Net invoice price		1,710

Tutorial note

Trade discount is always deducted in arriving at the invoice price. Early settlement discount is also deducted if the customer is expected to take advantage of the early settlement discount terms offered.

Task 2

Based upon the information available to you, complete the bank reconciliation as at 31 December 20X7: **(4 marks)**

	$	
Debit balance per bank statement	1,500	
Cheques not yet presented	2,400	
	————	
Sub-total	3,900	
Lodgments not yet cleared	3,400	
	————	
Balance per cash book	500	**Credit**
Cheque returned unpaid by customer's bank	1,000	
	————	
Updated balance per cash book	1,500	**Credit**
	————	

Tutorial note

Remember that a debit balance on the bank statement indicates that the customer owes money to the bank i.e. the bank balance is overdrawn. Consequently, the cash book balance in Cler Co's accounting records reflecting the same information would be a credit balance i.e. a liability.

Task 3

(a) **At what valuation should inventory be stated in the financial statements at 31 December 20X7?** **(1 mark)**

$190,871

Inventory is valued at the lower of cost of $4,000 and net realisable value of $4,500 ($6,000 − 1,500). This product will continue to be valued at cost of $4,000, so no change in required to the inventory valuation.

(b) **Complete the accounting policy disclosure note for inventory for inclusion in the financial statements for the year ended 31 December 20X7.** **(2 marks)**

Inventory is stated at the **lower** of cost and **net realisable value** for each separate item or product.

(c) **Complete the following table to state whether each of the following items should be included as part of the cost of inventory.** (3 marks)

		Included / excluded
(i)	Selling and administration expenses	Excluded
(ii)	Transport costs from supplier to Cler Co premises	Included
(iii)	Storage costs	Excluded

Tutorial note

Only those costs incurred in bringing inventory to its location and condition can be classified as part of the cost of inventory. Any post-production costs or storage costs cannot be regarded as part of cost of inventory.

(Total: 15 marks)

Marking scheme	
	Marks
Task 1 – Trade receivables and trade payables	5
Task 2 – Bank reconciliation	4
Task 3 – Accounting for inventory	6
	—
Total	**15**
	—

4   CARBON CO

Key answer tips

This question tests your knowledge of accounts preparation for a corporate entity.

In particular, you need to be able to apply the accounting requirements relating to revaluation of property, plant and equipment. Additionally, your knowledge of accounting for income tax and a rights issue is tested Ensure that you understand the difference between a rights issue and a bonus issue of shares. This question also tests your knowledge of preparing financial statements for a single entity by requiring you to identify relevant items for inclusion in the statement of changes in equity. Finally, there is a small task requirement dealing with interpretation of financial statements.

Task 1

(a) **State whether each of the following statements relating to accounting for property, plant and equipment are true or false:** **(3 marks)**

		True / False
(i)	When an entity does revalue its land and buildings, it is compulsory to make an annual transfer of 'excess depreciation' from revaluation surplus to retained earnings	False
(ii)	Any revaluation surplus arising on revaluation of property, plant and equipment is included in the statement of profit or loss in arriving at profit before tax	False
(iii)	The revaluation surplus is accounted for as an adjustment to cash inflows from operating activities	False

There is a choice of accounting policy to either make the annual transfer of 'excess depreciation', or not to make the annual transfer. Whichever policy is adopted, it should be applied consistently from year to year.

The revaluation surplus arising in the accounting period is disclosed as an item of 'other comprehensive income, and not as part of the statement of profit or loss.

Tutorial note

The revaluation surplus is not a relevant item for inclusion in the statement of cash flows. It does not affect profit before tax and nor is it a cash flow.

(b) **State the accounting entries required to account for the revaluation at 31 December 20X5.** **(3 marks)**

	$000	Credit / Debit
Freehold land and buildings	2,000	Debit
Depreciation charge for the year		
Accumulated depreciation provision	120	Debit
Revaluation surplus	2,120	Credit

Revaluation surplus - Land: $4m – $2.5m = $1.5m

Revaluation surplus - Buildings: $2m – (1.5m × 46/50) = ($2m - $1.38m) = $0.62m

Note that depreciation for four years is deducted to arrive at the carrying amount of the buildings immediately before accounting for the revaluation. This is because the revaluation was performed at 31 December 20X5.

Task 2

What was the income tax charge in the statement of profit or loss for the year ended 31 December 20X5? **(1 mark)**

$2,450,000

$2,400,000 + $50,000 under-provision relating to the previous year

Task 3

(a)   How many shares were issued as a result of making the rights issue?   (1 mark)

| 2,000,000 | 10,000,000 × 1/5 = 2,000,000 |

Tutorial note

Note that the trial balance is dated 31 December 20X5, i.e. after the rights issue has been made. Foe every four shares that were in issue, following the rights issue, there will now be five shares. Therefore, you need to reduce the number of shares by 4/5 to calculate the number of shares that were in issue prior to the rights issue. You can then apply the rights fraction of 1/4 to calculate the number of shares issued.

(b)   What were the total proceeds raised as a result of making the rights issue? (1 mark)

| $5,000,000 | 2,000,000 × $2.50 = $5,000,000 |

(c)   What was the balance on the share premium account as a result of making the rights issue?   (1 mark)

| $3,000,000 | 2,000,000 × ($2.50 - $1.00) = $3,000,000 |

Task 4

Identify whether or not each of the following items would be presented in the statement of changes in equity.   (3 marks)

	Included / excluded
Depreciation charge for the year	Excluded
Share issue made in the year	Included
Proposed dividend due to be paid on 26 February 20X6	Excluded
Dividend paid on 28 October 20X5	Included

Task 5

Which one of the following statements could be a plausible reason for the increase in the gross profit margin during 20X5?   (2 marks)

		Selected answer
(i)	Distribution costs reduced during 20X5	
(ii)	Carbon Co sold more goods during 20X5 due to a successful marketing campaign early in the year	
(iii)	There was a change in the sales mix during 20X5, with Carbon Co selling proportionately fewer of its low-margin goods	Correct

Tutorial note

Distribution costs do not affect the calculation of gross profit. The sale of a greater quantity of goods may increase the gross profit, but not necessarily the margin made on those sales. A change in the sales mix, so that proportionately fewer of the lower-margin goods are sold will improve the gross profit margin.

(Total: 15 marks)

Marking scheme	
	Marks
Task 1 – Property, plant and equipment	6
Task 2 – Accounting for income tax	1
Task 3 – Rights issue	3
Task 4 – SOCIE	3
Task 5 – Interpretation of information	2
	――
Total	**15**
	――

5   MARCUS

Key answer tips

This question tests your knowledge of accounts preparation for a sole trader.

When dealing with account preparation for a sole trader, ensure that you understand the composition of the capital account, along with how withdrawals of cash and/or goods for personal use should be accounted for. Knowledge of bookkeeping is tested with the requirement to account for a return of goods to a supplier – have a clear understanding of the difference between returns inwards and returns outwards. Knowledge of accounting for discounts is also tested in this question. Therefore, ensure that you understand the difference between a trade discount and an early settlement discount. Also, ensure that you understand how to account for early settlement discount offered to credit customers, depending upon whether or not they are expected to take advantage of the discount terms offered.

Task 1

State the accounting entries required to record the return of goods to the supplier. (2 marks)

	$000	*Credit / Debit*
Revenue		
Returns inwards		
Returns outwards (100/120 × $300)	250	Credit
Sales tax (20/120 × $300)	50	Credit
Trade payables' ledger control account	300	Debit
Trade receivables' ledger control account		

Task 2

State the accounting entries required to record withdrawal of goods from the business by Marcus for personal use. **(3 marks)**

	$000	Credit / Debit
Drawings	15	Debit
Trade payables' ledger control account		
Purchases	15	Credit
Revenue		

Task 3

State whether each of the following statements is true or false. **(3 marks)**

		True / False
(i)	Trade discount allowed to customers should be included as an expense in the statement of profit or loss	False
(ii)	Early settlement discount allowed to credit customers should be deducted from the invoice value at the point of sale when the customer is not expected to take advantage of the early settlement discount terms offered	False
(iii)	Early settlement discount earned from suppliers should be included in the statement of profit or loss	True

Tutorial note

Trade discount is never recognised in the financial statements. It is always deducted by the seller at the point of sale when preparing the invoice. Early settlement discount offered to a credit customer is only deducted from the invoice price at the point of sale when the customer is expected to take account of the early settlement discount terms offered.

Task 4

Complete each of the following three statements in relation to the information contained in this Task. **(3 marks)**

Accounting for the insurance **prepayment** will **increase** the profit for the year ended 30 April 20X5.

Accounting for the legal fees **accrual** will **reduce** the profit for the year ended 30 April 20X5.

The net effect upon the profit for the year ended 30 April 20X5 as a result of accounting for the accrual and/or prepayment required for insurances and legal fees will be to **increase** profit for the year by **$6,000**.

Insurance prepayment = 8/12 × $18,000 = $12,000 = increase profit for the year.

Legal fees accrual = $6,000 = reduction in profit.

Task 5

Identify whether each of the following items is relevant or not to reconcile and clear the suspense account (4 marks)

		Relevant / Not relevant
(i)	Sales returns listed as a debit balance in the trial balance	Not relevant
(ii)	Discounts received were recorded in the cash received book and credited to the Discounts received account in the general ledger	Relevant
(iii)	The total of the purchases day book for March was debited to the Trade payables' ledger control account and credited to the Purchases account	Not relevant
(iv)	The cost of a machine purchased during the year was debited to the Repairs account as $8,080 and credited to the Cash account as $8,800	Relevant

Sales returns are a debit balance, so there is not an error. Omission of transactions from the purchases' day book will not cause a difference in the trial balance totals.

The cash received book is a book of prime entry, with the totals posted periodically into the general ledger. The double-entry for discounts received is: Debit Trade payables' ledger control account and Credit Discounts received.

Only one part of the double-entry has been posted and this will cause a difference in the trial balance totals.

For the purchase of the machine, an unequal value of debits and credits has been posted into the general ledger. This will cause a difference to arise in the trial balance. **(Total: 15 marks)**

Marking scheme	
	Marks
Task 1 – Accounting for return of goods	2
Task 2 – Accounting for drawings	3
Task 3 – True or false statements = 1 mark for each correct statement	3
Task 4 – Accruals and prepayments – 1 mark for correctly completed statement	3
Task 5 – Suspense account statements - 1 mark per correct answer	4
	—
Total	**15**
	—

6   **FIREWORK CO**

Key answer tips

Ensure that you are familiar with the pro-forma of a standard statement of cash flows – it will help you to complete relevant extracts in an examination question. In particular, ensure that you understand the cash flows that may be included within each of the three standard classifications of cash flows. Note that the question tests your understanding of whether the statement begins with profit before tax or after tax.

Firework Co – Statement of cash flows for the year ended 30 June 20X5

	$000		Marks
Cash flows from operating activities			
Profit before tax	31,000		
Adjustments for:			
Depreciation charge	15,000	Add	0.5
Loss on sale of plant and equipment	2,000	Add	0.5
Interest payable	750	Add	0.5
Increase in inventories ($36,000 – $30,000)	(6,000)	Subtract	1.0
Increase in trade receivables ($40,000 – $35,000)	(5,000)	Subtract	1.0
Increase in trade payables ($36,500 – $30,000)	6,500	Add	1.0
	———		
Cash generated from operations	44,250		
Interest paid	(750)	Subtract	0.5
Income taxes paid (W3)	(9,500)	Subtract	1.0
	———		
	34,000		
Cash flows from investing activities			
Cash purchase of property, plant and equipment (W1)	(40,000)	Subtract	1.0
Disposal proceeds of plant and equipment (W2)	8,000	Add	1.0
	———		
	2,000		
Cash flows from financing activities			
Repayment of bank loan (W4)	(10,000)	Subtract	1.0
Proceeds of share issue ($5,000 + $5,000) (W5)	10,000	Add	2.0
Dividend paid (W6)	(14,000)	Subtract	2.0
	———		
Decrease in cash and cash equivalents	(12,000)		
($10,000 + $2,000)			1.0
Cash and cash equivalents at start of year	10,000	Add	0.5
	———		
Cash and cash equivalents at end of year	(2,000)	Net overdraft	0.5
	———		———
			15.0

Workings:

(W1) PPE additions in the year

	$000
PPE CA bal b/fwd	93,000
Less: CA of disposals ($8,000 + $2,000 loss)	(10,000)
Less: depreciation charge	(15,000)
Revaluation in year	2,000
Cash paid for PPE additions (bal fig)	40,000
	———
PPE CA bal c/fwd	110,000
	———

Tutorial note

When preparing the reconciliation of property, plant and equipment movements in the year, don't forget to include any revaluation surplus recognised in the year. You will find the relevant information either in the notes to the question or, as in this case, by identifying the revaluation surplus recorded as an item of 'other comprehensive income' within the statement of profit or loss and other comprehensive income.

(W2) Loss on disposal of plant and equipment

	$000
PPE CA of disposals ($8,000 + $2,000) (bal fig)	10,000
Less: loss on disposal in cost of sales	(2,000)
	———
Disposal proceeds received	8,000
	———

(W3) Income tax paid

	$000
Income tax liability b/fwd	10,000
Income tax charge for the year per P&L	6,000
Cash paid in year	(9,500)
	———
Income tax liability c/fwd	6,500
	———

(W4) Bank loan – amount repaid

	$000
Bank loan b/fwd	17,000
Cash paid	(10,000)
	———
Bank loan c/fwd	7,000
	———

(W5) Issue of shares in the year

	Share capital $000	Share premium $000
Balance b/fwd	15,000	3,000
Proceeds of share issue in year	5,000	5,000
	———	———
Balance c/fwd	20,000	8,000
	———	———

(W6) Dividend paid

	$000
Retained earnings b/fwd	85,000
Profit after tax for the year	25,000
Cash paid	(14,000)
	———
Bank loan c/fwd	96,000
	———

Marking scheme	
	Marks
Statement of cash flows (per answer)	15
	——
Total	**15**
	——

7   CRACKER CO

Key answer tips

Ensure that you understand which items are classified under each of the standard headings in a statement of cash flows. It will help you to complete relevant parts of a question efficiently. Begin with cash flows from operating activities, with the first item as 'profit before tax' from the statement of profit or loss. Use standard workings to calculate the required values for inclusion in the statement of cash flows.

Cracker Co – Statement of cash flows for the year ended 31 March 20X1

	$000		Marks
Cash flows from operating activities			
Profit before tax	11,650		
Adjustments for:			
Depreciation charge	500	Add	0.5
Gain on disposal of plant and equipment	(300)	Subtract	0.5
Investment income	(320)	Subtract	0.5
Interest payable	2,150	Add	0.5
Increase in inventories ($27,500 – $25,500)	(2,000)	Subtract	1.0
Increase in trade receivables ($37,500 – $33,000)	(4,500)	Subtract	1.0
Decrease in trade payables ($31,900 – $29,450)	(2,450)	Subtract	1.0
	———		
Cash generated from operations	4,730		
Interest paid	(2,150)	Subtract	0.5
Income taxes paid (W3)	(2,310)	Subtract	1.0
	———		
	270		
Cash flows from investing activities			
Investment income	320	Add	0.5
Cash purchase of property, plant and equipment (W1)	(3,800)	Subtract	1.0
Disposal proceeds of plant and equipment (W2) (Item 1)	1,100	Add	1.0
	———		
	(2,110)		
Cash flows from financing activities			
Proceeds of loan raised (W4)	3,500	Add	1.0
Proceeds of share issue ($1,000 + $610)(W5) (Item 2)	1,610	Add	2.0
	———		
Net change in cash and cash equivalents for the year	3,000	Increase	1.0
Cash and cash equivalents at start of the year	1,250	Add	1.0
	———		
Cash and cash equivalents at end of the year	4,250		1.0
	———		———
			15.0

Item 1: Disposal proceeds of plant and equipment (all figures in $000):

		Selected answer
(i)	$800 - $300	
(ii)	$800 + $300	Correct
(iii)	$800	

Item 2: Proceeds of the share issue (all figures in $000):

		Selected answer
(i)	$11,000 - $10,000	
(ii)	$11,000 - $10,000 + $610	Correct
(iii)	$!!,000 - $10,000 - $610	

Workings

(W1) PPE additions in the year

	$000
PPE CA bal b/fwd	70,500
Less: CA of disposals	(800)
Less: depreciation charge	(500)
Cash paid for PPE additions	3,800
	————
PPE CA bal c/fwd	73,000
	————

(W2) Gain on disposal of plant and equipment

	$000
PPE CA of disposals	800
Add: profit on disposal per P&L	300
	————
Disposal proceeds received	1,100
	————

Tutorial note

The SP&L includes the profit on disposal of plant and equipment, and the notes to the question specify the carrying amount of the items disposed of. From this, you can identify the disposal proceeds received. Also, don't forget to remove the carrying amount of the items disposed of within the property, plant and equipment reconciliation.

(W3) Income tax paid

	$000
Income tax liability b/fwd	2,310
Income tax charge for the year per P&L	2,900
Cash paid in year	(2,310)
	————
Income tax liability c/fwd	2,900
	————

(W4) Loan finance – additional loan finance raised

	$000
10% debenture Loan liability b/fwd	20,000
Cash received – additional loan finance	3,500
	————
10% debenture Loan liability c/fwd	23,500
	————

(W5) Issue of shares in the year

	Share capital $000	Share premium $000
Balance b/fwd	10,000	Nil
Proceeds of share issue in year	1,000	610
Balance c/fwd	11,000	610

Marking scheme	
	Marks
Statement of cash flows (per answer)	15
Total	15

8   SPARKLER CO

Key answer tips

IAS 7 *Statement of cash flows* permits inclusion of items under the classification of investing activities and financing activities respectively in any order, provided that they are within the appropriate classification - there is not a defined sequential order. Similarly, many of the items within operating activities can also be included in any order, although it should begin with 'profit before tax' and the final items being 'interest paid' and 'tax paid'. However, in a computer-based examination, the sequence in which items are included within each heading is likely to be pre-determined.

Sparkler Co – Statement of cash flows for the year ended 30 September 20X9

	$000		Marks
Cash flows from operating activities			
Profit before tax	18,000		0.5
Adjustments for:			
Depreciation charge (W1)	12,500	Add	0.5
Profit on sale of plant and equipment	(500)	Subtract	0.5
Interest payable	2,700	Add	0.5
Decrease in inventories ($36,000 – $30,750)	5,250	Add	1.0
Decrease in trade receivables ($45,000 – $39,250)	5,750	Add	1.0
Decrease in trade payables ($38,500 – $35,000)	(3,500)	Subtract	1.0
Cash generated from operations	40,200		
Interest paid (W7) (Item 1)	(2,575)	Subtract	1.0
Income taxes paid (W3)	(4,000)	Subtract	1.0

Cash flows from investing activities

Cash purchase of property, plant and equipment (W1)	(21,000)	Subtract	*1.0*
Disposal proceeds of plant and equipment (W2)	2,000	Add	*1.0*

Cash flows from financing activities

Proceeds of loan raised (W4)	5,000	Add	*1.0*
Proceeds of share issue ($6,000 + $2,000)(W5)	8,000	Add	*2.0*
Dividend paid (W6) (Item 2)	(20,125)	Subtract	*1.0*
Net change in cash and cash equivalents ($4,500 + $3,000)	7,500	Increase	*1.0*
Cash and cash equivalents b/fwd	(4,500)	Subtract	*0.5*
Cash and cash equivalents c/fwd	3,000		*0.5*
			15.0

Item 1: Interest paid: Choose the correct calculation of interest paid (all figures in $000):

		Selected answer
(i)	$2,700 - $625 - $500	
(ii)	$2,700 + $500 + $625	
(iii)	$2,700 + $500 - $625	Correct

Item 2: Dividend paid: Choose the correct calculation of dividend paid in the year:

		Selected answer
(i)	Retained earnings b/fwd + Profit after tax – Retained earnings c/fwd	Correct
(ii)	Retained earnings b/fwd + Total comprehensive income – Retained earnings carried forward	
(iii)	Retained earnings b/fwd – Profit after tax + Retained earnings c/fwd	

Workings:

(W1) PPE additions in the year

	$000
PPE CA bal b/fwd	85,000
Less: CA of disposals	(1,500)
Revaluation in year	3,000
Less: depreciation charge	(12,500)
Cash paid for PPE additions	21,000
PPE CA balVc/fwd	95,000

(W2) Gain on disposal of plant and equipment

	$000
PPE CA of disposals	1,500
Add: profit on disposal per P&L	500
Disposal proceeds received	2,000

(W3) Income tax paid

	$000
Income tax liability b/fwd	4,000
Income tax charge for the year per P&L	3,500
Cash paid in year	(4,000)
Income tax liability c/fwd	3,500

(W4) Loan finance – additional loan finance raised

	$000
10% debenture Loan liability b/fwd	20,000
Cash received – additional loan finance	5,000
10% debenture Loan liability c/fwd	25,000

(W5) Issue of shares in the year

	Share capital	Share premium
	$000	$000
Balance b/fwd	24,000	8,000
Proceeds of share issue in year	6,000	2,000
Balance c/fwd	30,000	10,000

(W6) Dividend paid in the year

	$000
Retained earnings b/fwd	66,500
Profit after tax for the year	14,500
Dividend paid in the year	(20,125)
Retained earnings c/fwd	60,875

Tutorial note

The dividend paid in the year can be calculated by reconciling the movement in retained earnings from the start of the year to the end of the year. Remember to include the profit after tax from the statement of profit or loss as part of your calculations. Note – do not include any revaluation surplus arising in the year (as included as an item of 'other comprehensive income' as this is not part of retained earnings.

(W7) Interest paid in the year

	$000
Interest payable b/fwd	500
P&L charge for the year	2,700
Interest paid in the year	(2,575)
	———
Interest payable c/fwd	625
	———

Marking scheme	
	Marks
Statement of cash flows per answer	15
	——
Total	**15**
	——

9 OUTFLOW CO

Key answer tips

IAS 7 *Statement of cash flows* permits you to include items under the classification of investing activities and financing activities respectively in any order, provided that they are within the appropriate classification - there is not a defined sequential order. Note that this question includes a loss before tax in the statement of profit or loss. There is also a revaluation of property, plant and equipment, so ensure that you understand how this affects the statement of cash flows. The revaluation surplus for the year does not affect profit (or loss) before tax, so should be excluded from the statement. Other items, such as the annual depreciation charge and the gain or loss on disposal should be accounted for as usual within the statement.

Outflow Co – Statement of cash flows for the year ended 30 April 20X2

	$000		Marks
Cash flows from operating activities			
Loss before tax	(4,300)		1.0
Adjustments for:			
Depreciation charge (W2)	11,000	Add	0.5
Loss on scrapped assets (W1)	1,000	Add	0.5
Interest payable	1,000	Add	1.0
Decrease in inventories ($33,000 – $30,000)	3,000	Add	1.0
Decrease in trade receivables ($52,000 – $48,750)	3,250	Add	1.0
Decrease in trade payables ($27,500 – $26,300)	(1,200)	Subtract	1.0
	———		
Cash generated from operations	13,750		
Interest paid	(1,000)	Subtract	1.0
Income taxes paid (W3)	(5,000)	Subtract	1.0
	———		
Cash flows from investing activities			
Cash purchase of PPE (W2) (Item 1)	(20,000)	Subtract	1.0
	———		
Cash flows from financing activities			
Proceeds of loan raised (W4)	7,500	Add	1.0
Proceeds of share issue ($4,000 + $1,000)(W5) (Item 2)	5,000	Add	2.0
Dividend paid (W6)	(1,000)	Subtract	1.0
	———		
Net change in cash and equivalents in the year	(750)	Decrease	1.0
Cash and cash equivalents b/fwd	(3,250)	Net overdraft	0.5
	———		
Cash and cash equivalents c/fwd	(4,000)	Net overdraft	0.5
	———		——
			15.0

Item 1: Additions to property, plant and equipment in the year (all figures in $000)

		Selected answer
(i)	$110,000 + $2,000 - $100,000 + $11,000 + $1,000	
(ii)	$110,000 - $100,000 + $11,000	
(iii)	$110,000 - $2,000 - $100,000 + $1,000 + $11,000	Correct

Item 2: Proceeds of the share issue (all figures in $000):

		Selected answer
(i)	$40,000 + 4,000 - $44,000	
(ii)	$44,000 + $5,000 - $40,000 - $4,000	Correct
(iii)	$44,000 - $40,000	

Workings:

(W1) Loss on disposal of scrapped assets

	$000
Disposal proceeds received	Nil
PPE CA of scrapped items	1,000
Loss on disposal	1,000

(W2) PPE additions in the year

	$000
Carrying amount b/fwd	100,000
Additions in year (bal fig)	20,000
Depreciation charge	(11,000)
Disposals in year	(1,000)
Revaluation in year	2,000
Carrying amount bal c/fwd	110,000

(W3) Income tax paid

	$000
Income tax liability b/fwd	5,000
Income tax recoverable per P&L	(500)
Cash paid in year (bal fig)	(5,000)
Income tax recoverable (asset) c/fwd	(500)

(W4) Bank loan – additional loan finance raised

	$000
Bank loan liability b/fwd	8,000
Cash received – additional loan finance (bal fig)	7,500
Bank loan liability c/fwd	15,500

(W5) Issue of shares in the year

	Share capital $000	Share premium $000
Balance b/fwd	40,000	4,000
Proceeds of share issue in year (bal fig)	4,000	1,000
Balance c/fwd	44,000	5,000

Tutorial note

Calculate the total cash proceeds received from the share issue by identifying movements in both the share capital and share premium accounts.

(W6) Dividend paid in the year

	$000
Retained earnings b/fwd	77,250
Loss after tax for the year	(3,800)
Dividend paid in the year (bal fig)	(1,000)
	──────
Retained earnings c/fwd	72,450
	──────

Marking scheme	
	Marks
Statement of cash flows (per answer)	15
	──
Total	**15**
	──

10 PATTY AND SELMA

Key answer tips

This question deals with the mid-year acquisition of a subsidiary. Ensure that you pro-rate the calculation of each item of income and expense in the subsidiary's statement of profit or loss as part of your consolidation workings.

Look for any intra-group trading to remove it from the consolidated statement, ensuring that you have also identified and adjusted properly for any unrealised profit on closing inventory. Remember that intra-group trading will always be post-acquisition.

Task 1

Complete the following consolidated statement of profit or loss for the year ended 31 December 20X1. (8 marks)

	$000	Marks
Revenue ($987 + ($567 × 8/12) – $120 (W1))	1,245	1.5
Less: Cost of sales ($564 + ($336 × 8/12) – $120 (W1) + $5 (W1)) (Item 1)	(673)	1.5
Gross profit	572	
Less: Administrative expenses ($223 + ($123 × 8/12))	(305)	1.0
Operating profit	267	
Less: Finance costs ($50 + ($30 × 8/12)) (Item 2)	(70)	1.0
Profit before taxation	197	
Less: Income tax expense ($40 + ($24 × 8/12))	(56)	1.0
Profit after tax for the year	141	
Profit after tax attributable to:		
Owners of Patty (bal fig)	130.2	
Non-controlling interest (W2) (Item 3)	10.8	2.0
	141.0	8.0

Item 1: Choose the correct calculation for cost of sales8

	All figures are in $000	Selected answer
(i)	$564 + ($336 × 8/12) - $120 - $5	
(ii)	$564 + ($336 × 8/12) + $120 - $5	
(iii)	$564 + ($336 × 8/12) - $120 + $5	Correct

Item 2: Choose the correct calculation for finance costs

	All figures are in $000	Selected answer
(i)	$50 – ($30 × 8/12)	
(ii)	$50 + ($30 × 8/12)	Correct
(iii)	$50 + $30	

Item 3: Choose the correct formula to calculate the non-controlling interest share of the consolidated profit for the year

		Selected answer
(i)	(Subsidiary profit before tax × 8/12) + NCI share of unrealised profit on inventory	
(ii)	(Subsidiary profit after tax × 8/12) - NCI share of unrealised profit on inventory	
(iii)	NCI% × Subsidiary profit after tax × 8/12	Correct

Workings:

(W1) Intra-group transactions and PURP

Remember to remove intra-group sales and purchases of $120k in the calculations. Note that these transactions do not need to be pro-rated as the question states that they are all post-acquisition.

Profit earned on intra-group sales = $120k × (20/120) = $20k

The proportion of this profit remaining in inventory must be eliminated:

$20k × 25% = $5k. The double entry to adjust for this is:

Dr Cost of sales (P&L) $5k, and Cr Inventory (SoFP) $5k

The parent bears all of the unrealised profit adjustment as the parent made the sales to the subsidiary.

Tutorial note

Ensure that you can identify whether sales have been made on a 'cost-plus' basis or based upon sales margin as this will affect the calculation of the provision for unrealised profit.

(W2) Non-controlling interest share of consolidated profit after tax

	$000
NCI % of S's PAT × 8/12 = 30% × ($54 × 8/12)	10.8

Note that the non-controlling interest does not bear any part of the unreaslised profit on inventory adjustment as the parent made the sale.

Task 2

State whether each of the following statements is true or false. (3 marks)

		True / False
(i)	Accounting for the acquisition of a subsidiary always includes recognition and accounting for a non-controlling interest	False
(ii)	Accounting for the acquisition of a subsidiary can be achieved by using equity accounting	False
(iii)	The share capital and share premium account balances of a subsidiary are not included in the consolidated statement of financial position	True

The first statement is false as control could be obtained by acquisition of all of the shares in a subsidiary – there would be no non-controlling interest to account for in this situation. The second statement is false as equity accounting is used to account for an interest in an associate.

Task 3

(a) **Using the individual entity financial statements, calculate the following ratios for Patty and Selma for the year ended 31 December 20X1.** **(2 marks)**

Marks

Gross profit margin

Patty: (423/987 × 100) = 42.9%   *0.5 mark*

Selma: (231/567 × 100) = 40.7%   *0.5 mark*

Operating profit margin:

Patty: (200/987 × 100) = 20.3%   *0.5 mark*

Selma: (108/567 × 100) = 19.0%   *0.5 mark*

(b) **What conclusion could you arrive at regarding the relative financial performance of the two entities?** **(2 marks)**

		Selected answer
(i)	Patty is relatively better at minimising distribution costs and administration expenses than Quartz	Correct
(ii)	Quartz is relatively better at minimising distribution costs and administration expenses than Patty	
(iii)	It is not possible to arrive at a conclusion regarding which entity is relatively better at minimising distribution costs and administration expenses	

(Total: 15 marks)

Marking scheme	
	Marks
Task 1 - Consolidated statement of profit or loss per answer	8
Task 2 – 1 mark for each correct answer	3
Task 3a – 0.5 mark per ratio calculated correctly	2
Task 3b – 2 marks for correct answer	2
	___
Total	15
	___

11   PENTAGON AND SQUARE

Key answer tips

Task 1 of this question r tests your knowledge of how to calculate goodwill on acquisition. Task 2 deals with preparation of a consolidated statement of profit or loss, including a mid-year acquisition. Ensure that you pro-rate the subsidiary's items of income and expense to consolidate only the post-acquisition element.

To answer this question fully, you also need to understand how to account for intra-group transactions and unrealised profit, together with calculation of the non-controlling interest share of the result for the year.

Task 1

(a)   Calculate the fair value of consideration paid to acquire the shares in Square. (1 mark)

	$	
Fair value of consideration paid:	N/A	
Cash paid	150,000	
FV of shares issued (75% × 40,000 × 4/3 × $2,50)	100,000	Add
	——	
	250,000	
	——	

(b)   State the accounting entries required by Pentagon to record the issue of shares used as part of the consideration to acquire control of Square.   (2 marks)

	$	Credit / Debit	
Investment in Square	100,000	Debit	0.5 mark
Issued share capital	40,000	Credit	0.5 mark
75% × 40,000 × 4/3 × $1			
Retained earnings			
Revaluation surplus			
Share premium	60,000	Credit	1 mark
75% × 40,000 × 4/3 × $1.50			

Tutorial note

Note that the loan from the parent to the subsidiary was mad part-way through the accounting year. Therefore, you need to calculate the interest receivable by the parent from the subsidiary. This then needs to be eliminated from interest receivable and interest payable upon consolidation, just like any other transaction between the parent and subsidiary during the accounting period.

(a)   Choose the correct formula to calculate goodwill arising upon acquisition of Square.

(1 mark)

		Selected answer
(i)	Fair value of consideration paid	
	Plus: Fair value of non-controlling interest at acquisition	
	Plus: Fair value of net assets at acquisition date	
(ii)	Fair value of consideration paid	
	Less: Fair value of non-controlling interest at acquisition	
	Plus: Fair value of net assets at acquisition date	
(iii)	Fair value of consideration paid	Correct
	Plus: Fair value of non-controlling interest at acquisition	
	Less: Fair value of net assets at acquisition date	

Task 2

State the amounts that each of the following items should be included in the consolidated statement of financial position as at 31 December 20X4.   **(6 marks)**

	$	$000	
Property, plant and equip't	454,000	205 + 179 + 70 (W2)	2 marks
Inventories	127,000	80 + 50 – 3 (W1)	2 marks
Trade and other receivables	159,000	60 + 99	1 mark
Cash and cash equivalents	51,000	0 + 51	1 mark

Workings:

(W1) Provision for unrealised profit

Profit earned on intra-group sales = $30,000 × 30% = $9,000

The proportion of this profit remaining in inventory must be eliminated:

1/3 × $9,000 = $3,000. The double entry to adjust for this is:

Dr Cost of sales (P&L)$3,000, and Cr Inventory (SOFP) $3,000

(W2) Fair value adjustment

FV of land = $170,000 less carrying amount $100,000 = $70,000

Task 3

Choose the correct calculation of the non-controlling interest to include in the consolidated statement of financial position as at 31 December 20X4.   **(2 marks)**

	All figures are in $	Selected answer
(i)	(25% × $75,000) + (25% × ($279,000 – $120,000))	
(ii)	$75,000 + (25% × ($279,000 + $120,000))	
(iii)	$75,000 + (25% × ($279,000 – $120,000))	Correct

Task 4

(a)   Using the individual financial statements, calculate the quick (acid test) ratio for Pentagon and Square as at 31 December 20X4.   **(2 marks)**

Pentagon	1.0 :1
Square	3.0 :1

(60 + 8) / 60   1 mark

(99 + 51) / 50   1   mark

(b)   Complete the following statement relating to the quick (acid test) ratio.   **(1 mark)**

The quick (acid test) ratio is a measure of **liquidity**. A quick (acid test) ratio of 0.75:1 indicates that an entity has a **lower** value of current assets than current liabilities. For the purposes of this ratio, inventories are **excluded** within the definition of current assets.

(Total: 15 marks)

Marking scheme	
	Marks
Task 1 – Goodwill calculation	4
Task 2 – Consolidated statement of financial position assets	6
Task 3 – Calculate NCI to include in SOFP	2
Task 4a – Ratio calculations	2
Task 4b – Interpretation of financial statements	1
	—
Total	**15**
	—

12   PIKE AND SALMON

Key answer tips

This question tests your knowledge of how to deal with a mid-year acquisition – you need to pro-rate the retained earnings for the year into pre- and post-acquisition elements. Ensure that you know how to account for intra-group transactions; in particular, (a) unrealised profits when the subsidiary sells to the parent, (b) cancellation of intra-group balances for receivables and payables and (c) cancellation of intra-group loans from parent to subsidiary.

Task 1

(a)   Choose the correct calculation of Salmon's retained earnings at the date of acquisition.   **(2 marks)**

	All figures are in $000	*Selected answer*
(i)	$6,090 + $240 + (3/12 × $240)	
(ii)	$1,290 – $240 + (9/12 × $240)	Correct
(iii)	$1,290 – $240 + (3/12 × $240)	

(b) Choose the correct calculation of the fair value of net assets of Salmon at the date of acquisition. **(2 marks)**

	All figures are in $000	Selected answer
(i)	$4,800 + $1,290 + $1,000	
(ii)	$4,800 - $1,230 + (3/12 × $240) + $1,000	
(iii)	$4,800 + $1,290 – (3/12 × $240) + $1,000	Correct

(c) Choose the correct calculation of goodwill at acquisition. **(2 marks)**

	All figures are in $000	Selected answer
(i)	$9,720 + $2,400 - $7,030	
(ii)	$8,720 + $2,400 - $7,030	Correct
(iii)	$8,720 + $2,400 - $6,030	

Task 2

(a) What amount should be included in the consolidated statement of financial position for the 5% Loan notes as at 31 March 20X6? **(2 marks)**

$26,620,000 $16,440 + $11,180 - $1,000 (intra-group)

(b) What amount should be included in the consolidated statement of financial position for retained earnings at 31 March 20X6? **(2 marks)**

$12,495,000 $12,480 + (75% × $60) – (75% × $40) PURP

Task 3

Complete the following table to state at what amount each of the following items should be included in the consolidated statement of financial position at 31 March 20X6. **(5 marks)**

		$000		
(i)	Non-current assets	40,950	$26,280 + 13,670 + $1,000 (FVA)	1 mark
(ii)	Current assets	9,480	$4,760 + $5,010 - $250 (IC) - $40 (PURP)	1.5 marks
(iii)	Current liabilities	3,800	$2,640 + $1,410 - $250 (IC)	1 mark
(iv)	Non-controlling interest	2,405	$2,400 + (25% × $60) - (25% × $40 (PURP))	1.5 marks

Tutorial note

For non-current assets, remember to include the increase in the fair value of land as at the date of acquisition (i.e. $170,000 - $100,000).

For current assets, remember remove the unrealised profit of $40,000 (80% × $50,000).within closing inventory.

Also, remember to eliminate the intra-group receivable and payable. Half of the invoice value of intra-group sales is still outstanding i.e. $250,000.

Tutorial note

For non-controlling interest remember to deduct their share of the unrealised profit on inventory of $10,000 ($50,000 × 80% × 25%). This must be done as the subsidiary sold goods to the parent at a profit and not all of it has been realised by the reporting date.

(Total 15 marks)

Marking scheme	
	Marks
Task 1 – Goodwill calculation	6
Task 2 – Consolidated statement of financial position items	4
Task 3 – Consolidated statement of financial position items	5
	——
Total	**15**
	——

13 PLATE AND SAUCER

Key answer tips

This question requires you to deal with preparation of a consolidated statement pf profit or loss. Ensure that you know how to deal with elimination of intra-group sales and purchases, along with unrealised profit arising on those transactions. There is also an additional aspect of intra-group trading as the parent has made a loan to the subsidiary – there is loan interest receivable and payable eliminate from the consolidated statements. Note that the loan was made part-way through the accounting year. You therefore need to calculate the interest payable by the subsidiary to the parent on a pro-rated basis. Then you need to cancel this intragroup item of income and expense as part of the consolidated process.

Task 1

Complete the following consolidated statement of profit or loss for the year ended 31 December 20X4. **(9 marks)**

Consolidated statement of profit or loss for the year ended 31 December 20X4.

	$000	Marks
Revenue ($1,500 + $700 - $150 (IC))	2,050	2.0
Less: Cost of sales ((775 + $370 – $150 (IC) + $5 (W1)) (Item 1)	1,000	2.0
	———	
Gross profit	1,050	
Less: Administrative expenses ($317 + $135)	452	1.0
	———	
Operating profit	598	
Add: Interest receivable ($15 + $0 - ($1,000 × 6% × 3/12) (IC))	Nil	1.0
Less: Finance costs ($60 + $20 – ($1,000 × 6% × 3/12)) (item 2)	65	1.0
	———	
Profit before taxation	533	
Less: Income tax expense ($96 + $45)	141	0.5
	———	
Profit after tax for the year	392	
	———	
Profit after tax attributable to:		
Owners of Plate (bal fig)	N/A	
Non-controlling interest (W2)	Item 3	1.5
	———	———
	N/A	**9.0**
	———	———

Tutorial note

Note that the loan from the parent to the subsidiary was mad part-way through the accounting year. Therefore, you need to calculate the interest receivable by the parent from the subsidiary. This then needs to be eliminated from interest receivable and interest payable upon consolidation, just like any other transaction between the parent and subsidiary during the accounting period.

Item 1: Choose the correct calculation for cost of sales

	All figures are in $000	Selected answer
(i)	$775 + $370 + 150 - $5	
(ii)	$775 + $370 – $150 + $5	Correct
(iii)	$775 + $370 - $150 - $5	

Item 2: Choose the correct calculation for finance costs

	All figures are in $000	Selected answer
(i)	$60 – $20 + ($1,000 × 6% × 9/12)	
(ii)	$60 + $20 - ($1,000 × 6%)	
(iii)	$60 + $20 – ($1,000 × 6% × 3/12)	Correct

Item 3: Choose the correct formula to calculate the non-controlling interest share of the consolidated profit for the year

		Selected answer
(i)	(NCI% × Subsidiary profit after tax) – (NCI share of unrealised profit on inventory)	Correct
(ii)	(NCI% × Subsidiary profit after tax) + NCI share of unrealised profit on inventory	
(iii)	(NCI% × Subsidiary profit before tax) - NCI share of unrealised profit on inventory	

Task 2

Select which one of the following is the correct accounting treatment for an associate in the consolidated statement of financial position. **(2 marks)**

		Selected answer
(i)	All assets and liabilities of the associate are cross-cast on a line-by-line basis with all other assets and liabilities of the group	
(ii)	The group share of the net assets of the associate are cross-cast on a line-by-line basis with all other assets and liabilities of the group	
(iii)	The net interest in the associate is included as a one-line entry as a non-current asset investment	Correct

Task 3

(a) **Using the individual entity financial statements of Plate and Saucer, calculate the operating profit margin for each entity for the year ended 31 December 20X4.**

(2 marks)

Plate	27.2%	408 / 1,500	1 mark

Saucer	27.9%	195 700	1 mark

(b) **State whether each of the following statements is true or false** **(2 marks)**

		True / False	
(i)	The operating profit margin will be affected by a change in the value of closing inventory, if all other factors remain unchanged	True	1 mark
(ii)	The operating profit margin is not affected by interest and finance charges incurred during the accounting period	True	1 mark

(Total: 15 marks)
(Total: 15 marks)

Workings:

(W1) PURP

$150,000 /120 × 20 = $25,000

The proportion of this profit remaining in inventory must be eliminated:

$25,000 × 1/5 = $5,000

The double entry to adjust for this is:

Dr Cost of sales (P&L) $5,000, Cr Inventory (SOFP) $5,000

(W2) Non-controlling interest

	$000
NCI % of S's PAT (30% × $130,000)	39,000
NCI % of PURP (30% × $5,000 (W1))	(1,500)
	———
	37,500
	———

(Total 15 marks)

Marking scheme	
	Marks
Task 1 – Consolidated statement of profit or loss	9
Task 2 – Accounting for an associate	2
Task 3 – Ratio calculations and interpretation of financial statements	4
	——
Total	**15**
	——

14   PORT AND STARBOARD

Key answer tips

This question comprises five tasks. Task 1 requires the calculation and accounting classification of goodwill. Tasks 2 and 3 require you to calculate individual items for inclusion in the consolidated statement of financial position. Task 4 deals with accounting for an associate and Task 5 tests your understanding of the current ratio of a business.

Task 1:

(a)   Choose the correct calculation of goodwill at acquisition of Starboard.   (2 marks)

		Selected answer
(i)	$300,000 + $80,000 – ($60,000 + $150,000 + $30,000)	
(ii)	$300,000 + $80,000 – ($70,000 + $150,000 + $30,000)	Correct
(iii)	$300,000 + $80,000 – ($70,000 + $150,000 - $30,000)	

(b) Identify which one of the following wold be the correct classification for goodwill in the consolidated statement of financial position. **(1 mark)**

		Selected answer
(i)	A tangible non-current asset	
(ii)	A current asset	
(iii)	An intangible non-current asset	Correct

Task 2

Complete the following table to state at what amount each of the following items should be included in the consolidated statement of financial position at 31 December 20X6.

(5 marks)

		$000	$000	
(i)	Property, plant and equip't	645	$350 + $265 + $30 (FVA)	1 mark
(ii)	Inventories	184	$109 + $80 - $5 (PURP)	1 mark
(iii)	Trade receivables	144	$79 + $95 - $30 (IC)	1 mark
(iv)	Trade and other payables	185	$155 + 60 - $30 (IC)	1 mark
(v)	7% Bank loan 20X9	385	$300 + $85	1 mark

Tutorial note

When cross-casting the net assets at the reporting date, don't forget to include any fair value adjustments for land and buildings within non-current assets. In addition, remember to eliminate any unrealised profit on closing inventory and any receivables/payables balances outstanding between parent and subsidiary at the reporting date.

Task 3

(a) What amount should be included in the consolidated statement of financial position for the non-controlling interest as at 31 December 20X6? **(2 marks)**

| $100,000 | See (W1) |

(b) What amount should be included in the consolidated statement of financial position for retained earnings at 31 December 20X6? **(2 marks)**

| $370,000 | See (W2) |

Workings:

(W1) Non-controlling interest

	$000
FV of NCI at acquisition	80
20% × (250 - 150)	20
	────
	100
	────

(W2) Retained earnings

	$000
Port	295
Starboard 80% × (250 -150)	80
Less: PURP ($50 × 25% × 40%)	(5)
	———
	370
	———

Note that the calculation of the provision for unrealised profit is based upon 40% of the intra-group sales still held within inventory. The question provides the proportion of those goods that had been sold, rather than unsold, by the reporting date.

Task 4

Which TWO of the following factors would be relevant when accounting for an associate?

(1 mark)

		Selected answer	
(i)	Control of Astern		
(ii)	Exercising significant influence over Astern	Correct	0.5 mark
(iii)	Owning the majority of the ordinary shares of Astern		
(iv)	Owning between 20% and 50% of the ordinary shares of Astern	Correct	0.5 mark
(v)	Accounting for goodwill		
(vi)	Accounting for the non-controlling interest in Astern		

Task 5

State whether each of the following statements is true or false.   **(2 marks)**

		True / False	
(i)	If the gross profit margin of a business improves, then the current ratio will also improve	False	1 mark
(ii)	If a bonus issue of shares is made, this will have no impact upon the current ratio	True	1 mark

(Total 15 marks)

Marking scheme	
	Marks
Task 1 – Accounting for goodwill	3
Task 2 – Items to include in consolidated SOFP	5
Task 3 – Items to include in consolidated SOFP	4
Task 4 – Accounting for an associate	1
Task 5 – Interpretation of financial statements	2
	——
Total	**15**
	——

15 HIDE AND SEEK

Key answer tips

This question requires you to calculate goodwill on acquisition (an item included in the consolidated statement of financial position) and also to complete the consolidated statement of profit or loss. Note that this was a mid-year acquisition, and the results of the subsidiary will need to be pro-rated accordingly. There is also intra-group trading (by definition, this will be post-acquisition) along with accounting for unrealised profit on inventory.

Task 1

Calculate goodwill arising on acquisition of Seek by Hide. (3 marks)

	$000	$000	
Fair value of consideration paid:			
Cash paid	24,000	3,000 × $8	1 mark
	———		
Fair value of the NCI at acquisition	4,000	1,000 × $4	1 mark
	———		
Fair value of net assets at acquisition:			
Share capital	4,000		
Retained earnings (Item 1)	20,000	$9,500 + (9/12 × $14,000)	1 mark
Fair value adjustment	2,000		
	———		
	26,000		
	———		
Goodwill on acquisition (Item 2)	2,000		
	———		

Item 1: Choose the correct calculation of retained earnings at the date of acquisition

	All figures are in $000	Selected answer
(i)	$9,500 + (3/12 × $14,000)	
(ii)	$9,500 + $14,000	
(iii)	$9,500 + (9/12 × $14,000)	Correct

Item 2: Choose the correct calculation for goodwill

		Selected answer
(i)	Fair value of consideration paid plus fair value of non-controlling interest at acquisition date plus fair value of net assets at acquisition	
(ii)	Fair value of consideration paid plus fair value of non-controlling interest at acquisition date minus fair value of net assets at acquisition	Correct
(iii)	Fair value of consideration paid minus fair value of non-controlling interest at acquisition date + fair value of net assets at acquisition	

Task 2

Consolidated statement of profit or loss for the year ended 30 June 20X6

	$000	Marks
Revenue ($200,000 + (3/12 × $100,000) – $12,500 (W1))	212,500	2.0
Cost of sales ($110,000 + (3/12 × $50,000) – $12,500 + $1,000 (W1)) (Item 1)	(111,000)	2.5
	────────	
Gross profit	101,500	
Distribution costs ($20,000 + (3/12 × $10,000))	(22,500)	1.0
Administrative expenses ($40,000 + (3/12 × $20,000))	(45,000)	1.0
	────────	
Profit before tax	34,000	
Income tax expense ($10,500 + (3/12 × $6,000))	(12,000)	1.5
	────────	
Profit after tax	22,000	
	────────	
Profit attributable to:		
Owners of Hide (bal fig)	21,375	
Non-controlling interest (W2) (item 2)	625	2.0
	────────	────
	22,000	10.0
	────────	────

Tutorial note

As this was a mid-year acquisition, remember to split each item of revenue and expense in the subsidiary P&L between pre-acquisition (9/12) and post-acquisition (3/12). Only the post=acquisition element is cross-cast into the consolidated statement of P&L on a line-by-line basis.

Item 1: Choose the correct calculation of cost of sales

	All figures are in $000	Selected answer
(i)	$110,000 + (3/12 × $50,000) – $12,500 - $1,500	
(ii)	$110,000 + (3/12 × $50,000) – $12,500 + $1,000	Correct
(iii)	$110,000 + (3/12 × $50,000) + $12,500 + $1,500	

Item 2: Choose the correct calculation for the non-controlling interest share of group profit after tax.

		Selected answer
(i)	Non-controlling interest share of Seek's profit for the year minus provision for unrealised profit on inventory	
(ii)	Non-controlling interest share of Seek's post-acquisition profit for the year, plus non-controlling interest share of provision for unrealised profit on inventory	
(iii)	Non-controlling interest share of Seek's post-acquisition profit for the year, minus non-controlling interest share of provision for unrealised profit on inventory	Correct

Workings:

(W1) Intra-group sales and PURP

	$000
Cost of goods sold by Seek to Hide	10,000
Add: 25% mark up	2,500
	———
Selling price of goods	12,500
	———
PURP = $2,500 × 40% in inventory	1000
	———

(W2) Non-controlling interest

	$000
NCI share of PAT: 25% × ($14,000 × 3/12)875	
NCI share of PURP: 25% × $1,000	(250)
	———
	625
	———

Task 3

Based upon the individual financial statements of Hide and Seek, Hide has a lower gross profit margin than Seek.

Which one of the following statements could be a plausible explanation for this situation?

(2 marks)

		Selected answer
(i)	Seek has lower levels of inventory than Hide at the start and end of the reporting period	
(ii)	Seek is able to purchase cheaper materials and has a lower wastage rate of material than Hide	Correct
(iii)	Seek has lower distribution costs and administrative expenses than Hide	

(Total: 15 marks)

Marking scheme	
	Marks
Task 1 – Accounting for goodwill	3
Task 2 – Items to include in consolidated SOP&L	10
Task 3 – Interpretation of financial statements	2
	–––
Total	15
	–––

16   PUSH AND SHOVE

Key answer tips

This question is a challenge as it requires you to prepare selected figures for both the statement of financial position and statement of profit or loss. Consequently, it is not time-efficient to adopt the standard approach of working through the normal consolidation workings. You should therefore try to o prepare specific workings for each individual figure required in the question.

Task 1

(a)   **State the accounting entries required to account for the issue of shares by Push upon acquisition of Shove.**   **(2 marks)**

	$000	Credit / Debit
Revaluation surplus		
Issued share capital (60% × 4,000 × 5/6 × $1)	2,000	Credit
Investment in Shove (60% × 4,000 × 5/6 × $6)	12,000	Debit
Retained earnings		
Share premium (60% × 4,000 × 5/6 × $5)	10,000	Credit

(b) **Calculate goodwill on acquisition of Shove** (3 marks)

	$000	
Fair value of consideration paid (Item 1) (60% × 4,000 × 5/6 × $6)	12,000	1 mark
	———	
Fair value of the NCI at acquisition (40% × 4,000 × $3.50)	5,600	0.5 mark
	———	
Fair value of net assets at acquisition:		
Share capital	4,000	0.5 mark
Retained earnings (Item 2)	12,400	1 mark
	———	
	16,400	
	———	
Goodwill on acquisition (Item 3)	1,200	
	———	

Item 1: Choose the correct calculation of the fair value of consideration paid

	All figures are in $000	Selected answer
(i)	4,000 × 60% × $6	
(ii)	4,000 × 60% × 5/6 × $1	
(iii)	4,000 × 60% × 5/6 × $6	Correct

Item 2: Choose the correct calculation for retained earnings of Shove at the date of acquisition.

	All figures are in $000	Selected answer
(i)	$16,500	
(ii)	$16,500 - $4,100	Correct
(iii)	$35,400 - $4,100	

Item 3: Choose the correct calculation for goodwill

		Selected answer
(i)	Fair value of consideration paid plus fair value of non-controlling interest at acquisition date plus fair value of net assets at acquisition	
(ii)	Fair value of consideration paid minus fair value of non-controlling interest at acquisition date + fair value of net assets at acquisition	
(iii)	Fair value of consideration paid plus fair value of non-controlling interest at acquisition date minus fair value of net assets at acquisition	Correct

Tutorial note

As the parent gained control of the subsidiary on the first day of the accounting period, the profit after tax of the subsidiary must all be post-acquisition. Any retained earnings prior to that date must have been earned up to the date of acquisition.

	$000
Subsidiary retained earnings at reporting date	16,500
Less: profit after tax for the year (from P&L)	4,100
Retained earnings up to date of acquisition	12,400

Task 2

Calculate the following figures for inclusion in the consolidated statement of financial position: **(3 marks)**

		$000	$000
(i)	Non-current assets	63,200	40,600 + $22,600
(ii)	Current assets	21,350	$16,000 + $6,600 - $1,000 (W1) - $250 (W1)
(iii)	Current liabilities	11,900	$8,200 + $4,700 - $1,000 (W1)

(W1) Intra-group sales and PURP

	$000
Cost of goods sold by Shove to Push (100%)5,000	
Add: 20% mark-up	1,000
Selling price of goods by Shove to Push (120%)	6,000
PURP = $1,000 × 25% in inventory	250

Note – as Shove was the seller, the PURP is allocated between the controlling group and NCI based upon their respective shareholdings.

Group share = 60% × $250 = $150 and NCI share = 40% × $250 = $100.

This information will be relevant for the calculation of retained earnings and non-controlling interest at the reporting date.

Task 3

Choose the correct calculation of each of the following items for inclusion in the consolidated statement of financial position: **(4 marks)**

(a)   Non-controlling interest at the reporting date

	All figures are in $000	Selected answer
(i)	(4,000 × 40% × $1) + (40% × (4,100 + 250))	
(ii)	(4,000 × 40% × $3.50) + (40% × (4,100 – 250))	Correct
(iii)	(4,000 × 40% × $6) + (40% × (4,100 + 250))	

(b) **Retained earnings at the reporting date**

	All figures are in $000	Selected answer
(i)	$35,400 - (60% × (4,100 + 250))	
(ii)	$45,400 - (60% × (4,100 – 250))	
(iii)	$35,400 + (60% × (4,100 – 250))	Correct

Task 4

Choose the correct calculation of each of the following items for inclusion in the consolidated statement of financial position: **(3 marks)**

(a) **Revenue**

	All figures are in $000	Selected answer
(i)	$85,000 + $42,000 - $6,000	Correct
(ii)	$85,000 + (40% × ($42,000 - $6,000)	
(iii)	$85,000 + $42,000 + $6,000	

(b) **Cost of sales**

	All figures are in $000	Selected answer
(i)	$63,000 + $32,000 - $6,000 - $250	
(ii)	$63,000 + $32,000 - $6,000 + $250	Correct
(iii)	$63,000 + (40% × ($32,000 - $6,000 + $250))	

(Total 15 marks)

Marking scheme	
	Marks
Task 1 – Accounting for goodwill	5
Task 2 – Items to include in consolidated SOFP	3
Task 3 – Retained earnings and NCI for SOFP	4
Task 4 – Revenue and cost of sales for SP&L	3
	——
Total	**15**
	——

Section 6

ANSWERS TO LONG-FORM QUESTIONS

1   CARBON

Statement of profit or loss for the year ended 31 December 20X5

	$	Marks
Revenue ($450,000 − $1,000 (W1))	449,000	1.0
Cost of sales (W2)	(210,000)	2.0
	————	
Gross profit	239,000	
Administrative expenses (W3)	(162,500)	1.5
Distribution costs	(56,000)	0.5
	————	
Operating profit	20,500	
Finance costs ($50,000 × 8% × 3/12)	(1,000)	1.0
	————	
Profit before tax	19,500	
Income tax charge	(5,000)	1.0
	————	————
Profit after taxation	14,500	7.0
	————	————

Statement of financial position as at 31 December 20X5

	$	
Non- current assets		
Property, plant and equipment	96,000	1.5
($150,000 − $30,000 − $24,000 (W2))		
Current assets		
Inventories	27,000	0.5
Receivables (W4)	30,000	1.5
Cash and cash equivalents	5,000	0.5
	————	
Total assets	158,000	
	————	

Equity

Ordinary share capital	10,000	0.5
Retained earnings ($25,500 + $14,500 (P/L)	40,000	0.5
Non-current liabilities		
8% Loan	50,000	0.5
Current liabilities		
Trade and other payables ($32,000 + $1,000 loan interest)	33,000	1.0
Tax payable	5,000	0.5
Provision	20,000	1.0
	————	———
Total equity and liabilities	158,000	8.0
	————	———

Workings

(W1) Sales return

A sales return has not been accounted for. The correcting entry is:

Dr Revenue $1,000

Cr Receivables $1,000 (W4)

(W2) Cost of sales

	$
Opening inventory	33,000
Purchases	180,000
Depreciation	24,000
(($150,000 – $30,000) × 20%)	
Closing inventory	(27,000)
	————
	210,000
	————

(W3) Administrative expenses

	$
Per trial balance	140,000
Irrecoverable debt (W4)	1,500
Increase in allowance for receivables (W4)	1,000
Provision – defective goods claim	20,000
	————
	162,500
	————

(W4) Receivables

	$
Per trial balance	36,000
Allowance per trial balance	(2,500)
Increase in allowance required (W3)	(1,000)
Irrecoverable debt (W3)	(1,500)
Sales return (W1)	(1,000)
	30,000

Marking scheme	
	Marks
Statement of profit or loss	7.0
Statement of financial position	8.0
Total	**15.0**

2 MARKUS

Statement of profit or loss for the year ended 30 April 20X3

	$	*Marks*
Revenue	230,000	0.5
Cost of sales (W1)	(94,550)	2.0
Gross profit	135,450	
Administrative expenses (W2)	(65,500)	1.5
Distribution costs (W3)	(31,550)	1.0
Operating profit	38,400	
Finance costs ($300 + $135 (W4))	(435)	1.0
Profit for the year	37,965	6.0

Statement of financial position as at 30 April 20X3

	$	Marks
Non- current assets		
Property, plant and equipment	39,950	1.5
($72,000 – $25,000 – $7,050 (W1))		
Current assets		
Inventories (W1)	16,250	1.0
Trade receivables (W5)	16,750	1.5
Prepayment	400	0.5
	———	
Total assets	73,350	
	———	
Capital account		
Balance at 1 May 20X2	30,000	0.5
Profit for the year	37,965	
Less: Cash drawings	(18,000)	0.5
Goods for own use	(5,000)	1.0
	———	
	44,965	
Non-current liabilities		
6% Loan	3,000	0.5
Current liabilities		
Trade payables	17,500	0.5
Accruals ($135 (W4) + $350 (W3))	485	1.0
Bank overdraft	7,400	0.5
	———	———
	73,350	9.0
	———	———

Workings

(W1) Cost of sales

	$
Opening inventory	18,750
Purchases for resale ($90,000 – $5,000 own use)	85,000
Depreciation	7,050
(($72,000 – $25,000) × 15%)	
Closing inventory ($17,500 – ($5,000 – $3,750))	(16,250)
	———
	94,550
	———

(W2) Administrative expenses

	$
Per trial balance	65,800
Irrecoverable debt (W5)	600
Reduction in allowance for receivables (W5)	(500)
Less: Insurance prepaid	(400)
	65,500

(W3) Distribution costs

	$
Per trial balance	31,200
Freight and delivery accrual	350
	31,550

(W4) Loan interest accrual

	$
$3,000 \times 6\% \times 9/12$	135

(W5) Trade receivables

	$
Per trial balance	20,000
Allowance per trial balance	(3,150)
Reduction in allowance required	500
Irrecoverable debt (W2)	(600)
	16,750

Marking scheme	Marks
Statement of profit or loss	6.0
Statement of financial position	9.0
Total	**15.0**

3   FIREWORK

Key answer tips

Ensure that you remember the proforma presentation of a statement of cash flows – it will help you to complete relevant extracts in an examination question.

Firework – Statement of cash flows for the year ended 31 March 20X1

	$000		Marks
Cash flows from operating activities			
Profit before tax	31,000		
Adjustments for:			
Depreciation charge	15,000	Add	0.5
Loss on sale of plant and equipment	2,000	Add	0.5
Interest payable	750	Add	0.5
Increase in inventories ($36,000 – $30,000)	(6,000)	Subtract	1.0
Increase in trade receivables ($40,000 – $35,000)	(5,000)	Subtract	1.0
Increase in trade payables ($36,500 – $30,000)	6,500	Add	1.0
Cash generated from operations	44,250		
Interest paid	(750)	Subtract	0.5
Income taxes paid (W3)	(9,500)	Subtract	1.0
Cash flows from investing activities			
Cash purchase of property, plant and equipment (W1)	(40,000)	Subtract	1.0
Disposal proceeds of plant and equipment (W2)	8,000	Add	1.0
Cash flows from financing activities			
Repayment of bank loan (W4)	(10,000)	Subtract	1.0
Proceeds of share issue ($5,000 + $5,000) (W5)	10,000	Add	2.0
Dividend paid (W6)	(14,000)	Subtract	2.0
Decrease in cash and cash equivalents	(12,000)		
($10,000 + $2,000)			1.0
Cash and cash equivalents at start of year	10,000	Add	0.5
Cash and cash equivalents at end of year	(2,000)	Net overdraft	0.5
			15.0

Workings

(W1) PPE additions in the year

	$000
PPE CV bal b/fwd	93,000
Less: CV of disposals ($8,000 + $2,000 loss)	(10,000)
Less: depreciation charge	**(15,000)**
Revaluation in year	2,000
Cash paid for PPE additions	**40,000**
PPE CV bal c/fwd	110,000

(W2) Loss on disposal of plant and equipment

	$000
PPE CV of disposals ($8,000 + $2,000)	10,000
Less: loss on disposal in cost of sales	**(2,000)**
Disposal proceeds received	8,000

(W3) Income tax paid

	$000
Income tax liability b/fwd	10,000
Income tax charge for the year per P/L	6,000
Cash paid in year	**(9,500)**
Income tax liability c/fwd	6,500

(W4) Bank loan – amount repaid

	$000
Bank loan b/fwd	17,000
Cash paid	**(10,000)**
Bank loan c/fwd	7,000

(W5) Issue of shares in the year

	Share capital $000	Share premium $000
Balance b/fwd	15,000	3,000
Proceeds of share issue in year	**5,000**	**5,000**
Balance c/fwd	20,000	8,000

(W6) Dividend paid

	$000
Retained earnings b/fwd	85,000
Profit after tax for the year	25,000
Cash paid	**(14,000)**
Bank loan c/fwd	96,000

Marking scheme	
	Marks
Statement of cash flows (per answer)	15
	——
Total	**15**
	——

4   PEDANTIC

(a)   Consolidated statement of profit or loss for the year ended 30 September 20X8

	$000
Revenue (85,000 + 42,000 – 6,000 intra-group sales)	121,000
Cost of sales (w (i))	(89,250)
	———
Gross profit	31,750
Distribution costs (4,000 + 3,500)	(7,500)
Administrative expenses (8,000 + 1,000)	(9,000)
Finance costs (600 + 400)	(1,000)
	———
Profit before tax	14,250
Income tax expense (2,162 + 1,000)	(3,162)
	———
Profit for the year	11,088
	———
Attributable to:	
Equity holders of the parent	9,548
Non-controlling interest	
((4,100 – 250 PURP) × 40%)	1,540
	———
	11,088
	———

(b)   Consolidated statement of financial position as at 30 September 20X8

Assets	
Non-current assets	
Property, plant and equipment	
(40,600 + 12,600)	53,200
Goodwill (W3)	9,100
	———
	62,300
Current assets (W8)	21,350
	———
Total assets	83,650
	———
Equity and liabilities	
Equity attributable to owners of the parent	
Equity shares of $1 each (10, 000 + 1,600 (W3))	11,600
Share premium (W3)	8,000
Retained earnings (W5)	37,710
	———
	57,310
Non-controlling interest (W4)	7,440
	———

Total equity	64,750
Non-current liabilities	
10% loan notes (3,000 + 4,000)	7,000
Current liabilities (8,200 + 4,700 – 1,000 intra-group balance)	11,900
Total equity and liabilities	83,650

Workings (figures in brackets in $000)

(W1) Group structure

Pedantic

60%

Sophistic

Investment acquired on the first day of the accounting period – 1 October 20X7. Therefore Pedantic has exercised control over Sophistic for the full year.

(W2) Net assets of Sophistic

	At acquisition	At reporting date
	$000	$000
Share capital	4,000	4,000
Retained earnings	2,400	6,500
PURP on inventory (W6)		(250)
	6,400	10,250

Tutorial note

As the parent gained control of the subsidiary on the first day of the accounting period, the profit after tax of the subsidiary must all be post-acquisition. Any retained earnings prior to that date must have been earned up to the date of acquisition.

	$000
Subsidiary retained earnings at reporting date	*6,500*
Less: profit after tax for the year (from P/L)	*4,100*
Retained earnings up to date of acquisition	*2,400*

(W3) Goodwill

	$000
Parent holding (investment) at fair value:	
Share exchange ((4,000 × 60%) × 2/3 × $6)	9,600
NCI value at acquisition (given)	5,900
	———
	15,500
Less:	
Fair value of net assets at acquisition (W2)	(6,400)
	———
	9,100
	———

Tutorial note

The share consideration given on the acquisition of Sophistic has not been recorded. Therefore share capital should be increased by ((4,000 x 60%) × 2/3 × $1) $1,600 and share premium should be increased by ((4,000 × 60%) × 2/3 × $5) $8,000.

(W4) Non-controlling interest

	$000
NCI value at acquisition	5,900
NCI share of post-acquisition reserves	1,540
((10,250 – 6,400) (W2) × 40%)	
	———
	7,440
	———

(W5) Consolidated retained earnings

	$000
Pedantic	35,400
Sophistic ((10,250 – 6,400) × 60%)	2,310
	———
	37,710
	———

(W6) Provision for unrealised profit on inventory

The unrealised profit (PURP) in inventory is calculated as ($6 million/1.2 × 20% = $1 million. Unrealised profit = $1 million × 25% = $250,000.

(W7) Cost of sales

	$000
Pedantic	63,000
Sophistic	32,000
Intra-group sales	(6,000)
PURP in inventory (W6)	250
	89,250

(W8) Current assets

	$000
Pedantic	16,000
Sophistic	6,600
PURP in inventory (W6)	(250)
Intra-group balance	(1,000)
	21,350

Marking scheme		Marks
(a)	Statement of profit or loss	6
(b)	Statement of financial position	9
	Total	**15**

Section 7

SPECIMEN EXAM QUESTIONS

SECTION A

ALL 35 questions are compulsory and MUST be attempted

Each question is worth 2 marks.

1   Which one of the following calculates a sole trader's net profit for a period?

    A   Closing net assets - drawings + capital introduced – opening net assets

    B   Closing net assets – drawings - capital introduced – opening net assets

    C   Closing net assets + drawings + capital introduced – opening net assets

    D   Closing net assets + drawings - capital introduced – opening net assets

2   Which one of the following statements best explains the imprest system of operating petty cash?

    A   All expenditure out of the petty cash must be properly authorised

    B   Regular equal amounts of cash are transferred into petty cash at intervals

    C   The exact amount of expenditure is reimbursed at intervals to maintain a fixed float

    D   Weekly expenditure cannot exceed a set amount

3   Which of the following statements are TRUE about limited liability companies?

    (1)   The company exposure to debt and liability is limited

    (2)   Financial statements must be produced

    (3)   A company continues to exist regardless of the identity of its owners

    A   1, 2 and 3

    B   1 and 3 only

    C   2 and 3 only

    D   1 and 2 only

4 Annie is a sole trader who does not keep full accounting records. The following details relate to her transactions with credit customers and suppliers for the year ended 30 June 20X6:

	$
Trade receivables, 1 July 20X5	130,000
Trade payables, 1 July 20X5	60,000
Cash received from customers	686,400
Cash paid to suppliers	302,800
Discounts received	2,960
Contra between payables and receivables ledgers	2,000
Trade receivables, 30 June 20X6	181,000
Trade payables, 30 June 20X6	84,000

What figure should appear in Annie's statement of profit or loss for the year ended 30 June 20X6 for purchases?

$ [   ]

5 **Which TWO of the following errors would cause the total of the debit column and the total of the credit column of a trial balance not to agree?**

	Selected answer
A cheque received from a customer was credited to cash and correctly recognised in receivables	
A purchase of non-current assets was omitted from the accounting records	
A transposition error was made when entering a sales invoice into the sales day book	
Rent received was included in the trial balance as a debit balance	

6 At 31 December 20X5 the following require inclusion in a company's financial statements:

(1) On 1 January 20X5 the entity made a loan of $12,000 to an employee, repayable on 1 January 20X6, charging interest at 2% per year. On the due date the employee repaid the loan and paid the whole of the interest due on the loan to that date.

(2) The entity paid an annual insurance premium of $9,000 in 20X5, covering the year ending 31 August 20X6.

(3) In January 20X6 the entity received rent from a tenant of $4,000 covering the six months to 31 December 20X5.

For these items, what total figures should be included in the entity's statement of financial position as at 31 December 20X5?

A   Current assets $10,240   Current liabilities $nil

B   Current assets $22,240   Current liabilities $nil

C   Current assets $16,240   Current liabilities $6,000

D   Current assets $10,000   Current liabilities $12,240

7   A company's statement of profit or loss for the year ended 31 December 20X5 showed a net profit of $83,600. It was later found that $18,000 paid for the purchase of a motor van had been debited to the motor expenses account. It is the company's policy to depreciate motor vans at 25% per year on the straight-line basis, with a full year's charge in the year of acquisition.

What would the net profit be after adjusting for this error?

$

8   Xena has the following working capital ratios:

	20X9	20X8
Current ratio	1·2:1	1·5:1
Receivables days	75 days	50 days
Payables days	30 days	45 days
Inventory turnover	42 days	35 days

Which of the following statements about Xena is CORRECT?

A   Xena is suffering from a worsening liquidity position in 20X9

B   Xena is taking longer to pay suppliers in 20X9

C   Xena is receiving cash from customers more quickly in 20X9 than in 20X8

D   Xena's liquidity and working capital has improved in 20X9

9   **Are the following statements true or false?**

	True	False
A statement of cash flows prepared using the direct method produces a different figure to net cash from operating activities from that produced if the indirect method is used		
Rights issues of shares do not feature in a statement of cash flows		
A surplus on revaluation of a non-current asset will not appear as an item in a statement of cash flows		
A profit on the sale of a non-current asset will appear as an item under cash flows from investing activities in the statement of cash flows		

10 An entity receives rent from a significant number of properties. The total received in the year ended 30 April 20X6 was $481,200.

The following were the amounts of rent in advance and in arrears at 30 April 20X5 and 20X6:

	30 April 20X5	30 April 20X6
	$	$
Rent received in advance	28,700	31,200
Rent in arrears (all subsequently received)	21,200	18,400

What amount of rental income should appear in the company's statement of profit or loss for the year ended 30 April 20X6?

A $475,900

B $501,500

C $486,500

D $460,900

11 **Which TWO of the following are differences between sole traders and limited liability companies?**

	Selected answer
A sole trader's financial statements are private; a company's financial statements are sent to shareholders and may be publicly filed	
Only companies have capital invested into the business	
A sole trader is fully and personally liable for any losses that the business might make	
Revaluations can be carried out in the financial statements of a company, but not in the financial statements of a sole trader	

12 **Which of the following statements is TRUE?**

	Selected answer
An entity's management will not assess an entity's performance using financial ratios	
The analysis of financial statements using ratios provides useful information when compared with previous performance or industry averages	
The interpretation of an entity's financial statements using ratios is only useful for potential investors	
Ratios based on historical data can predict the future performance of an entity	

13 A company's motor vehicles cost account at 30 June 20X6 is as follows:

Motor vehicles – cost

	$		$
Balance b/f	35,800	Disposal	12,000
Additions	12,950	Balance c/f	36,750
	————		————
	48,750		48,750
	————		————

What opening balance should be included in the following period's trial balance for Motor vehicles (at cost) at 1 July 20X6?

A $48,750 Dr

B $48,750 Cr

C $36,750 Cr

D $36,750 Dr

14 Which TWO of the following items must be disclosed in the note to the financial statements for intangible assets?

	Selected answer
A description of the development projects that have been undertaken during the period	
The useful lives of intangible assets capitalised in the financial statements	
A list of all intangible assets purchased or developed in the period	
Impairment losses written off intangible assets during the period	

15 Which of the following statements are correct?

(1)   Capitalised development expenditure must be amortised over a period not exceeding five years.

(2)   Capitalised development costs are shown in the statement of financial position under the heading of non-current assets.

(3)   If certain criteria are met, research expenditure must be recognised as an intangible asset.

A   2 and 3

B   1 only

C   1 and 3

D   2 only

16 The following transactions relate to Rashid's electricity expense ledger account for the year ended 30 June 20X9:

	$
Prepayment brought forward	550
Cash paid	5,400
Accrual carried forward	650

What amount should be charged to the statement of profit or loss in the year ended 30 June 20X9 for electricity?

A $5,300

B $6,600

C $5,400

D $5,500

17 At 30 June 20X5 a company's allowance for receivables was $39,000. At 30 June 20X6 trade receivables totalled $517,000. It was decided to write off debts totalling $37,000 and to adjust the allowance for receivables to the equivalent of 5% of the trade receivables based on past events.

What figure should appear in the statement of profit or loss for the year ended 30 June 20X6 for these items?

$

18 The total of the list of balances in Valley's payables' ledger was $438,900 at 30 June 20X6. This balance did not agree with Valley's payables' ledger control account balance. The following errors were discovered:

(1)   A contra entry of $980 was recorded in the payables' ledger control account, but not in the payables' ledger.

(2)   The total of the purchase returns day book was undercast by $1,000.

(3)   An invoice for $4,344 was posted to the supplier's account as $4,434.

What amount should Valley report in its statement of financial position for accounts payable at 30 June 20X6?

A $436,830

B $437,830

C $438,010

D $439,790

19 **According to IAS 2 Inventories, which TWO of the following costs should be included in valuing the inventories of a manufacturing company?**

	Selected answer
Carriage outwards	
Depreciation of factory plant	
Carriage inwards	
General administrative overheads	

20 Prisha has not kept accurate accounting records during the financial year. She had opening inventory of $6,700 and purchased goods costing $84,000 during the year. At the year-end she had $5,400 left in inventory. All sales were made at a mark-up on cost of 20%.

What is Prisha's gross profit for the year?

$ [   ]

21 At 31 December 20X4 a company's capital structure was as follows:

	$
Ordinary share capital	125,000
(500,000 shares of 25c each)	
Share premium account	100,000

In the year ended 31 December 20X5 the company made a rights issue of 1 share for every 2 held at $1 per share and this was taken up in full. Later in the year the company made a bonus issue of 1 share for every 5 held, using the share premium account for the purpose.

What was the company's capital structure at 31 December 20X5?

A   Ordinary share capital $212,500   Share premium account $262,500

B   Ordinary share capital $225,000   Share premium account $325,000

C   Ordinary share capital $225,000   Share premium account $250,000

D   Ordinary share capital $450,000   Share premium account $25,000

22 **Which of the following should appear in a company's statement of changes in equity?**

(1)   Total comprehensive income for the year

(2)   Amortisation of capitalised development costs

(3)   Surplus on revaluation of non-current assets

A   1 and 3 only

B   1 and 2 only

C   1, 2 and 3

D   2 and 3 only

23 The plant and machinery account (at cost) of a business for the year ended 31 December 20X5 was as follows:

Plant and machinery (at cost)

20X5	$	20X5	$
1 Jan Balance b/f	240,000	31 Mar Transfer to disposal account	60,000
30 Jun Cash purchase of plant	160,000	31 Dec Balance c/f	340,000
	400,000		400,000

The company's policy is to charge depreciation at 20% per year on the straight-line basis, with proportionate depreciation in the years of purchase and disposal.

What should be the depreciation charge for the year ended 31 December 20X5?

A $68,000

B $64,000

C $55,000

D $61,000

24 **The following extracts are from Hassan's financial statements:**

	$
Profit before interest and tax	10,200
Interest	(1,600)
Tax	(3,300)
Profit after tax	5,300

	$
Share capital	20,000
Reserves	15,600
	35,500
Loan liability	6,900
	42,500

What is Hassan's return on capital employed?

	%

25   Is each of the following statements about sales tax true or false?

	True	False
Sales tax is recorded as income in the accounts of the entity selling the goods		
Sales tax is an expense to the ultimate consumer of the goods purchased		

26   Q's trial balance failed to agree and a suspense account was opened for the difference. Q does not keep receivables' and payables' control accounts. The following errors were found in Q's accounting records:

(1)   In recording an issue of shares at par, cash received of $333,000 was credited to the ordinary share capital account as $330,000

(2)   Cash of $2,800 paid for plant repairs was correctly accounted for in the cash book but was credited to the plant asset account

(3)   The petty cash book balance of $500 had been omitted from the trial balance

(4)   A cheque for $78,400 paid for the purchase of a motor car was debited to the motor vehicles account as $87,400

Which of the errors will require an entry to the suspense account to correct them?

A   1 and 4 only

B   2 and 3 only

C   1, 2, 3 and 4

D   1, 2, and 4 only

27   Prior to the financial year end of 31 July 20X9, Cannon Co received a claim of $100,000 from a customer for providing poor quality goods which damaged the customer's plant and equipment. Cannon Co's lawyers have stated that there is a 20% chance that Cannon will successfully defend the claim.

Which of the following is the correct accounting treatment for the claim in the financial statements for the year ended 31 July 20X9?

A   Cannon should disclose a contingent liability of $100,000

B   Cannon should provide for the expected cost of the claim of $100,000

C   Cannon should provide for an expected cost of $20,000

D   Cannon should neither provide for nor disclose the claim

28 Gareth, a sales tax registered trader, purchased a computer for use in his business. The invoice for the computer showed the following costs related to the purchase:

	$
Computer	890
Additional memory	95
Delivery	10
Installation	20
Maintenance (1 year)	25
	———
	1,040
Sales tax (17.5%)	182
	———
Total	1,222
	———

How much should Gareth capitalise as a non-current asset in relation to this purchase?

$ [   ]

29 The following bank reconciliation statement has been prepared by a trainee accountant:

	$
Overdraft per bank statement	3,860
Less: Unpresented cheques	9,160
	———
	5,300
Add: Outstanding lodgements	16,690
	———
Cash at bank	21,990
	———

What should be the correct balance per the cash book?

A $3,670 overdrawn

B $3,670 balance at bank

C $21,990 balance at bank as stated

D $11,390 balance at bank

30 The IASB's Conceptual Framework for Financial Reporting identifies characteristics which make financial information faithfully represent what it purports to represent.

Which TWO of the following are examples of these characteristics?

	Selected answer
Accruals	
Completeness	
Going concern	
Neutrality	

31 The following ledger control account has been prepared by a trainee accountant:

Receivables' ledger control account

	$		$
Opening balance	308,600	Cash received from credit customers	147,200
Credit sales	154,200	Discounts allowed to credit customers	1,400
Cash sales	88,100	Interest charges on overdue debts	2,400
		Irrecoverable debts written off	4,900
Contras against credit balances in payables' ledger	4,600	Allowance for receivables	2,800
		Closing balance	396,800
	_____		_____
	555,500		555,500
	_____		_____

What should the closing balance be when all the errors made in preparing the receivables' ledger control account have been corrected?

A $309,500

B $307,100

C $304,300

D $395,200

32 Are the following material events after the reporting date and before the financial statements are approved adjusting events?

	Yes	No
A valuation of property providing evidence of impairment in value at the reporting date		
Sale of inventory held at the reporting date for less than cost		
Discovery of fraud or error affecting the financial statements		
The insolvency of a customer with a debt owing at the reporting date which is still outstanding		

33   A company values its inventory using the FIFO method. At 1 May 20X5 the company had 700 engines in inventory, valued at $190 each. During the year ended 30 April 20X6 the following transactions took place:

20X5

1 July	Purchased 500 engines at $220 each
1 November	Sold 400 engines for $160,000

20X6

1 February	Purchased 300 engines at $230 each
15 April	Sold 250 engines for $125,000

What is the value of the company's closing inventory of engines at 30 April 20X6?

A $188,500

B $106,000

C $166,000

D $195,500

34   Amy is a sole trader and had assets of $569,400 and liabilities of $412,840 on 1 January 20X8. During the year ended 31 December 20X8 she paid $65,000 capital into the business and withdrew $800 per month.

At 31 December 20X8, Amy had assets of $614,130 and liabilities of $369,770.

What was Amy's profit for the year ended 31 December 20X8?

$ [   ]

35   Bumbly Co extracted the trial balance for the year ended 31 December 20X7. The total of the debits exceeded the credits by $300.

Which of the following could explain the imbalance?

A   Discounts received of $150 was extracted to the debit column of the trial balance

B   The bank ledger account did not agree with the bank statement by a debit of $300

C   Discounts allowed of $150 was extracted to the debit column of the trial balance

D   Sales of $300 were omitted from the sales day book

(Total 70 marks)

SECTION B

BOTH questions are compulsory and MUST be attempted

36   Background

Keswick Co acquired 80% of the share capital of Derwent Co on 1 June 20X5. The summarised draft statements of profit or loss for Keswick Co and Derwent Co the year ended 31 May 20X6 are shown below:

	Keswick Co $000	Derwent Co $000
Revenue	8,400	3,200
Less: Cost of sales	(4,600)	(1,700)
Gross profit	3,800	1,500
Less: Distribution costs	(1,500)	(510)
Less: Administrative costs	(700)	(450)
Profit before tax	1,600	540
Less: Tax	(600)	(140)
Profit for the year	1,000	400

During the year, Keswick Co sold goods costing $1,000,000 to Derwant Co for $1,500,000. At 31 May 20X6, 30% of these goods remained in Derwent Co's inventory.

Task 1 (11 marks)

Use the information to complete the following financial statement:

∇ Drop down list for the title of the financial statement	Selection
Statement of profit or loss as at 31 May 20X6	
Statement of profit or loss for the year ended 31 May 20X6	
Consolidated statement of profit or loss for the year ended 31 May 20X6	
Consolidated statement of profit or loss as at 31 May 20X6	

∇ Drop down list for Revenue calculation	Selection
8,400 + 3,200 + 1,500	
8,400 + (80% × 3,200) - 1,500	
8,400 + 3,200	
8,400 + 3,200 − 1,500	
8,400 + 3,200 − 1,000	

∇ Drop down list for Cost of sales calculation	Selection
4,600 + 1,700 − 1,000	
4,600 + (80% × 1,700) − 1,500	
4,600 + 1,700 − 1,500 + (30% × 500)	
4,600 + (80% × 1,700)	
4,600 + 1,700 − 1,500 + (30% × 500)	

Gross profit ———

Less: Distribution costs

Less: Administrative costs

Profit before tax ———

Less: Tax

Profit for the year ———

Attributable to:

∇ Drop down list for Equity owners of Keswick Co	Selection
Keswick Co profit after tax	
Group profit after tax - NCI	
Group profit after tax + NCI	
Group profit after tax	

Non-controlling interest ———

Task 2 (4 marks)

Does each of the following factors illustrate the existence of a parent – subsidiary relationship?

	Yes	No
Control		
Non-controlling interest		
Greater than 50% of the equity shares held by an investor		
50% Of all shares and debt being held by an investor		
Greater than 50% of the preference shares being held by an investor		
Greater than 50% of preference shares and debt being held by an investor		
Significant influence		
100% of the equity shares being held by an investor		

(Total 15 marks)

37 Background

Malright, a limited liability company, has an accounting year end of 31 October. The accountant is preparing the financial statements as at 31 October 20X7. A trial balance has been prepared.

Task 1 (4 marks)

Do each of the following items belong on the statement of financial position (SOFP) as at 31 October 20X7?

	Dr	Cr	Yes / No
	$000	$000	
Buildings at cost	740		
Buildings accumulated depreciation at 1 November 20X6		60	
Plant at cost	220		
Plant accumulated depreciation at 1 November 20X6		110	
Bank balance		70	
Revenue		1,800	
Net purchases	1,140		
Inventory at 1 November 20X6	160		
Cash	20		
Trade payables		250	
Trade receivables	320		
Administrative expenses	325		
Allowance for receivables at 1 November 20X6		10	
Retained earnings at 1 November 20X6		130	
Equity shares, $1		415	
Share premium account		80	
	———	———	
	2,925	2,925	
	———	———	

Task 2 (3 marks)

The allowance for receivables is to be increased to 5% of trade receivables. The allowance for receivables is treated as an administrative expense.

The year-end journal for allowance for receivables is given below. Prepare the double entry by selecting the correct option for each row.

	Debit	Credit	No debit or credit
Trade receivable			
Administrative expenses			
Allowance for receivables			
Revenue			

Complete the following:

The amount included in the statement of profit or loss after the allowance is increased to 5% of trade receivables is:

$	'000

Task 3 (5 marks)

Plant is depreciated at 20% per annum using the reducing balance method and buildings are depreciated at 5% per annum on their original cost. Depreciation is treated as a cost of sales expense.

The year-end journal for buildings and plant depreciation is given blow. Using the information above, prepare the double entry by selecting the correct option for each one.

	Debit	Credit	No debit or credit
Administrative expenses			
Cost of sales			
Buildings cost			
Plant cost			
Buildings accumulated depreciation			
Plant accumulated depreciation			

Calculate the depreciation charge calculated for the year ended 31 October 20X7. Use the information above to help you.

Buildings	$	'000
Plant	$	'000

Task 4 (1.5 marks)

Closing inventory has been counted and is valued at $75,000.

Ignoring the depreciation charge calculated earlier, what is the cost of sales for the year?

$	'000

Task 5 (1.5 marks)

An invoice of $15,000 for energy costs relating to the quarter ended 30 November 20X7 was received on 2 December 20X7. Energy costs are included in administrative expenses.

Complete the following statements.

The double entry to post the year end adjustment for energy costs is:

	Debit	Credit
Accrual		
Administrative expenses		

The amount to be posted within the year end adjustment double entry above is:

$ '000

(Total 15 marks)

Section 8

ANSWERS TO SPECIMEN EXAM QUESTIONS

SECTION A

1   D

Closing net assets + drawings - capital introduced - opening net assets

2   C

The exact amount is reimbursed at intervals to maintain a fixed float.

3   B

Items (2) and (3) only are true. Only the members (i.e. shareholders) of a company have limited liability.

4 $331,760

Payables' ledger control account

	$		$
Cash paid to suppliers	302,800	Balance b/fwd	60,000
Discount received	2,960	Purchases (bal fig)	331,760
Contra	2,000		
Balance c/fwd	84,000		
	———		———
	391,760		391,760
	———		———

5

	Selected answer
A cheque received from a customer was credited to cash and correctly recognised in receivables	✓
A purchase of non-current assets was omitted from the accounting records	
A transposition error was made when entering a sales invoice into the sales day book	
Rent received was included in the trial balance as a debit balance	✓

6   B

Current assets $22,240 and current liabilities $nil

7 $97,100

	$
Net profit	83,600
Reduce motor expenses for cost of car	18,000
Depreciation charge ($18,000 × 25%)	(4,500)
Adjusted net profit	97,100

8   A

Xena is suffering from a worsening liquidity position in 20X9.

9

	True	False
A statement of cash flows prepared using the direct method produces a different figure to net cash from operating activities from that produced if the indirect method is used		✓
Rights issues of shares do not feature in a statement of cash flows		✓
A surplus on revaluation of a non-current asset will not appear as an item in a statement of cash flows	✓	
A profit on the sale of a non-current asset will appear as an item under cash flows from investing activities in the statement of cash flows		✓

10 A

	$
Balance b/f (advance)	28,700
Balance b/f (arrears)	(21,200)
Cash received	481,200
Balance c/f (advance)	(31,200)
Balance c/f (arrears)	18,400
	————
Rental income receivable	475,900
	————

11

	Selected answer
A sole trader's financial statements are private; a company's financial statements are sent to shareholders and may be publicly filed	✓
Only companies have capital invested into the business	
A sole trader is fully and personally liable for any losses that the business might make	✓
Revaluations can be carried out in the financial statements of a company, but not in the financial statements of a sole trader	

12

	Selected answer
An entity's management will not assess an entity's performance using financial ratios	
The analysis of financial statements using ratios provides useful information when compared with previous performance or industry averages	✓
The interpretation of an entity's financial statements using ratios is only useful for potential investors	
Ratios based on historical data can predict the future performance of an entity	

13 D

14

	Selected answer
A description of the development projects that have been undertaken during the period	
The useful lives of intangible assets capitalised in the financial statements	✓
A list of all intangible assets purchased or developed in the period	
Impairment losses written off intangible assets during the period	✓

15   D

Capitalised development costs are shown in the statement of financial position under the heading of non-current assets.

16   B

	$
Balance b/f	550
Expense incurred (cash)	5,400
Accrual c/f	650
	─────
	6,600
	─────

17 $22,000

	$	$
Debts written off		37,000
Closing allowance: (517 – 37) × 5%	24,000	
Less: opening allowance	39,000	
	─────	(15,000)
		─────
P&L charge		22,000
		─────

18   B

	$
Balance per ledger	438,900
Less: contra	(980)
Posting error	(90)
	─────
Corrected balance	437,830
	─────

Note: Adjustment 2 affects only the control account and does not affect the payables' ledger list of balances.

19

	Selected answer
Carriage outwards	
Depreciation of factory plant	✔
Carriage inwards	✔
General administrative overheads	

20 **$17,060**

$(6,700 + 84,000 - 5,400) \times 20\% = \$17,060$

21 **C**

	Ordinary share capital	Share premium account
	$	$
Balance b/f	125,000	100,000
Rights issue	62,500	187,500
Bonus issue	37,500	(37,500)
Balance c/f	225,000	250,000

22 **A**

Amortisation of development costs is charged to profit or loss as an expense.

23 **C**

Depreciation	$	
Jan – Mar	12,000	$(240,000 \times 20\%) \times 3/12$
Apr – Jun	9,000	$(240,000 - 60,000) \times 20\% \times 3/12$
Jul – Dec	34,000	$(180,000 + 160,000) \times 20\% \times 6/12$
	55,000	

24 **24%**

$(10,200/42,500) \times 100 = 24\%$

25

	True	False
Sales tax is recorded as income in the accounts of the entity selling the goods		✔
Sales tax is an expense to the ultimate consumer of the goods purchased	✔	

26 C

27 B

It is probable (80% chance) that Cannon Co will lose the case. As it is probable and results from a past transaction or event and can be reliably measured provision for the full amount should be made.

28 $1,015

$1,040 – $25 maintenance = $1,015.

Note that, as the business is registered to account for sales tax, they cannot be capitalised as part of the cost of the computer. The maintenance cost cannot be capitalised – that is written off to profit or loss over the period of the maintenance contract.

29 B

	$
Overdraft per bank statement	(3,860)
Less: unpresented cheques	(9,160)
Add: outstanding lodgements	16,690
Cash at bank	3,670

30

	Selected answer
Accruals	
Completeness	✓
Going concern	
Neutrality	✓

31 B

Receivables' ledger control account

	$		$
Opening balance	308,600	Cash	148,600
Credit sales	154,200	Contras	4,600
Interest charged on overdue accounts	2,400	Irrecoverable debts	4,900
		Closing balance	307,100
	465,200		465,200

32

	Yes	No
A valuation of property providing evidence of impairment in value at the reporting date	✓	
Sale of inventory held at the reporting date for less than cost	✓	
Discovery of fraud or error affecting the financial statements	✓	
The insolvency of a customer with a debt owing at the reporting date which is still outstanding	✓	

33   A

Closing inventory	$
50 × $190	9,500
500 × $220	110,000
300 × $230	69,000
	188,500

34 $32,400

	$
Opening net assets ($569,400 - $412,840)	156,560
Capital introduced	65,000
Drawings ($800 × 12)	(9,600)
Profit for the year (bal fig)	32,400
Closing net assets ($614,130 - $369,770)	244,360

35   A

Discount received is a form of income and should be a credit balance. By including this item as a debit balance in the trial balance, the credit column is understated by $150 and the debit column is overstated by $150 – i.e. a total imbalance of $300.

SECTION B

36   Task 1   **(11 marks)**

Use the information to complete the following financial statement:

∇ Drop down list for the title of the financial statement	Selection
Statement of profit or loss as at 31 May 20X6	
Statement of profit or loss for the year ended 31 May 20X6	
Consolidated statement of profit or loss for the year ended 31 May 20X6	✓
Consolidated statement of profit or loss as at 31 May 20X6	

∇ Drop down list for Revenue calculation	Selection
8,400 + 3,200 + 1,500	
8,400 + (80% × 3,200) - 1,500	
8,400 + 3,200	
8,400 + 3,200 − 1,500	✓
8,400 + 3,200 − 1,000	

∇ Drop down list for Cost of sales calculation	Selection
4,600 + 1,700 − 1,000	
4,600 + (80% × 1,700) − 1,500	
4,600 + 1,700 − 1,500 + (30% × 500)	
4,600 + (80% × 1,700)	
4,600 + 1,700 − 1,500 + (30% × 500)	✓

Gross profit	5,150
Less: Distribution costs (1,500 + 510)	(2,010)
Less: Administrative costs (700 + 450)	(1,150)
Profit before tax	1,990
Less: Tax (600 + 140)	(740)
Profit for the year	1,250

Attributable to:

∇ Drop down list for Equity owners of Keswick Co	Selection
Keswick Co profit after tax	
Group profit after tax − Non-controlling interest	✓
Group profit after tax + Non-controlling interest	
Group profit after tax	

Non-controlling interest (20% × 400)	80

Task 2 (4 marks)

Does each of the following factors illustrate the existence of a parent – subsidiary relationship?

	Yes	No
Control	✓	
Non-controlling interest	✓	
Greater than 50% of the equity shares held by an investor	✓	
50% 0f all shares and debt being held by an investor		✓
Greater than 50% of the preference shares being held by an investor		✓
Greater than 50% of preference shares and debt being held by an investor		✓
Significant influence		✓
100% of the equity shares being held by an investor	✓	

(Total 15 marks)

37   Task 1 (4 marks)

Do each of the following items belong on the statement of financial position (SOFP) as at 31 October 20X7?

	Dr $000	Cr $000	Yes / No
Buildings at cost	740		✓
Buildings accumulated depreciation at 1 November 20X6		60	No
Plant at cost	220		✓
Plant accumulated depreciation at 1 November 20X6		110	No
Bank balance		70	✓
Revenue		1,800	No
Net purchases	1,140		No
Inventory at 1 November 20X6	160		No
Cash	20		✓
Trade payables		250	✓
Trade receivables	320		✓
Administrative expenses	325		No
Allowance for receivables at 1 November 20X6		10	No
Retained earnings at 1 November 20X6		130	No
Equity shares, $1		415	✓
Share premium account		80	✓
	2,925	2,925	

Note: the accumulated depreciation balances as at 1 November 20X6 would not appear on the statement of financial positon as at 31 October 20X7. Those balances would need to be updated for the depreciation charge for the year ended 31 October 20X7, along with any adjustment that may be required for additions and/or disposals in the year. Similarly, the allowance for receivables as at 1 November 20X6 would need to be adjusted to the circumstances existing at 31 October 20X7.

Task 2 (3 marks)

The year-end journal for allowance for receivables is given below. Prepare the double entry by selecting the correct option for each row.

	Debit	Credit	No debit or credit
Trade receivable			✓
Administrative expenses	✓		
Allowance for receivables		✓	
Revenue			✓

Complete the following:

The amount included in the statement of profit or loss after the allowance is increased to 5% of trade receivables is:

$6	'000	(5% × 320,000) – 10,000

Task 3 (5 marks)

The year-end journal for buildings and plant depreciation is given blow. Using the information above, prepare the double entry by selecting the correct option for each one.

	Debit	Credit	No debit or credit
Administrative expenses			✓
Cost of sales	✓		
Buildings cost			✓
Plant cost			✓
Buildings accumulated depreciation		✓	
Plant accumulated depreciation		✓	

Calculate the depreciation charge calculated for the year ended 31 October 20X7. Use the information above to help you.

Buildings	$37	'000	5% × 740,000
Plant	$22	'000	20% × (220,000 – 110,000)

Task 4 (1.5 marks)

Ignoring the depreciation charge calculated earlier, what is the cost of sales for the year?

$1,225	'000	160,000 + 1,140,000 – 75,000

Task 5 (1.5 marks)

Complete the following statements.

The double entry to post the year end adjustment for energy costs is:

	Debit	Credit
Accrual		✓
Administrative expenses	✓	

The amount to be posted within the year end adjustment double entry above is:

$10	'000	2/3 × 15,000

(Total 15 marks)

Section 9

REFERENCES

The Board (2016) *Conceptual Framework for Financial Reporting*. London: IFRS Foundation.

The Board (2015) *ED/2015/3: Conceptual Framework for Financial Reporting*. London: IFRS Foundation.

The Board (2015) *ED/2015/8: IFRS Practice Statement: Application of Materiality to Financial Statements*. London: IFRS Foundation.

The Board (2016) *IAS 1 Presentation of Financial Statements*. London: IFRS Foundation.

The Board (2016) *IAS 2 Inventories*. London: IFRS Foundation.

The Board (2016) *IAS 7 Statement of Cash Flows*. London: IFRS Foundation.

The Board (2016) *IAS 16 Property, Plant and Equipment*. London: IFRS Foundation.

The Board (2016) *IAS 27 Separate Financial Statements*. London: IFRS Foundation.

The Board (2016) *IAS 28 Investments in Associates and Joint Ventures*. London: IFRS Foundation.

The Board (2016) *IAS 37 Provisions, Contingent Liabilities and Contingent Assets*. London: IFRS Foundation.

The Board (2016) *IAS 38 Intangible Assets*. London: IFRS Foundation.

The Board (2016) *IFRS 3 Business Combinations*. London: IFRS Foundation.

The Board (2016) *IFRS 10 Consolidated Financial Statements*. London: IFRS Foundation.

The Board (2016) *IFRS 15 Revenue from Contracts with Customers*. London: IFRS Foundation.